# FACTORIES IN THE FIELD

# FACTORIES IN THE FIELD

## THE STORY OF MIGRATORY FARM LABOR IN CALIFORNIA

### CAREY McWILLIAMS

*"Bring me men to match my mountains."*
— SCROLL ON THE STATE CAPITOL
IN SACRAMENTO

Peregrine Publishers, Inc.
SANTA BARBARA AND SALT LAKE CITY
1971

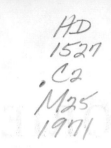

*HD*
*1527*
*.C2*
*M25*
*1971*

ISBN: 0–87905–005–5
LIBRARY OF CONGRESS CATALOG CARD NUMBER: 70–177593
PRINTED IN THE UNITED STATES OF AMERICA

# CONTENTS

# FOREWORD

*The Grapes of Wrath* and *Factories in the Field* were published in the spring of 1939 at approximately the same time, not through prearrangement and not quite by pure chance either. Both books, one might say, were cultural by-products of the dust bowl migration to California in the 1930s — one of the great migrations in our history in terms of volume, velocity, and distances travelled. While to some extent the so-called Okies and Arkies had been induced to move westward by misleading ads and notices, the great bulk of them were simply refugees from disaster — the disaster of dust and drought — moving in the only direction that seemed "open" or feasible, that is, westward. They came so rapidly and in such volume that by 1934 approximately half the farm labor supply in California was made up, for the first time, of native-born Americans, white, largely Protestant, and of Anglo-Saxon lineage. It seemed therefore, as I put it then, that "the jig is up," that is, at long last an historic confrontation was about to take place between large growers on the one hand and native-born workers on the other. The flare-up of large scale farm labor strikes in the middle 1930s was a clear indication that the larger employers of farm labor would not be able to deal with dust bowl migrants — a notably independent group of former yeoman farmers — as they had dealt with the foreign-born workers they had recruited and exploited for so many years. Steinbeck was struck by the drama of the confrontation that seemed to be shaping up as well as by the biblical overtones of the great migration — thousands of refugee families moving across the desert to a promised land.[1]

I too was impressed with the changes that began to take place in the farm labor scene in the late 1930s. I was also deeply

[1] For example, his article in *The Nation*, September 12, 1936 — incidentally his first published magazine article.

moved by the saga of farm labor in California, the recruitment of one group and then another and their trials and tribulations in the beautiful orchards and immense farm factories of the state. *Factories in the Field* was deliberately subtitled "The Story of Migratory Farm Labor in California" for I wanted to emphasize that I was telling a story as much as I was analyzing a problem. It was of course an old story in California by 1939 when the book was published. What gave it immediacy and dramatic interest was the dust bowl migration. In a sense the importance of the book was, and still is, that it was the first attempt to put together, as an ongoing narrative, the various chapters that constitute the fascinating saga of migratory farm labor in California.

Logically the story should have been told by someone more familiar with factory-style farming than I was in the 1930s. I was a fairly recent migrant to California myself, having moved to California from Colorado in the early 1920s. I got interested in farm labor more or less by chance. As a young lawyer in Los Angeles, I had been asked by the local A.C.L.U. on several occasions to defend Mexican citrus workers who had gone on strike. The experience was illuminating. I became quite curious about the structure of the citrus industry and what it was about it that produced such sharp employer-employee tensions in those seemingly placid citrus belt communities, outwardly so friendly, pious, and charming. The more I found out about labor in the citrus industry, the more curious I became about farm labor throughout the state. So I began to spend long hours in the library at nights and on weekends reading the files of the *Pacific Rural Press* and digging into other sources. And when I had a chance, I began to make forays into the San Joaquin Valley to see for myself just what went on in the fields and in the labor camps. Also I began to take an interest in the various ethnic minorities, Filipinos and Mexicans in particular, and to write about them. In July, 1933, for example, I did a piece for *The American Mercury* about the way in which Mexicans were being "repatriated" to Mexico in order to get them off the relief rolls. But my real education in farm labor began when I was appointed Chief, Division of Immigration and Housing in the state government. Someone had heard that I had written a book about farm labor — it had not yet been published — and so Governor Culbert L. Olson decided to appoint me to the post on the recommendation of George Kidwell, the San Francisco labor leader, and other political supporters. The appointment was made in January, 1939; *Factories in the Field* was not published until the spring of that year. The Division of Immigration and Housing was a unique agency that had been set up by Governor Hiram Johnson on the recommendation of Simon J. Lubin, a distinguished public figure with a longstanding interest in the problem of farm labor. The Division had several functions, one of which was to enforce the state labor camp act. So in the next four years I was exposed to every aspect of the farm labor problem as I set about trying — with some success — to enforce the labor camp act; no serious effort to enforce it had been made for many years. I visited virtually every county and township in the state, inspecting all kinds of labor camps, mining camps, railroad camps, lumber camps, and farm labor camps. At the height of the harvest season, the farm labor camps would, for short periods, contain a population of around 160,000 men, women and children. Inspecting these camps was a memorable experience. It changed my point of view about a number of things.

It so happened — to turn back a bit — that *Factories in the*

*Field* got caught up in the furious state-wide controversy that was touched off by publication of *The Grapes of Wrath*. The Associated Farmers, their friends and allies, were convinced that they were confronted by a left-wing conspiracy of some sort. They could not accept as fact the proposition that it was pure coincidence that the two books had been released at approximately the same time. As a matter of fact I never met John Steinbeck.[2] Nor could they accept my appointment to head the Division of Immigration and Housing as the accident it was. The truth is that I was appointed because I was the only person known to the Governor and his advisors who was even *supposed* to know something about farm labor. In any case, the fire that was directed against *The Grapes of Wrath* and *Factories in the Field* — and their authors — certainly stimulated the sale of both books but, more important, it put the farm labor problem high on the California — and national — agenda for the first time. Here and there both books were burned or banned and I became, in the agitational material of the Associated Farmers, "Agricultural Pest No. 1 in California, outranking pear blight and boll weevil."[3] But the discussion and controversy did serve an important public purpose if only because it was a factor — perhaps the decisive factor — in bringing the La Follette Committee to California. The hearings of this committee[4] so thoroughly exposed the anti-labor activities of the Associated Farmers that it never regained the power it had once exerted.

But for all the excitement of those years, the great confronta-

[2] See *The American West*, May, 1970, for details on our relationship.

[3] Two books contain careful documentation of all this fuss and fury: *A Companion to the Grapes of Wrath* edited by Warren French. 1963, and *A Casebook on The Grapes of Wrath* edited by Agnes McNeill Donohue, 1968.

[4] *Labor and Liberty: The La Follette Committee and the New Deal* by Jerold S. Auerbach, 1966.

tion that had been anticipated did not take place. World War II came along and the despised Okies and Arkies moved quickly into the shipyards and factories and, in no small degree, were responsible for the extraordinary economic expansion that took place. On October 12, 1942, Senator La Follette presented his report and recommendations on farm labor to the Senate but by that time no one was listening. The recommendations have been ignored from that day to this. What some of us had thought would be a climactic phase of the farm labor story turned out to be merely another chapter. And since then of course there have been other chapters — the Di Giorgio strike, the *bracero* program, and the emergence of Cesar Chavez and the movement he heads.

\* \* \*

The removal of Japanese-Americans at the outset of World War II, for so-called "security" reasons, created a demand for the return of the Mexicans who had been "encouraged" to "repatriate" by relief officials during the depression. Then too the influx of dust bowl migrants had made it difficult for Mexicans to find jobs during the late 1930s. But World War II had an enormous economic impact in California, more perhaps than in any other state. Between 1940 and 1944 it has been estimated that the federal government invested over a billion dollars in the state for aircraft plants, shipyards, steel plants, synthetic rubber plants, and other facilities. Agricultural production began to expand accordingly. For a variety of reasons, one being the necessity of maintaining at least the facade of "Good Neighbor" relations with Mexico, an executive agreement was entered into between the two countries in 1942 — supplemented by legislation in 1943 — the effect of which was to make possible the recruitment of Mexican labor by federal agencies for agricultural employment in California subject to certain "safeguards" and restrictions — the so-called *bracero* program. But despite these arrangements it was not long before illegal entrants or "wetbacks" began in large numbers to cross into California attracted by wartime wages. When the federal recruitment program expired in 1947, it was renewed but the new agreement permitted California farm employers to recruit contract labor without the intervention of a federal agency, whenever the Employment Service certified that a need existed for their service. These new post-1947 agreements, with the exception of the 1948 agreement, allowed employers to make contracts with illegal entrants or "wetbacks" who were already in the United States.[5] From then on, of course, the farm labor market became increasingly demoralized.

With Mexican labor surging in, and wartime demands beginning to abate, it was not long before reporters were describing a "new Grapes of Wrath" situation. For example, on March 17, 1950, Gladwin Hill reported in the New York *Times* that "The spectre of human misery again is striking the Grapes of Wrath country. Throughout the vast and fertile San Joaquin Valley, one of the nation's prime agricultural areas, where the trek of the Okies made history a dozen years ago, a new cycle of destitution among farm workers is under way." Newspapers in the San Joaquin Valley reported 28 deaths from hunger that winter and a grand jury inquiry turned up the startling fact that 11 infants had died of malnutrition in farm labor communities. When Earl Warren was elected Governor in 1942, he rather flamboyantly announced that his first official act would be to remove me from office (actually my term expired automatically

---

[5] "The Politics of the Mexican Labor Issue," by Ellis W. Hawley, *Agricultural History*, July, 1966.

the day he was sworn in). Now, confronted with the first farm labor crisis for which he was responsible — and it was a mini-crisis by contrast with those the Olson Administration had been forced to cope with — he proceeded to appoint a commission to inquire into the problem on March 1, 1950. Not surprisingly, the commission came up with recommendations strikingly similar to those that had emerged from a conference of state, county, and federal officials which I had called, with the approval of Governor Olson, in 1939.

As might have been expected, the pattern of events toward the end of the 1940s stimulated still another attempt to organize farm labor. On October 1, 1947, Local 218, AFL, went on strike at the huge Di Giorgio farms. A reporter for the San Francisco *Chronicle* once said — quite appropriately — that "Di Giorgio is to farming what Tiffany's is to jewelry." In the late 1940s, the Di Giorgio farms alone — there were subsidiaries — could harvest, process and ship 70 carloads of asparagus, 350 carloads of potatoes, 400 carloads of plums and 1,200 carloads of grapes. It owned the Klamath Lumber and Box Company, had a controlling interest in the Baltimore Fruit Exchange, and was a thoroughly "integrated" operation, from the fields to the eastern produce exchanges. The strike was savagely contested but by 1950 it had been broken, although phases of it dragged on for some time.[6] The Di Giorgio strike was, in effect, the link that connected the big farm labor strikes of the 1930s with the beginning of Cesar Chavez organizing activities in the San Joaquin Valley.

But once again the cycle took another spin as it had on so many occasions in the past. The Korean War had much the

[6] The story of the strike is told in detail in Ernesto Galarza's book *Spiders in the House and Workers in the Field*, 1970. I reported certain phases of it for *The Nation* in the issue of February 19, 1949.

same effect as World War II in stimulating a sharp upsurge of economic activity in California. By February 25, 1951, — just a year after his dismal stories of destitution — Gladwin Hill was reporting an acute farm labor shortage. Farm employers wanted to import Filipinos and Hawaiians. At one point they even discussed the possible use of Lithuanians and other "displaced persons" from Eastern Europe. Committees were set up to study the possibility of importing Japanese and South Koreans. In part what stimulated all this excitement was the fact that the last agreement with Mexico had expired and some new form of recruitment had to be arranged. Out of these negotiations came Public Law 78 (July, 1951), which for the next fourteen years formed the basis of labor recruitment from Mexico. It provided that labor could not be imported until the Secretary of Labor had certified that a need existed for them, and it had the usual "safeguards" and restrictions. But these provisions were largely window-dressing. The fact is that the Immigration Service, acting in cahoots with the large employers, permitted thousands of wetbacks to enter the country. Periodically it would then round them up and "parole" them to employers. In 1954, the President's Commission on Migratory Labor found that "Our government has thus become a contributor to the growth of an illegal traffic which it has responsibility to prevent." [7] In response to protests from Mexico that the "safeguards" were not being observed and mounting pressure from various groups and organizations in this country, the Justice Department — with splashy publicity — finally launched Operation Wetback in 1953 in an effort to reduce the traffic in wetbacks. Government spokesmen claimed that a million or more wetbacks had

---

[7] "Wetbacks, Growers and Poverty," by Sheldon L. Greene, *The Nation*, October 20, 1969. See also *Merchants of Labor* by Ernesto Galarza, 1966, *Los Mojados: The Wetback Story* by Julian Samora, 1971.

been rounded up and returned to Mexico. As a postscript it might be noted that under Public Law 78 about 94 percent of the workers imported from Mexico between 1951 and 1965 went to work for some 50,000 growers in five states where they were almost exclusively used in such crops as cotton, sugar beets, fruits and vegetables. Over 98 percent of the nation's commercial farmers made no use of this labor and did not benefit in any way from the program.

Statistics about the movement of Mexicans back and forth across the border, entering or leaving, legally or illegally, were for many years far from accurate and still leave much to be desired on this score. For example, a wetback can enter this country and be deported and then re-enter and be deported again, and the process can be repeated many times but the statisticians are continuing to count the same man. Even so it is possible to get some idea of the magnitude of the movement by Sheldon L. Greene's estimate that between 1942 and 1963, 4.5 million Mexicans entered this country for temporary employment. Whatever estimates are used, it is apparent that this migration has far exceeded the dust bowl migration of the 1930s and, for many years, it has been a continuing process nor has it wholly ceased. Yet it has never attracted the same public interest or concern in part of course because there was no John Steinbeck around to convey a feeling of the enormous human drama involved.

While it seemed at times as though Public Law 78 would be endlessly renewed, enough pressure was finally mobilized against it so that it was permitted to expire at the end of 1964. But there was tucked away in the Immigration and Nationality Act — Public Law 414 — a provision which was misused to continue labor importations, under one ruse or another, until 1968.

In August of that year Secretary of Labor W. Willard Wirtz denied a request of California growers for emergency labor and characterized the action as "a historic step towards healing the migrant worker sore in California and in the entire United States." Even so "wetbacks" continued to enter, work, and be deported, in a kind of annual ritual, although in declining numbers. But the expiration of P. L. 78 at the end of 1964, although it did not stop entirely the influx of Mexican labor, did set the stage for the emergence of Cesar Chavez and the movement he heads.

*   *   *

So much has been written about the Chavez Chapter in the history of farm labor that little need be said about it here.[8] But I can supply one or two missing links in the story.

Fred W. Ross is the person who discovered Chavez and Fred is quite a story in himself. A native Californian, a graduate of the University of Southern California, he is a man of exasperating modesty, the kind who never steps forward to claim his fair share of credit for any enterprise in which he is involved. Fred has a very rare gift: he is a natural born organizer. I say "natural born" because it is difficult to train people how to become organizers. Fred knows how.

I first met Fred when he was in the migratory camp program which was run by the Federal Farm Security Administration in the 1930s. I had many contacts with the FSA officials — and field personnel — and got to know many of them very well, Fred included. Later I had occasion to know Fred in another

---

[8] See *Sal Si Puedes* by Peter Mattiessen, 1969, *Forty Acres: Cesar Chavez and the Farm Workers*, by Mark Day, with an introduction by Cesar Chavez, 1971, *Delano: The Story of the California Grape Strike* by John Gregory Dunne, 1967, *So Shall Ye Reap, The Story of Cesar Chavez and The Farm Workers' Movement* by Joan London and Henry Anderson, 1970, *The Slaves We Rent* by Truman E. Moore, 1965, *La Causa: The California Grape Strike* by Paul Fusco and George D. Horwitz, 1970.

capacity, when he joined the staff of the War Relocation Authority, the agency set up to supervise the removal of Japanese-Americans from the West Coast during World War II. I got interested in the program — and the situation that led up to it — and did a book about Japanese-Americans.[9] Later I knew him when he was working with the American Council on Race Relations, experimenting with the first community service organizations (some references to him then may be found in *North from Mexico*). The American Council had to let him go for lack of funds, and the canny Saul Alinsky of the Industrial Areas Foundation, had the wit to take him on. In 1947 the Mexican-American community in Los Angeles asked Alinsky to help them organize the 100,000 or more persons of Mexican descent then living on the East Side of Los Angeles. Ross served as Alinsky's representative on this project. Out of the effort came the Community Service Organization which was responsible for registering thousands of Mexican-American voters and for carrying on a variety of community activities. Among other achievements, it was largely responsible for Edward Roybal's election to the Los Angeles City Council in 1949 — the first Mexican-American to hold that position. Later he was elected to Congress where he still serves. During this period I was able to be helpful in raising a fairly substantial sum, largely from my friends in the Los Angeles Jewish community, which made it possible for these early organizing activities to continue.

One night in 1952 — June 9th to be exact — Fred met Cesar Chavez in a San Jose barrio known as "Sal si Puedes" ("Get out if you can"). Ross was then trying to project the CSO on a state-wide basis. It was this meeting which first involved

[9] *Prejudice: Japanese-Americans, Symbol of Racial Intolerance*, 1944, re-issued in 1971.

Chavez in organizational activities. For four months the two of them worked in the barrio, mostly at nights. Gifted as he is, Chavez could not have had a better instructor in the delicate art of what to do and what not to do in trying to get people to act in their own self interest. Later, on March 15, 1954, Ross persuaded Alinsky to take Chavez on as an organizer and from then until 1958 Ross and Chavez carried the CSO movement into every large concentration of Mexican-Americans in California and Arizona. Eventually there were 35 chapters which then combined to form the National CSO which hired its own full-time secretary.

Toward the end of 1958, the Packing House Workers decided to try to organize farm workers through the agency of the National CSO and provided a grant of $20,000 with the understanding that Chavez would direct an organizing effort in Oxnard, California. Ralph Helstein, then president of the Packing House Workers — a union that he had organized — is a great friend of his fellow Chicagoan, Saul Alinsky, and both are old friends of mine. The strategy was to organize shed workers first and then to organize field workers. But farm workers, as Chavez learned, must organize themselves; they cannot be organized from the outside, so to speak. All the same Helstein, a good and gallant man, wanted to help and was able to induce the Packing House Workers to spend a large sum in this effort during the period from 1954 to 1961. There were some minor victories but, in general, the effort did not succeed. But it gave Chavez some first-hand trade-union organizing experience. Later, in 1960, he became director of the CSO and over the next two years tried to persuade its leaders that the organization should turn its full attention to the organization of farm workers. But he could not convince them and so he resigned in

April, 1962, and set out, with his rather meager savings, and with a wife and family to support, to build an organization of farm workers — from the ground up, without outside direction or assistance. He had enough experience by then to know that it would be folly to lead farm workers into a series of desperate strikes for which they were not prepared. So he spent three years in a slow and patient effort to build an organization. The first meeting of the organization, known as the National Farm Workers Association, was held in Fresno, California, in September 1962. By that time the movement had a credit union, a death benefit plan, a service center, and a weekly newspaper *El Malcriado* ("The Bad Boy").

Somewhat later the Filipino grape workers, members of the Agricultural Workers Organizing Committee (AFL-CIO) went on strike. Chavez would have been wary about calling a strike of this magnitude but once the Filipinos had gone on strike, the NFWA was virtually forced to join in. Thus began one of the largest, longest, and best reported farm labor strikes. It started in September, 1965, and did not terminate until 1970. In large part because of Chavez' talents as a leader, the strike quickly became, and remained, a national news story. It received strong support from the churches, from student activists, from a few politicians (Robert Kennedy was one), and from some trade union leaders, notably Walter Reuther. Some of the fervor of the civil rights movement and the "war on poverty" entered into the strike. The fact that Public Law 78 had expired at the end of 1964 helped even though wetback labor was still coming in. On March 17, 1966, Chavez — influenced no doubt by the civil rights movement — started out on the well-publicized march to Sacramento, which helped to keep the story of the strike alive and on the front pages. His fast, which began on February 14, 1968, had much the same effect and it also was influential in keeping the strike non-violent. The boycott of table grapes, which began in New York in January 1968, was skillfully conducted and was perhaps the decisive factor. Throughout this long struggle, Chavez' continued emphasis on non-violence was tactically wise and drew — and held — support which might have quickly dropped off had the union indulged in violence. All in all, the grape strike was a remarkable victory and marked the end of yet another chapter in the turbulent farm labor history of California.

So now what next? Are there still more chapters to come? Another chapter is unfolding now but it is difficult to see what role farm labor will play in it. Saul Alinsky puts his finger on the nub of the problem: "Let's face it," he told John Gregory Dunne, "the problem of the Mexican-Americans is an urban problem. There's one acid question you've got to ask yourself before you get involved in something like this: 'If we succeed, what have we got after we got it?' With the farm workers, you don't have much. It's like fighting on a constantly disintegrating bed of sand. The big problem is automation. In ten years, mechanization will make the historical farm workers obsolete. So what you've got to do is to retrain the Mexican-Americans for urban living." [10] Mechanization is indeed proceeding at a fast pace. Table grapes are, so to speak, one of the remaining islands of hand labor, but there are not too many. Curtis J. Sitomer, writing in the Christian Science *Monitor* (May 24, 1968) presents a picture of California agriculture in the future: "harvested by automation, and shipped, marketed and sold by ultramodern, perhaps data-processed, methods." Such projections should be taken with a grain of salt because so many un-

[10] Dunne, supra, p. 170.

expected developments can, and usually do, intervene. But the trends foreshadowed in *Factories in the Field* have continued in the last three decades and the end is not in sight.

Since 1939, of course, "factory farming" has become "agribusiness." The big farm factories I knew were, for the most part, just what they appeared to be: Large-scale corporate farms owned and directed by a single corporate ownership. Now the conglomerates have become actively interested in "farming" and may transform our concepts of it. Big corporate empires such as Purex, United Brands, Tenneco, Gulf & Western, Penn Central, W. R. Grace, Del Monte, Getty Oil, Montsanto, Union Carbide, Kaiser Aluminum, Aetna Life, Boeing, Dow Chemical and American Cyanamid have their eyes on "farming." [11] At the same time the number of farms in California has declined from 123,000 in 1954 to about 65,000 in 1969 (the same trend is reflected nationally). [12] Indeed the California story is being repeated nationally. In the United States the total farm population has decreased from more than 15 million in 1960 to about 10 million in 1968. An estimated 20 million persons have moved from farms and small towns to the cities since 1950. Today 70 per cent of the nation's population lives on 1 per cent of the land. In California urban expansion is forcing the sale of some of the best farm lands to subdividers and urban developers. On the national scene, the drain from rural areas has reached the point where thousands of towns and villages in the Mississippi Valley and the Rocky Mountain area no longer can function as economic units. [13] And the southern Great Plains is once again visited with dust and drought, the worst affliction of its kind

[11] *The New Republic*, June 22, 1971, p. 22.
[12] *Illinois Business Review*, September, 1969.
[13] *Life*, June 25, 1971 .

since the 1930s and a reminder that nature has not changed much since the Joads set out for California, "the promised land."

What all of this may mean is that the old-style migratory farm worker belongs to the past. His passing from the scene may have been symbolized by the Yuba City (California) tragedies where the number of bodies now recovered totals twenty-five. These men — all of them — were successors to a long line of single men, lonely, destitute, virtually anonymous, who were recruited by labor contractors each morning during the season from the skid-row sections of such towns as Marysville and Stockton to pick this crop or that. Most of the Yuba City dead could not be identified. They had no last known addresses and, in fact, their disappearances had not been noticed. The San Francisco *Chronicle* put the right headline on the story: "*Deaths of No One in Particular.*" They were no one in particular — just farm workers. But just think of the long line — the thousands on thousands of such workers — who have passed through those California skid-rows down the years. A pamphlet by Morrison I. Swift, "What a Tramp Learns in California," published in 1896, shows clearly enough that the Yuba City tragedies have a history. And one can press the inquiry back a step further. The San Francisco *Chronicle* of Sept. 8, 1875, wrote of farm laborers who seem to "have been thrown outside of social influence, and even if at the outset possessing good impulses and habits, they became, in a short time, desperate, degraded, or criminal and perhaps all three."

But regardless of what the next chapter brings, what Chavez and his farm workers have accomplished will not be undone. They have put an end once and for all to the desperate anonymity of "the farm worker." At the end of a long succession, they have forced a recognition of the fact that they too belong to the society along with farm labor contractors, shipper-growers, and agribiz tycoons. Their accomplishment is their own and theirs is the credit for it. They have finally forced a recognition of their worth and dignity and the importance of their contribution. Delano will long remain a symbol of what human effort and determination can accomplish against even the heaviest odds. As Chavez has written: "People are not going to turn back now. The poor are on the march: black, brown, red, everyone, whites included. We are now in the midst of the biggest revolution this country has ever known. It really doesn't matter, in the final analysis, how powerful we are, how many boycotts we win, how many growers sign up, or how much political clout we possess, if in the process we forget whom we are serving. We must never forget that the human element is the most important thing we have — if we get away from this, we are certain to fail."[14] Somehow one has a feeling that the farm workers will not fail because they will not forget.

CAREY MCWILLIAMS

New York, July 4, 1971.

[14] Day, supra, introduction.

# THE NOMAD HARVESTERS
### by
### *Marie De L. Welch*

The nomads had been the followers of flocks and herds,
Or the wilder men, the hunters, the raiders.
The harvesters had been the men of homes.

But ours is a land of nomad harvesters.
They till no ground, take no rest, are homed nowhere.
Travel with the warmth, rest in the warmth never;
Pick lettuce in the green season in the flats by the sea.
Lean, follow the ripening, homeless, send the harvest home,
Pick cherries in the amber valleys in tenderest summer.
Rest nowhere, share in no harvest;
Pick grapes in the red vineyards in the low blue hills.
Camp in the ditches at the edge of beauty.

They are a great band, they move in thousands;
Move and pause and move on.
They turn to the ripening, follow the peaks of seasons,
Gather the fruit and leave it and move on.
Ours is a land of nomad harvesters,
Men of no root, no ground, no house, no rest;
They follow the ripening, gather the ripeness,
Rest never, ripen never,
Move and pause and move on.

# FACTORIES IN THE FIELD

## CHAPTER I

# INTRODUCTION

IN THE saga of the States the chapter that is California has long fascinated the credulous and charmed the romantic. A fabled land, California, rich in the stuff of which legends are made. Proverbially it is a wealthy and indolent province, blessed with a miraculous climate and steeped in beauty. Here gold was discovered and the colorful pageant of '49 was enacted. The legends about this land at the rainbow's end thrilled a nation for decades. Even before the discovery of gold, California was the scene of a favorite chapter: the idyllic period of Spanish occupation "before the gringos came." Here, according to the fable, handsome Spanish grandees enjoyed a somnolent existence for generations and monks, famous for their courage and benevolence, trekked up and down "the fortune coast" founding missions, converting the Indians, creating the society of Alta California. Here, reads the fable, life has always been easier and abundance an acknowledged historical fact. Something of this legend, embellished by the fantasies of latter-day fabulists, has survived into the present. But there has long existed another California — a hidden California. Its tradition parallels the legend. The tradition dates from the ugly, but not generally known, records of Indian exploitation; it carries through the period of the ruthless American occupation; and, occasionally, it echoes in the violent history of racial exploitation which has long existed in the State. This book is designed as a segment — one of the chapters — in this hidden history. It is intended as a guide to the social history of California, an attempt to dispel a few of the illusions and to focus attention on certain unpleasant realities. It deals with the hidden history of the State's first industry, agriculture, and with the workers who have contributed to its establishment. "Agriculture" is a quiet word, but, in California, it has taken on new meaning and novel implications.

There is a surface placidity about the great inland farm valleys of California that is as deceptive as the legends in the books. Travelers along the highways pass through orchards that seem literally measureless and gaze upon vast tracts of farm land stretching away on either side of the road to the distant foothills, yet, curiously enough, there seem to be no farms in the accepted sense. One looks in vain for the incidents of rural life: the schoolhouse on the hilltop, the comfortable homes, the compact and easy indolence of the countryside. Where are the farmers? Where are the farmhouses? Occasionally the highway passes within view of a row of barracklike shacks which the traveler mistakenly identifies as, perhaps, the hovels of section hands. In the harvest seasons, the orchards are peopled with thousands of workers; and, in the great fields, an army of pickers can be seen trudging along, in the dazzling heat, in the wake of a machine. The impression gained is one of vast agricultural domains, huge orchard and garden estates, without permanent occupants.

These amazingly rich agricultural valleys — Imperial Valley, a vast truck garden reclaimed from the desert; the great San Joaquin Valley, an empire in itself; and the Valley of the Sacramento — withhold many secrets from a casual inspection. The richness of the soil and its staggering productivity, for example, are not readily apparent. Here a new type of agriculture has been created: large-scale, intensive, diversified, mechanized. The story of its evolution, quite apart from social implications, is a record of remarkable technical achievement. Because of peculiar soil and climatic conditions — the great variety of soils and the division of the seasons into two periods: a short rainy season and a long stretch of warm and rainless and sun-drenched days — it has been possible in California to evolve an agricultural economy without parallel in the United States. Over one hundred and eighty specialty crops are produced in the State. Crops are maturing, in some sections, throughout the year, a circumstance that has given rise to the boast of the agricultural industrialists that "we're green the year round." In 1929, California shipped 240,000 carloads of perishable agricultural products; today the production is much greater. The value of these products has risen steadily until today the annual value of agricultural production in California is close to a billion dollars. So far as fruits and vegetables are concerned, California could feed the nation. This great industry, moreover, has been created in a remarkably short period. It is a created industry and one that is, to a large degree, artificial. Deserts have been changed into orchards; wastelands and sloughs have been converted into gardens. California agriculture is a forced plant — the product of irrigation. Fifty years ago the great farm valleys were wastelands and deserts into whose reclamation has gone untold human suffering. Today it is impossible to visit these valleys without gaining an impression of vast power, of immense potentialities, and of the dramatic conflict between man and nature. But, beneath this surface conflict, which is everywhere apparent, are social conflicts no less dramatic and no less impressive.

Occasionally the urban Californian, the city dweller, catches an echo of these underlying social conflicts. From time to time, he reads in the newspapers strange stories about bloody riots, about great strikes, of fiery crosses burning on hilltops, of thousands of migratory workers starving in the off seasons, of vigilante terror. Although these stories have appeared with increasing frequency of late years, the city dweller is inclined to regard them as mere aberrations of the "heat counties" and to forget them, but gradually the State and the nation have become vaguely aware that California agriculture is charged with social dynamite. Eastern reporters have come out of Imperial Valley breathless with stories of beatings, violence, and intimidation. Social workers, intrigued by reports of unbelievable human misery, have gone on slumming expeditions along the canal banks and have penetrated into the shantytowns and jungle camps. Occasionally the entire State has been shocked by incidents of inexplicable wholesale violence. But, in general, the tendency has been to engage in excited moralization and to ignore the facts, so that the real story has not been told. Back of the surface manifestations of violence and unrest in California farm labor is a long and complicated history. To understand why the valleys are made up of large feudal empires; to know why it is that farming has been replaced by industrialized agriculture, the farm by the farm factory; to realize what is back of the terror and violence which breaks out periodically in the farm valleys, it is necessary to know something of the social history of California. It is this history which the latter-day commentators, busy recording impressions and giving vent to their indignation, have largely ignored.

It is, in many respects, a melodramatic history, a story of theft, fraud, violence and exploitation. It completely belies the sense of peace and lassitude that seems to hover over rural California. It is a story of nearly seventy years' exploitation of minority racial and other groups by a powerful clique of landowners whose power is based upon an anachronistic system of landownership dating from the creation, during Spanish rule, of feudalistic patterns of ownership and control. The most remarkable single circumstance pertaining to the entire record is the unbroken continuity of control. The exploitation of farm labor in California, which is one of the ugliest chapters in the history of American industry, is as old as the system of landownership of which it is a part. Time has merely tightened the system of ownership and control and furthered the degradation of farm labor. As far as the vast army of workers who operate these great tracts are concerned, their plight is nearly as wretched today as it was thirty years ago.

In all America it would be difficult to find a parallel for this strange army in tatters. It numbers 200,000 workers and a more motley crew was never assembled in this country by a great industry. Sources of cheap labor in China, Japan, the Philippine Islands, Puerto Rico, Mexico, the Deep South, and Europe have been generously tapped to recruit its ever-expanding ranks. As one contingent of recruits after the other has been exhausted, or has mutinied, others have been assembled to take their places. Although the army has been made up of different races, as conditions have changed and new circumstances arisen, it has always functioned as an army. It is an army that marches from crop to crop. Its equipment is negligible, a few pots and pans, and its quarters unenviable. It is supported by a vast horde of camp followers, mostly pregnant women, diseased children, and fleabitten dogs. Its transport consists of a fleet of ancient and battered Model T Fords and similar equipage. No one has ever been able to fathom the mystery of how this army supports itself or how it has continued to survive. It has had many savage encounters, with drought and floods and disease; and, occasionally, it has fought in engagements that can hardly be called sham battles, as its casualties have been heavy. Today the army has many new faces as recruits have swarmed in from the dust-bowl area eager to enlist for the duration of the crops at starvation wages. But, in substance, it is the same army that has followed the crops since 1870.

To those who have found the patterns of social behavior in California somewhat enigmatic, the story of this strange migratory army should be illuminating. It is a story with many ramifications. It is impossible, for example, to understand the early race riots, the fierce anti-Chinese campaigns of the seventies and nineties, and the hysterical "yellow peril" agitation against the Japanese at a later date, apart from a close study of the changing patterns of agricultural operations in the State. It is the farm-labor history of California that illuminates these social problems and that places them in proper perspective, and it is precisely this history that has remained unwritten and, in large part, unknown. Labor history in general has a tendency to remain unwritten, but the story of farm labor in California has been almost wholly neglected. To get at the facts, it is necessary to go back to contemporary newspaper files, to the early reports and documents, and, from this starting point, to piece together the fragments of a rich and dramatic story. It is likewise impossible to understand the social phenomenon known as "vigilantism" — a peculiarly Californian phenomenon — without some knowledge of the absorbing history of farm labor in the State. Here again it is necessary to push aside the official histories and to examine the facts. Vigilantism is not a peculiarity of the California climate. Its roots are to be found in the history of farm labor in the State.

Not only are the ramifications of this history interesting and varied, but its implications, with respect to the future, are of the utmost importance. California, in these critical times, should be the subject of close scrutiny. Here the mechanism of fascist control has been carried to further lengths than elsewhere in America; and both the reasons for this development, and the possibility of its still further extension, are, I believe, set forth in the following pages. On several occasions in the past serious riots, scarcely distinguishable from a variety of civil warfare, have swept the farm valleys of California. Today some 200,000 migratory workers, trapped in the State, eke out a miserable existence, intimidated by their employers, homeless, starving, destitute. Today they are restless but quiet; tomorrow they may be rebellious. Before these workers can achieve a solution of the problems facing them, they will have to work a revolution in California landownership and in the methods of agricultural operations which now prevail. When these circumstances are considered in the light of the entire background of farm labor in California, the necessity for a study of this character is immediately apparent.

Before proceeding with a study of landownership in California, a word of explanation is probably advisable. In the summer of 1935, in company with Herbert Klein, I made a trip through the San Joaquin Valley, inspecting some of the ranches, talking with workers, interviewing organizers who had been active in the strikes of 1933, and gathering material for a series of articles on farm labor. In collaboration with Mr. Klein, I wrote one article which appeared in *The Nation*; and, later, in March and April, 1936, six articles, presenting the work of such research and investigation as we had made up to that time, appeared in the *Pacific Weekly*, under the general title of "Factories in the Field." The present work, however, is based upon entirely new research. I think it should also be stated that the manuscript for this volume was forwarded to the publishers prior to the time that Mr. John Steinbeck's novel, *Grapes of Wrath*, was published. This fact will account for the circumstance that no reference is made in the text to Mr. Steinbeck's excellent book. It should also be pointed out that the research for *Factories in the Field* was concluded independently of the thoroughgoing research on migratory labor that has been performed by the Federal Writers' Project, Oakland, California. As my manuscript was finished prior to the time that I first inspected or knew of the Oakland Project, it was not possible for me to go over the material that the staff of the Project has so painstakingly assembled.

## CHAPTER II

## LAND MONOPOLIZATION

### 1. The Gold Rush Ends

BY 1860 the gold rush was at an end. To be sure, mining remained active; claims were discovered; a king's ransom continued to pour into San Francisco. But after 1860 the business of mining became not any man's game but the prerogative of those with fortunes large enough to enable them to battle in the arena of the Titans — Sharon, Flood, Tevis, Ralston, Sutro. As a consequence something of a recession set in and thousands of "miners" — mostly Eastern and Middle Western farmers — began to look about for land. The population of the State had increased from 92,000 in 1850 to 380,000 in 1860, and an active demand for locally grown food products had arisen. Later, in 1869, the transcontinental railroad was completed and farming for out-of-State shipment became feasible. Many of the Forty-Niners began to realize that California was primarily an agricultural state, a farming territory of vast potentialities. Few of them realized, however, the extent of the State's agricultural resources. Few of them realized, for example, that, in the San Joaquin Valley and the Sacramento Delta, they gazed upon lands of almost fabulous fertility, lands that, in truth, can only be compared with those of the Nile

Valley and the other great river-valley gardens of the world. But, beginning with 1860, the expatriated Easterners and Middle Westerners began to leave the creek beds and badly scarred hillsides of the Mother Lode and to look about for farms. There was land to burn: untenanted, undeveloped, unoccupied. From 1860 to 1870 the settlers were engaged in the business of trying to occupy this land, of attempting to find farms. But, with a great wave of indignation, they began to discover, by 1870, that, just as they had been pushed out of the Mother Lode by a few mining barons, so they were being excluded from the great farming empire that was California. In 1863 Hittell pointed out that of 39,000,000 tillable acres in the State, only 1,000,000 or less were in cultivation. Part of this tillable acreage was not readily accessible; it was subject, also, to other drawbacks; but the richness of the general farming domain was echoed in every survey of the period. Yet, as early as 1860, the good lands were pre-empted. What had happened to the land during that feverish decade from 1850 to 1860? What forces blocked its settlement and improvement?

## 2. Grants That Float

In a remarkably shrewd tract published in 1871, Henry George referred to the Mexican land grants in California as "a history of greed, of perjury, of corruption, of spoliation and high-handed robbery for which it will be difficult to find a parallel." The statement is conservative. Through the instrumentality of the Mexican land grants the colonial character of landownership in Spanish-California was carried over, and actually extended, after the American occupation. By the terms of the cession of California to the United States it was provided that previously issued Mexican land grants would be respected. Under Spanish rule only about thirty land grants had been made, but, in 1846, when the United States took possession, over eight million acres of California land were held by some eight hundred Mexican grantees. The connivers, Mexican and American, had rushed through huge grants on the eve of American occupation. Most of these grants were vague, running merely for so many leagues within certain natural boundaries, and, in the confusion of the period, they were imperfectly registered. Many of the grants had never been surveyed, and thus the bars were down for all manner of fraud. Speculators emerged from dusty archives with amazing documents. The grants, purporting to be conveyed by these documents, assumed all sorts of fantastic shapes — for the purpose of roping in the improvements of settlers and the best land. George described one of these grants as looking, on the map, like a tarantula. For thirty years the land titles of the State were involved in litigation, both in the State and Federal courts, over disputes which arose in connection with these grants. The owner of the grant, usually by assignment from a Mexican settler who had sold an empire for little or nothing, would sit idly by while settlers entered upon the grant and made extensive improvements. He would then come forward with his grant, usually forged, ask for its confirmation, and then evict the settlers. Although most of these grants were known to be fraudulent, and have since been acknowledged as such, the majority of them were confirmed by the courts.

The brigandage was, indeed, awful to behold. John

Charles Frémont, patron saint of California, had a Mexican grant re-surveyed in such a manner that it included, within its bounds, the valuable Ophir mine upon which an English company had spent over $100,000 for improvements after repeated assurances from the owner of the grant that no claim was made to the mine. A survey of Los Nogales grant was made in 1861, under a decree for one league of land and no more, but a new survey was immediately pushed through for 11,000 acres. In surveying grants after the American occupation, the surveys were habitually for an area vastly in excess of the original grant and the courts frequently confirmed the survey for an area which included the mysterious accretion. In Santa Barbara one José Dominguez sold a Mexican grant for one dollar. A speculator later petitioned Congress in the name of Dominguez — although Dominguez swore he never signed the petition — to confirm the grant for 208,742 acres (the celebrated Los Prietos Y Najalayegua rancho case). This was a typical California bargain of the time: one dollar for 208,742 acres of land. At one time a rake by the name of Limantour, under the guise of a bogus Mexican grant, laid claim to the entire city of San Francisco and came very nearly making his claim good. In court decisions, Government reports, and later investigations the story of these Mexican grants has been told in detail and the processes by which most of the grants were validated have been repeatedly denounced as fraudulent,[1] yet the monopolistic character of land ownership in California today is, in large part, based upon these very grants.

[1] See *Fraudulent California Land Grants*, 1926, by Clinton Johnson; Report of the Commissioners of the General Land Office, 1885.

The point about the Mexican land grants is, however, not that settlers were swindled and huge profits made, but that the grants were not broken up. These vast feudal holdings, which should have been purchased by the Government and held as part of the public domain, were never disrupted. Some of them are intact to this day. The ownership changed from Mexican grantee to American capitalist; the grant, as such, remained. This factor has had important social consequences in California. In 1919, W. J. Ghent made a survey of large landholdings in Southern California and found that "the dominant form of large holdings is the tract which has held the greater part of its boundaries undisturbed from Mexican times . . . the large holdings in Southern California are an inheritance from Spanish-Mexican times."

In almost any direction, then, that the prospective farmer turned in California in 1860, he ran into a Mexican land grant. The State was covered with them: vast principalities, embracing millions of acres of the best lands in the State (the bona fide grants alone embraced between nine and ten million acres), with water, timber, and excellent resources, miniature self-contained empires. The monopolization of land in California through the medium of the forged, bogus, or "floating" Mexican land grant was, moreover, but one of the means by which ownership was centralized and the settler excluded.

### 3. The Railroad Grants

By 1870 the railroads held some 20,000,000 acres of land in California. This land was granted, of course, in the form of alternate sections of Government land along the various rights of way, but the justification, if any, for the grants was very slight, for, in most cases, the Government had made actual cash subsidies to the railroads in amounts that were more than adequate for all purposes. Here, again, the uncertainty of the grant opened the door to the grossest fraud. Settlers would occupy and improve land only to discover that it was located on one of the unsurveyed alternate sections belonging to the railroad. In fact, the railroad actually encouraged such mistaken settlement, for the purpose of appropriating the improvements. In one famous instance, the Mussel Slough affair, the settlers rebelled against the railroad and something very like civil war resulted. In 1871 a group of settlers, at the direct invitation of the Southern Pacific Railroad, settled in the San Joaquin Valley. Their occupancy was known to the railroad. Once the land was sufficiently improved, however, the Southern Pacific stepped in and claimed the land and ordered a wholesale eviction of the settlers. A fight occurred, as a consequence, at a place called Mussel Slough, in which seven men were killed: five ranchers and two deputy marshals. Seventeen leaders of the Settlers Land League, an organization formed to protect the rights of the settlers, were indicted and convicted, although they had no participation in the fight whatever, their "guilt" being that of "conspirators." On one petition sent to President Hayes in Washington asking for a pardon for these men, 47,000 names appeared, yet, as one of the leaders remarked at the time, "not one of these petitions was considered any more than if it had been a piece of blank brown paper." And, of course, the railroad, which had promised in its prospectuses to sell the land to the settlers for $2.50 an acre, if they would come to the San Joaquin Valley and improve the land, forced these same settlers, in the long run, to pay a hundred times this amount and then, as a final irony, robbed them, by exorbitant freight rates, for the next fifty years. This story is part of the social history of California and is chronicled in Frank Norris' *The Octopus*, which follows, in fairly close detail, the history of the struggle against the Southern Pacific in California.[2] There is no more shameful chapter in the history of corporate swindling in the United States than this story. For every dollar that the Southern Pacific took from the settlers on its lands, it took a thousand dollars from the people of the State. It took the Californians fifty years to break the dominance of the Southern Pacific over the State Government, and one of the important props, at all times, of the railroad's great power was its landownership within the State. The Ghent survey, above referred to, shows that in 1919 the Southern Pacific was still the chief landowner in the State, owning 2,598,775 acres in Southern California alone, including 642,246 acres in one county.

It did not take the settlers long to discover, in 1860, that approximately 16 per cent of the entire area of land owned by the Government in California, which would otherwise have been open for settlement, had been given to the railroads, and that, if they wished to settle on this land, they would have to buy it from the railroads, at the latter's terms, or else move on.

[2] See, also, a forgotten novel of California life by Josiah Royce: *The Feud of Oakville Creek*.

### 4. Land Speculation

The process of land monopolization in California was given early impetus by a carelessly conceived State land policy, by the wholesale corruption of State land officials, and through the instrumentality of so-called "scrip locations."

The management of State lands was notoriously wasteful after the admission of California to the Union. For example, the Federal Government granted to the State about 3,381,-691 acres of swamp land; and, in addition, about 7,421,804 acres of general Government land within the State. "These large donations," wrote George, "have proved an evil rather than a benefit to the people of California; for in disposing of them, the State has given even greater facilities for monopoly than has the Federal Government." The grant of swamp land was vague: it depended upon the nature of the land, i.e. whether it was in fact swamp land. Speculators purchased swamp land from the State for virtually nothing — a dollar an acre and less — nor was there any limitation on the amount of swamp land one man might acquire. By 1866 most of this swamp land had been given away, yielding the State practically nothing, and by this means speculators were able to monopolize thousands of acres of the most valuable lands in California, and, of course, to rob settlers.

The greediness of these speculators almost exceeds comprehension. For example, one of them contended that Sierra Valley in Plumas County, in the heart of the Sierra Mountains, was "swamp" land. Similarly a beautiful 46,000-acre tract near Sacramento was seized upon as falling within this classification, and, in respect to general lands donated by the Federal Government, the State was a party to the grossest frauds worked on settlers by a small group of speculators. One member of this group acquired title to the town of Amador, and all improvements, including the valuable Keystone Mine, because of technical deficiencies in the State act which were in large part attributable to the administrators of the act. Open brigandage was frequently practised. In Lake County one firm seized 28,000 acres of Government land, open by the laws of the United States to pre-emption by actual settlers, enclosed it by a board fence, and held it by armed force until the compliant State courts upheld its title. In less than a decade most of the Government land had been given away, including all of the swamp lands, some of which are today the most valuable farming properties in the State. In the course of a few years, it became apparent that ownership of this vast domain had become concentrated in the hands of a few large speculators. In the whole sickening story of land fraud in the United States there is no more sordid chapter than the methods by which, in less than a decade, California and its settlers were robbed of millions of acres of valuable land, land intended for individual settlement, for homes and farms. By 1871 George could write that "the land of California is already to a great extent monopolized by a few individuals, who hold thousands and hundreds of thousands of acres apiece. Across many of these vast estates a strong horse cannot gallop in a day, and one may travel for miles and miles over fertile ground where no plough has ever struck, but which is all owned," and "on which no settler can come to make

himself a home, unless he pays such tribute as the lord of
the domain chooses to exact."

### 5.  Who Got the Land?

Who were the beneficiaries of this largess? In 1871, 516
men in California owned 8,685,439 acres of land; in Fresno
County, 48 owners had more than 79,000 acres each. Sixteen men in California each controlled 84 square miles of
land. By taking the Government grant away from his own
railroad company and then transferring the road itself to
another concern, minus the grant, McLaughlin of the Western Pacific Railway managed to grab about 400,000 acres
for himself. William S. Chapman, the celebrated "scrip land
speculator," acquired some 350,000 acres by buying Half
Breed scrip, issued by the Government in exchange for
Indian lands, which gave the holder the right to select lands
elsewhere in the Government domain; some of this scrip
was purchased by Chapman, and others, on the basis of
$.50 and $1.25 an acre. In 1871 it was revealed that ex-State
Surveyor General Houghton had emerged from office with
350,000 acres of land. Ex-United States Surveyor General
Beale had about 300,000 acres, a large part of it being the
famous Tejon Ranch now owned by Mr. Harry Chandler,
publisher of the *Los Angeles Times*. Miller and Lux, of
whom more later, owned 450,000 acres in 1871. Other individual listings in the 1871 report of the Board of Equaliza-
tion are: Bixby, Flint & Co., 200,000 acres; George W.
Robert & Co., 120,000 acres; Isaac Friedlander, 100,000
acres; Throckmorton, 146,000 acres; the Murphy family, in
Santa Clara, 150,000 acres; John Foster of Los Angeles,

120,000 acres; Thomas Fowler, 200,000 acres in Fresno, Tulare, and Kern Counties; Abel Stearns, of Los Angeles, 200,000 acres. "Our land system," said Governor Haight, "seems to be mainly framed to facilitate the acquisition of large blocks of land by capitalists or corporations either as donations or at nominal prices." Nor does the brief listing of holdings which I have given include the enormous railroad grants. The fact that a few individuals swindled the State out of most of its best land for nominal prices would, of itself, be interesting but not particularly significant, if these holdings had ever been broken up and sold. But such has not been the case. The huge holdings, acquired in the manner I have indicated, are, in most cases, still intact. In 1919, W. J. Ghent, in the survey mentioned above, found that in Southern California most of the large holdings were still concentrated in a few hands. Paul Taylor, writing in 1935, states that "Of all farms in the United States whose product is valued at $30,000 or above, nearly 37 per cent are found in our own State. California has within its borders 30 per cent of the large-scale cotton farms of the country, 41 per cent of the large-scale dairy farms, 44 per cent of the large-scale general farms, 53 per cent of the large-scale poultry farms, and 60 per cent of the large-scale fruit farms of the United States."

The ownership patterns established by force and fraud in the decade from 1860 to 1870 have become fixed; the social structure of the State is, in large part, based upon these patterns. California more than once has been referred to as a colonial empire, and, by and large, the description is accurate. The irrational character of California agriculture — its topheaviness and lack of balance; its social irresponsibility (of which more later) — may be traced to the fact that the lands of the State were monopolized before they were settled, that a few individuals and concerns got possession of the agricultural resources of the State at the very moment when the State was thrown open for settlement and that the types of ownership thus established have persisted. The ownership itself has changed, but the fact of ownership remains. The character of farm ownership, established at the outset, is at the root of the problem of farm labor in California and has long been recognized, guardedly, as the key issue involved. "In California," wrote Walter V. Woehlke, in *Sunset Magazine*, October, 1920, "the safety valve of free land or cheap land became useless long before it quit functioning in the other Far Western states. Wheat and cattle barons controlled the bulk of the fertile land in large tracts, having acquired their principalities through purchase of the old Spanish grants or through evasion of the laws protecting the public domain." The land barons refused to sell, in many cases, and thus there was developed "a class of landless tenants and drifting homeless farm laborers before the last of the Dakota and Nebraska homestead land had been pre-empted." The process of land monopolization in California, wrote one observer, was achieved with "peculiar directness," not by evolution or change in the forms of ownership, but at the outset, by acquisition.

What were the immediate consequences of the process of land monopolization in California? Certain social consequences have at all times been apparent. In the first place, there is the ugly fact of expropriation. Literally thousands of settlers were robbed of their lands by trickery of one kind or another; and the improvements which they had made were appropriated, and they themselves were forced out of ownership, either to become tenants or to move on. The hardship and havoc worked in this manner is reflected in the bitter landlaw reform agitation of the seventies. "If 600 men," wrote an editorial writer in the *Sacramento Union*, "out of 600,000 own half the land in this State, refusing to partition it out and sell it at reasonable rates, and conspiring from year to year to prevent its being taxed so as to yield its share of the burdens of government, nothing is clearer to our minds than that the 599,400 of landless citizens and small and overtaxed farmers have the right to lay such taxes upon the estates of the land monopolists as will compel them either to support the Government or to divide up and sell their vast estates." Provisions along this line were actually written into the "radical" constitution of 1879, but were soon nullified. Nor were the great estates ever taxed: forty ranchos in San Diego, including over 600,000 acres of land, were taxed for years at seventy-five cents an acre. The whole problem can be summarized in one statement: In 1870, 1/500 of the population of California owned one half or more of the available agricultural lands of the State. Although the squatters and settlers protested and even rioted, they accomplished little.[3] "There is no state in the Union," wrote George, "in which settlers in good faith have been so persecuted, so robbed, as in California. Men have grown rich, and men still make a regular business of blackmailing settlers upon public land, or of

[3] For a rather romantic version of the squatter riots, see a novel by Charles Duff Stuart, *Casa Grande*, 1906.

appropriating their homes, and this by power of the law and in the name of justice." It was not by chance that Henry George and his single-tax theory made their appearance in California. George knew something of land monopolization, and its social consequences, from firsthand observation.

Another consequence should be noted. The growth of the State, its quick and prosperous settlement, was seriously retarded by land monopolization. After 1860, and for years, residents complained of a "general stagnation" which had set in, robbing the great decade, 1850–1860, of its exceptional promise. Had there been any measure of democracy in land settlement, the brisk movement of '49 would have continued through the century. But a kind of dry rot set in after 1860. "The whole country is poverty-stricken," wrote one observer; "the farmers are shiftless, and crazy on wheat. I have seen farms cropped for eighteen years with wheat, and not a vine, tree, shrub or flower on the place. The roads are too wide, and are unworked, and a nest for noxious weeds. The effect of going through California is to make you wish to leave it, if you are poor and want to farm." "Californians," wrote Charles Howard Shinn, "were once the most magnificently liberal race of men on earth; now they are determined to become the most miserly." A blight had fallen on the State, the blight of monopolization.

Moreover, the wasteful character of California agriculture, a character which it still retains, was fixed by reason of the pattern of landownership. "California," wrote George in 1871, "is not a country of farms, but a country of plantations and estates. Agriculture is a speculation."

"California," wrote William Godwin Moody in 1880, "is noted for its great farms of tens of thousands of acres, and the great extent of its acres cultivated by tenantry." In 1871 George called attention to the typical California tenant: overworking the land, hiring cheap labor, neglecting the property, living in a hovel; and also to the California farmers, "the lords of California, lords as truly as ever were ribboned Dukes or belted Barons," who resided in San Francisco hotels and drove "spanking teams over the Cliff House road," and who spent most of their time in Europe. Nor has the pattern changed to any considerable extent. If anyone thinks the problem of migratory farm labor in California is a new problem, let him consult Henry George. Migratory labor, it has been said, is a result of the character of California agriculture, but the character of California agriculture is, in turn, a consequence of the type of land-ownership in California.

But listen to George (he is speaking of the farm laborers of California of 1871, the progenitors of the hordes of migratory workers today): "And over our ill-kept, shade-less, dusty roads, where a house is an unwonted landmark, and which run frequently for miles through the same man's land, plod the tramps, with blankets on back, the labourers of the California farmer, looking for work, in its seasons, or toiling back to the city when the ploughing is ended or the wheat crop is gathered." No one knows who these tramps were; they became a fixture of the California landscape and were accepted and taken for granted. Were they squatters or the sons of squatters? They came back year after year, these "blanket" or "bindle" stiffs, to work in the fields, and, after the season was over, they obligingly disappeared —

into the flophouses of San Francisco — to come back next season like so many ragged crows.

I could write a volume on the complacent acceptance of this army of workers — it has always been of army proportions — by the Californians. A theory was evolved at an early date to rationalize the existence of these countless tramps: They were "tramps," shiftless fellows who actually *preferred* "the open road" and the jolly camaraderie of the tramp jungle to a settled and decent life; chaps who adored lice and filth and vermin, and long marches (in pre-hitchhiking days) through scorchingly hot valleys, and the drizzle and cold of early fall rains. There was nothing you could do with these insouciant and light-hearted boys: you couldn't even pay them a decent wage for they would "drink it up right away." As for providing them with shelter or a bed — why, they loved the open air and would rather die than take a bath. The attitude I describe is not obsolescent: Responsible farm groups in California, at meetings which I have attended, have protested the installation of private privies and showers in labor camps on the ground that they are a needless luxury for the farm laborer.

Nor was Henry George the only observer to note the phenomenon of the California tramp. I quote from Stephen Powers' travel book, *Afoot and Alone* (1872): "One of the notable phenomena of California is the multitude of its tramps, the so-called blanket men. I seldom met less than a dozen or fifteen a day." Later he writes: "I did not see ten honest, hard-fisted farmers in my whole journey. There are plenty of city-haunting old bachelors and libertines, who own great ranches and lease them; and there are enough crammers of wheat, crammers of beans, crammers of mulberries, crammers of anything that will make their fortune in a year or two, and permit them to go and live and die in 'Frisco. Then, for laborers, there are runaway sailors, reformed street thieves, bankrupt German scene-painters, who carry sixty pounds of blankets, old soldiers who drink their employers' whiskey and fall into the ditch which they dug for a fence row; all looking for jobs." Powers, moreover, took a look into the future: "It is not unlikely," he wrote, "that within two centuries California will have a division of population something like that of ancient Greece, to-wit: merchants, artisans, and many great lords of the soil, in the cities; and in the country a kind of peasantry of goatherds, shepherds, tough, little black-haired, lazy farmers, and the like, to whom the cities will be unwelcome resorts." The details of the description are inaccurate, but the fact of the division — "great lords of the soil" on the one hand and "a kind of peasantry" on the other — is sound, and it has been achieved, not in two centuries, but within the last fifty years.

**CHAPTER III**

## *EMPIRES AND UTOPIAS*

A GENERAL description, such as I have given in the preceding chapter, of land monopolization in California, does not of itself convey an accurate impression of the social forces which provided the dynamics of centralization. To see these forces in actual operation, it is necessary to examine two samples of the process. The two case histories which I have selected for this purpose — the growth of the Miller and Lux empire and the utopian society known as the Kaweah Co-operative Colony — reveal the basic social pattern which obtained throughout the period of land monopolization. It should be pointed out, however, that both stories have more than illustrative significance. Henry Miller belongs in the saga of the Robber Barons. Rich in social significance, his career is almost without parallel in the history of land monopolization in America. He must be considered as a member of the great brotherhood of buccaneers: the Goulds, the Harrimans, the Astors, the Vanderbilts. The Kaweah Colony, on the other hand, forms an important chapter in the neglected history of early co-operative experiments in America. One of the largest and most significant co-operative colonies ever launched in the United States, it has been wholly ignored by the one or two historians who have concerned themselves with utopian experiments. Into the story of the cruel butchering of this genuinely progressive idea it is possible to read a phase of the social history, not only of California, but of the nation. If the Kaweah experiment had been permitted to succeed — the success of the colony was demonstrated at the time — the subsequent history of California might have been entirely different. Kaweah has, indeed, tragic significance. When the bright promise of this prophetic experiment was blotted out, the cause of Socialism in California was retarded for two generations.

### 1. Miller and Lux

Heinrich Alfred Kreiser, later to be known as Henry Miller, was born in Brackenheim, Germany, July 15, 1827. The son of a butcher, he quickly mastered the trade of his father which he was to follow intermittently throughout his career. A monument to the memory of this master butcher stands in Brackenheim today. He came to America in 1847, and, in 1850, an American acquaintance whose name was Henry Miller gave him a steamship ticket to California. Some sentiment seems to have attached to the name, for, in 1858, the legislature of the State of California formally changed the name of Heinrich Alfred Kreiser to Henry Miller.

Miller arrived in San Francisco with exactly six dollars in his pocket. At that time the mining excitement was at its height and the agricultural resources of the State remained unexplored. Miller's biographer [1] accurately describes the California of 1850 as "vast, undeveloped, agri-

[1] Edward F. Treadwell, *The Cattle King*, 1931.

culturally undiscovered, swamped in parts." For some years, Miller operated a butcher shop in San Francisco. Soon he began to buy and to sell cattle. As the community grew, the demand for native cattle increased. Looking about for cattle, Miller became interested in a great section of land known as the San Joaquin Valley. He began to make excursions into the valley on horseback from San Francisco, inspecting the land and interviewing its occupants. It was not long before he had purchased, at prices such as $1.15 an acre, most of the Spanish grants lying between San Francisco and the San Joaquin: Rancho Santa Rita (48,000 acres), Buri Buri, Salispuedes, Juristac, La Laguna, Bolsa de San Felipe, San Justo, Las Lomarias Muertas, Aromitas y Agua Caliente, San Antonio, San Lorenzo, Orestimba, Las Animas, and Tesquesquito. One of the numerous tricks used by Miller in acquiring his initial holdings was to buy out one or more of the Spanish heirs to whom ownership of a grant had descended by inheritance. Ownership of this interest gave Miller a right, as tenant in common, to range his cattle over the entire grant. For all practical purposes, he would soon be in complete possession of the grant and the heirs would be forced to sell out to him at his own price. The canniest of traders and a shrewd practical politician, he usually kept the local officials, particularly the county assessors, in his debt. He followed this method of indirect bribery for years, so that his vast holdings might escape taxation. On one occasion he was pulled about a great tract of land in an improvised boat, — with a team of horses hitched to it, — so that he might swear that the land was so-called "swamp land" and thus eligible for entry under the swamp-land legislation of the period. A large portion of his empire was acquired through the purchase of land scrip which he bought from land speculators who, a few years previously, had obtained the scrip when they, while in the employ of the United States Government as surveyors, had carved out vast estates for themselves. Through the purchase of land scrip at the ratio of $1.25 per acre, Miller was able to acquire thousands of acres of the richest land in the San Joaquin Valley, being assisted in these operations by his partner, Charles Lux, an Alsatian emigrant.

Most of Miller's vast holdings in the San Joaquin Valley were, at the time of their acquisition, arid lands. He watched, therefore, with great interest the formation of the San Joaquin and Kings River Canal Company in 1871, a company which had ambitious plans for irrigating a vast section of the valley. Miller co-operated with the company to a degree, but managed, in doing so, to get a contract for water, the right to all overflow waters (a rich concession), and other lucrative perquisites. Later, when the company was on the verge of bankruptcy and after it had invested an enormous amount of money in the project, Miller stepped in and purchased a controlling interest for one third of its original cost and thus found himself in control of a company which supplied water to over a hundred and fifty thousand acres of land most of which he owned or controlled. Stepping into control, as he did, during one of those periodic "depressions" which have proved so helpful to shrewd manipulators in this country, he was able to complete most of the canal work in the nineties at a time when labor could be hired for practically nothing. "Men were tramping the country," writes

Mr. Treadwell, "almost in armies looking for work. Miller employed as many as possible and did all the work possible during the period of low prices."

In most of his land-grabbing operations Miller, characteristically, was to be found in the secondary line of attack. He purchased land scrip from the original speculators who at least had gone to the trouble of having the land surveyed and located, and who had worked out the legal machinery for its acquisition. Miller, like the scavenger he was, merely stepped in and purchased the reward of their efforts at a low figure. Likewise with the swamp lands. He let others, for the most part, buy the land from the State, spend money and endless toil in an effort to improve it, and then he would intervene and purchase it from them for less than they had paid the State ($1.25 an acre) with the improvements added. By these methods, he acquired a continuous strip of land along the San Joaquin River over a hundred miles in length and a tract along the Kern River fifty miles in length containing over one hundred thousand acres. It was not long before Miller and Lux owned an empire in California as large as the Kingdom of Belgium. Whenever any question was raised which affected the title to the lands which they had acquired by such dubious methods, Miller and Lux never had the slightest difficulty in getting special acts passed by the Legislature validating their countless thefts.

Their spectacular march to empire was not, however, without opposition. Miller never had any difficulty with the small settlers — he brushed them aside like flies — but when Haggin and Tevis, a rival group of buccaneers, challenged his dominion over the entire San Joaquin Valley, a sensational war to the death was launched. The issue was joined over the question of water rights, with the entire San Joaquin Valley, an empire in itself, as the stakes. Both forces recruited armies to protect their canals and the valley was dotted with the camps and patrols of the rival claimants. The fight hinged on the question of whether the doctrine of the common law, riparian rights, i.e. the idea of water being attached to the land through which it runs, or the doctrine of appropriation, i.e. that the ownership of water should be influenced by considerations of its use, should prevail. The doctrine of riparian rights had arisen in England, where irrigation was not a problem, and its application to the arid lands of the West was a tragedy of legalistic confusion, but, after pushing the Supreme Court of California around for nearly a decade, Miller finally managed to have the doctrine of riparian rights upheld. In effect what happened was as follows: He lost the first decision; then prevailed upon the Supreme Court to reconsider its decision pending an election; and, finally, by a four to three decision, managed to make his will prevail. The decision was bitterly opposed by the people and it created a major scandal in California at the time, but Miller won out and his victory left him in undisputed mastery of an empire. The doctrine of appropriation was obviously the only sensible rule to insure the fairest and most economical and the fullest use of an inadequate water supply. It was based upon an equitable idea and a practical consideration. It is interesting to note that, after the lapse of over fifty years, it has come to be the established rule in California, the Miller and Lux decision having been modified a few years ago.

At the time the Miller and Lux decision prevailed, however, it operated to the decided advantage of those who had located land along river courses. The practical effect of the decision was to force hundreds of small landowners to sell to Miller at his own price or to make their peace with him, and he was about as easy to negotiate with as Bismarck, whom he knew and greatly admired. The decision, in effect, legalized theft and encouraged blackmail. It operated to take rights from one group, numerically the overwhelming majority of settlers, and to confer these rights, which were more valuable than the land itself, upon a single individual whose claim to them was socially and legally indefensible. The decision was unquestionably one of the chief weapons which Miller used in building up his immense holdings. But there is more to the story. Miller soon began to acquire large holdings in Nevada and there, since he was a later comer, so to speak, it suited his interests to advocate the doctrine of appropriation versus the doctrine of riparian rights. As part of his Nevada campaign, he obtained a decision from the United States Supreme Court to the effect that the State of Nevada had the power to determine questions of water rights involving streams which arose in California but which flowed through Nevada. Then he proceeded, in the Nevada courts, to have his rights validated on the theory of prior use or appropriation. Thus, by two utterly inconsistent positions, he was able to acquire and to consolidate his immense holdings in two States, using the doctrine of riparian rights in California and the doctrine of appropriation in Nevada, to force others to sell to him or to knuckle under to his power. If one looks at the substance, rather than the form, of these transactions, it is apparent that if Miller had used a shotgun instead of the courts, his methods could not have been more ruthless, or essentially more illegal, than they were.

The upshot of all this conniving was that by the turn of the century Miller and Lux owned over a million acres of land and over a million head of cattle. Miller liked to boast that he could ride on horseback from Canada to Mexico and sleep every night in one of his own ranches. Naturally, being the land baron that he was, Miller exerted great political power in California. He once told William Herrin, counsel for the Southern Pacific Railroad and political boss of California for fifty years, that "Bismarck got rid of all the little kings and princes in Germany, and I would like to get rid of all the little bosses in California." He was a close political ally of the Southern Pacific and the alliance was mutually profitable. Mr. Miller's sympathetic biographer sets forth the facts unblushingly: "The practice of giving rebates on trainload and carload lots made Henry Miller hundreds of thousands of dollars. No one profited more than he by rebates and drawbacks, which were in vogue in these years. The railroad was, in effect, his partner." Through the same political channels, Miller was able to keep his taxes at a ridiculously low level. "Thus did he build," writes Mr. Treadwell, "his business into the political institutions of the state. Assessors could not over-assess him. Legislatures could not impose excessive taxes upon him." And from this sordid story Mr. Treadwell, of course, draws the moral that private business is more efficient and economical than government operation. Yet, by his own statement, it was the State that gave Miller his

Workers on the "Dirty Plate Route" in California.

Blanket partitions used to form rooms in California labor camp.

Agricultural laborer's home near Fresno, California.

land; confirmed his thefts; insured his possessions; permitted a railroad to discriminate in his favor; failed to assess his property; and otherwise acted as a co-conspirator in the creation of his vast empire. Miller, in the words of his biographer, "passed to the great beyond" on October 14, 1916. Prior to his death, however, he had managed to beat the heirs of his deceased partner, Charles Lux, out of their interest in the estate.

Because of the vast extent of their holdings, and because of the fact that most of the early settlers had been squeezed out, Miller and Lux always had difficulty in recruiting labor. In a report of the Commission on Industrial Relations (Vol. VI), it is stated that the Miller and Lux payroll changed every month; the labor turnover being as high as 40 per cent. In order to obtain a steady supply of labor, Miller and Lux encouraged the movement of "tramps" and "hoboes" along the vast reaches of their empire. "By these means," to quote from the report mentioned above, "they keep a stream of men flowing through the country all the time, and they are able to keep labor on their farms. If they did not do that, having such a vast territory, no laboring man, no tramp, would go through the territory at all." The route which they thus established — and it constitutes the beginning of migratory farm labor in California — came to be known as the "Dirty Plate Route."

Miller had a theory about these homeless and landless men. They were apt to cause trouble, but, at the same time, they were absolutely essential, particularly during harvests. Therefore, they must be kept on the move. Yet, in order to keep a steady stream of labor moving through the territory at all times, it was necessary to give them some encouragement. In the mornings, in Bakersfield, the tramps, who had jumped off the train, would line up in front of the bank when they saw Henry Miller enter. When he emerged from the bank, it would generally be with a large bag of coins — two-bit pieces. As Miller shuffled out of the bank, he would hand each man two bits, while he, hat in hand, would murmur, "Thank you, Mr. Miller," or "God bless you, sir." All the foremen on the Miller and Lux ranches received definite written instructions from Henry Miller as to how they were to treat tramps and hoboes. "Never refuse a tramp a meal, but never give him more than one meal. A tramp should be a tramp and keep on tramping. Never let the tramps eat with the other men. Make them wait until the men are through, and then make them eat off of the same plates." These were a few of his personal instructions to the foremen. Mr. Treadwell implies that the tramps loved Henry Miller and that, awed by his generosity (as I have described it) they called him Santa Claus. In writing of these tramps, Mr. Treadwell echoes some of the prejudices of his client, Henry Miller. The tramps, he writes, "were mostly old, decrepit, and unkempt. They were the first tourists to learn the value of California's winter climate. They were beset with the idea that society owed them a living" — a strange obsession, indeed. Once, shortly before his death, Miller said: "If I took everything I could get, it wouldn't be safe for me to go through the country." Consequently, being a man of great foresight, he devised the system of giving an occasional two-bit piece to the tramps and of allowing them one meal, provided it was eaten from a dirty plate.

Other observers of the "Dirty Plate Route," however,

had a different theory about these homeless men. H. A. Van Coenen Torchiana, who was once a foreman on one of the Miller and Lux ranches, has much to say on the subject in his novel *California Gringos* (1930), in which the character Carpenter is a thinly disguised portrait of Henry Miller. "It was not wanderlust," he writes, "or laziness which had driven the tramp to places away from family and friends, but a desire to find work. In those days jobs were generally to be had, for the fast-growing development of the West was far ahead of the normal growth of population. The West demanded then and demands now a large army of temporary workers at different places and at different periods of the year." As to the living conditions provided for this army of workers on the Miller and Lux ranches, he writes: "There were not sufficient rooms, nor were there accommodations for the ordinary decencies of life; there was almost always a shortage of sleeping quarters, and those were often lousy and foul. Bathing facilities were unknown, washing facilities inadequate. Often the men slept on manure piles to keep warm during the frosty nights, with only discarded dry-goods boxes or sugar barrels to separate the sleeper from the steaming, stinking refuse." Miller and Lux, he notes, always farmed the good land themselves. The balance of the land they rented to tenants who turned over a fourth of the crop as rental; or, in some cases, they would sell undesirable tracts and take back a mortgage which provided for 12 per cent interest. Local constables were paid a fee to round up tramps and hoboes, by driving them from the freight cars or by raiding jungle camps, who were given vagrancy sentences and ordered to work it out on the ranches. "The

whole system," he writes, "was vicious, and bred industrial oppression on a large scale." Miller, "the Clemenceau
of the Plains," was, he believes, primarily responsible for
the system.

## 2. Kaweah

To understand fully the development of the Miller and
Lux empire, it is necessary to contrast it with the story of
the Kaweah Co-operative Colony. In many respects the
two stories represent a conflict between two types of
development, between land development under capitalism
and land development under socialism. The two developments took place in the same area, within the same State,
and at the same time. The creation of the Miller and Lux empire was furthered at every step in its development by the
State and the agencies of the State; the Kaweah experiment
was consistently opposed and, finally, stabbed in the back by
the State. Today the holdings of the Miller and Lux empire
constitute the basis for most of the large ranches, or farm
factories, in the San Joaquin Valley, while Kaweah is only
a name, the name of an experiment that remains unchron-
icled and forgotten. Kaweah, as a symbol, has, however,
lasting significance and may yet come to be remembered
long after Miller and Lux are forgotten.

During the eighties in San Francisco the labor movement had considerable vitality. One of its leaders was a
young lawyer, Burnette G. Haskell, a man of some elo-
quence and imagination. He was quite active in the labor
movement between 1882 and 1885 and, in fact, was instru-
mental in organizing the first section of the International

Workingmen's Association in the United States. He came to think, along with a small group of associates, that, from his experience in the labor movement, he had discovered the answer to most social problems. "We were of the opinion," he wrote, "that the abolition of poverty, if accomplished, meant the happiness of the people. When answered that 'human nature' itself was the gate that shut out heaven, we retorted, in our pride, that this selfish nature was but the product of conditions, and that when these were altered human disposition would change." The "we" of this group, most of whom had been active in the labor struggles in San Francisco (Mr. J. J. Martin, for example, had been one of the founders of the Sailors' Union) came to think that some experiment should be undertaken outside the sphere of the labor movement itself, an experiment that would illustrate and validate the premises upon which the labor movement was based. The genesis of this particular notion seems to have been Laurence Gronlund's book, *The Co-operative Commonwealth*, first issued in 1884. The first camp or settlement at Kaweah was called Camp Gronlund (later "Advance"), and subsequent editions of *The Co-operative Commonwealth*, one of the most influential Socialist tracts of the time, contain references to the Kaweah settlement. To some degree, also, the colonists seem to have been influenced by Edward Bellamy. Encouraged by the idealistic and utopian philosophy of Bellamy and Gronlund, these San Francisco labor leaders determined to found an experimental co-operative colony in California, and to put their principles to the test of reality.

In the northwest corner of Tulare County, in the San

Joaquin Valley, and about thirty miles from the town of Visalia, they found a magnificent tract of land which, for the most part, was heavily wooded. As Government land, it had long been open for settlement, but, because of its inaccessibility, it had remained unoccupied. The colonists were fairly realistic. They wanted, for example, to make their colony semi-industrial, i.e. they wanted, in addition to farming, to have a product to sell. The product, in this case, was lumber, for which there was an active demand in the San Joaquin Valley, then undergoing rapid development. The colonists made a careful survey of the project, particularly of the feasibility of building a road to the property. The road presented a real problem as the country between Visalia and the tract was rough and mountainous. Finally determining that the project was feasible, they filed some forty-three separate entries for the tract (it embraced, in area, about six hundred acres) and organized the Kaweah Co-operative Colony. Through various contracts, they corresponded with people all over the world, mostly utopian socialists, and, at one time or another, approximately five hundred people were interested in the colony, the formal organization of which was launched November 9, 1894. The work of building the road, however, had been commenced at an earlier date: October 8, 1886. The road, eighteen miles in length, winding around the hills and through the canyons to attain an elevation of eight thousand feet, was completed four years later, in June, 1890. An average of twenty men worked at the task continuously during this period, without proper tools, powder or equipment. The road was an excellent piece of engineering and construction; in fact, it is in use today. If it had been built by private construction at the time, it would have cost not less than $8,000 a mile or a total of about $150,000. The colonists spent about $50,000, which they raised by subscription, and issued labor checks for about $150,000.

When the road was finished, the town of Kaweah was established. The number of inhabitants varied, with as few as fifty living in the community to as many as three hundred. The town of Advance or Camp Gronlund, a tent city, was the home of the colonists from April, 1887, to December, 1889. Many severe hardships were suffered by the colonists prior to the time when the town of Kaweah was established. There they laid out a town site and built homes. Settlers were allotted fifty-five square yards for home sites. No money was issued and all labor was "requited by checks drawn on time," i.e. based upon the number of hours actually engaged in work for the community. These checks were convertible at the community store. William Carey Jones, of the University of California, visited the colony in 1892. He found about 150 people living there at the time and was favorably impressed with the entire enterprise. The colonists were, he found, an exceptionally fine aggregation of people. For the most part, they had come to Kaweah because they wanted to be "free from the competitive world." Mr. Jones, who was a hard-headed realist, states that he found many brilliant and charming people at Kaweah. The place had an atmosphere of culture; there were no churches, but many homes had books and paintings and they had been furnished in good taste. The colonists enjoyed music and sponsored concerts and lectures. "A home-like air," Mr. Jones wrote, "pervades the settlement." The setting was superb. "No more suitable spot could have been chosen for a new experiment in living," wrote a correspondent for Charles Dickens' magazine *All-the-Year-Round* in 1892. The land was finely timbered; there were "lovely fertile nooks and rich pastures"; the colonists had laid out fruit trees and gardens. "As a social scheme," wrote the same correspondent, "Kaweah seems to have been a distinct success." Most of the evidence confirms this conclusion. During the four years the colony was in existence, there was not a single crime committed; the authorities at Visalia later admitted that, during this period, not a single misdemeanor had been reported. By 1890 the colony owned 600 acres of land; it had constructed a model road eighteen miles in length; it owned a property worth conservatively $600,000; and it did not owe a cent. In addition to these assets, the colony had in operation a saw mill which represented an investment of about $10,000; it had a fifteen horse power tractor and a 300 horse power turbine, with equipment available to construct a planing mill, a shingle mill, and a woolen mill; and a site for the development of water power had been selected and the plans for its use worked out in detail. Besides these items, the colonists had much additional property: houses, furnishings, horses, wagons, equipment. They had constructed a ferry which was operated automatically by the use of the river current. The colony boasted the best equipped printing office in the state, operated by steam power; it had the first printing press established in Tulare County, and it published a weekly magazine which was distributed to subscribers in nearly every State in the union and throughout the world. In

1885–1886 arrangements had been made to incorporate the Giant Forest and Tulare Valley Railroad. Rights of way had been acquired and a survey completed.

The first hostile act against Kaweah dates, in fact, from the time when it began to be rumored that the colony intended to build a railroad from the settlement to Visalia. The troubles of the colonists date from this announcement. In the last days of the 1890 session of Congress, a bill was introduced and hurriedly passed creating the Sequoia National Park out of the lands embraced within the filings of the original Kaweah colonists. The act was based upon the assumption that there had been some technical deficiencies in the filings. In response to the outcry of the colonists, United States Commissioner Lewis A. Groff was sent West to investigate. His report, filed in Washington, February 25, 1891, vindicated the colonists in every respect. He found, for example, that they had had no intention of exploiting the timber. "The purpose of these colonists," he wrote, "is of a lawful and laudatory nature; and that instead of damaging the lands or destroying the giant trees thereon, they have expended about $100,000 in improving the lands and adding to their value, and have guarded and protected the giant trees for over five years, saving them from damage and possible destruction from forest fires on many occasions." The colonists had, in fact, made careful and detailed plans for reforestation; it was their intention to plant two trees for every one that they cut down. Mr. Groff went on to state, in his report, that "on the face all the claims appear to be bona fide, and to have been made in absolute good faith, and the requirements of the law fully complied with, so far as the applicants are concerned."

It will be recalled that, in the previous chapter, I have pointed out the manner in which outrageous thefts of the public domain were quickly sanctioned by the courts and the Government, the "vested rights" of the occupants seldom being disturbed. But despite the Government's vindication of the Kaweah settlers, the act of Congress stood, and the settlers were evicted. One of their saw mills was located on privately owned land, yet, when the settlers refused to vacate, they were rounded up and driven from the property by a company of United States Cavalry. Nor did the heavy irony of the whole affair cease at this point. On the contrary, the leaders of the colony were tried in the courts and convicted of cutting timber on Government property; later they were arrested and charged with using the mails to defraud. When they came on for trial, on the latter charges, in Los Angeles, on May 6, 1892, United States District Judge Erskine Ross ordered their acquittal. In doing so, he stated: "There is no testimony to show that these defendants entered into a fraudulent scheme; there is no evidence going to show that there was fraud on their part; nothing to show that they appropriated any of the funds or intended to do so." For many years afterward, the colonists petitioned Congress again and again for redress, asking for an appropriation to cover the cost of the improvements which they had made, particularly for the value of the road which they had built and which had been taken over by the Government. All of these petitions were denied and the settlers were never allowed one cent by way of indemnification, despite the fact that a later congressional committee, appointed to investigate the matter, recommended that some relief be allowed them. After investigating this high-handed action, the anonymous correspondent for *All-the-Year-Round* wrote that "the truth seems to be that as a presumed 'Socialist' experiment the colony was not in good odour with the powers that be, while it was decidedly obnoxious to the private adventure lumbering or timber-felling companies which were its neighbors and competitors." In like manner, William Carey Jones wrote: "I can come to no other conclusion than that a great injustice has been done. When it is notorious that thousands of acres of the most valuable timber and agricultural land in California has been illegally absorbed by individual corporations and by corporations with almost the connivance of the government, it seems unpardonably harsh and cruel that these men, most of whom are indubitably honest, who have given their energy and life to this undertaking, should be made the victims of even the government's repentance."

The Kaweah experiment was not forgotten immediately; it was kept alive for demonstrative purposes. With fetid hypocrisy, the newspapers of California, from 1892 on, continued to use the Kaweah experiment as a stock illustration of the "inevitable failure" of Socialism. On August 29, 1893, the *Los Angeles Times*, after admitting that "no section in the United States is so well adapted to co-operative farm work as California," pointed out that the Kaweah Colony had "demonstrated" that all such co-operative ventures "must fail." The word Kaweah, if it has any meaning in the State today, has become associated with the notion of a cockeyed and irrational Socialism. The *Fresno Bee*, as late as July 3, 1928, ran a series of articles on the Kaweah Colony to illustrate "the follies of socialism."

The colonists were, of course, driven from the land. Haskell died in absolute poverty in San Francisco: one of the most idealistic and socially enlightened men of his generation in California. J. J. Martin, secretary of the colony, tried once more to establish the "co-operative commonwealth." He rallied a few of the original settlers and took them to Tasmania, where, on the eve of the World War, a new venture was launched. After being promised unstinted support by the local parliament, private interests intervened and the whole enterprise collapsed. Now eighty-four years of age, Mr. Martin lives at San Luis Obispo, California, and is still vocal in his belief in socialism and in his effort to keep the injustice done the Kaweah colonists alive. On August 11, 1935, Mr. Burns Mantle, the dramatic critic, visited Sequoia, "and found many of the traditions of the original Kaweah Colony, which was both socialistic and co-operative, still obtaining."

## CHAPTER IV

## THE PATTERN IS CUT

IN NO other state has farming so quickly lost its traditional character and become an established industry as in California. Today, "farming" in its accepted sense can hardly be said to exist in the State. The land is operated by processes which are essentially industrial in character; the importance of finance, in all of the 180 or more crops produced in California, has steadily increased as more and more emphasis has been placed on financial control; the "farm hand," celebrated in our American folklore, has been supplanted by an agricultural proletariat indistinguishable from our industrial proletariat; ownership is represented not by physical possession of the land, but by ownership of corporate stock; farm labor, no longer pastoral in character, punches a time clock, works at piece or hourly wage rates, and lives in a shack or company barracks, and lacks all contact with the real owners of the farm factory on which it is employed.

To understand how farms have become factories in California, it is necessary to trace the rise of typically capitalistic patterns of industrial operation in California agriculture. The first consideration on this score is, as I have pointed out, the early monopolization of the best land by a few owners. Concentration of ownership made large-scale operations feasible, but other considerations must be

carefully weighed. The use to which the land has been
put has always conditioned not only methods of operation,
but the type of labor employed. From the outset, the
history of California agriculture has been dynamic; it has
developed by a series of revolutionary changes in land use.
Each transition in use has precipitated a change in the type,
and amount, of labor employed. Underlying each upheaval
in farm labor has been a basic shift in agricultural operations.
Agriculture has developed into a specialized industry in
California, not by a process of gradual transition, but by
a series of major dislocations in methods of operation. The
changes which have occurred have been spasmodic in
character, the violent and chaotic history of farm labor in
the State being paralleled by the various phases which have
marked the development of the industry itself. The early
phases of this march toward industrialization of agriculture
in California are traced in the following sections.

### 1. The Bonanza Farms

Prior to 1860, farming in California was pastoral in
character, i.e. chiefly the work of cultivating the fields set
out by the missions. But, after 1860, farming became a
large-scale industry. The immense acreage, which by 1860
had come into the control of a relatively small number of
individuals, was immediately subjected to intensive exploitation. No effort was made to cultivate the land scientifically or with any regard to its social use, but solely to
get money out of the land as quickly as possible. The
methods used by the missions were promptly jettisoned by
the land buccaneers who came into power with the Ameri-

can conquest. They were not interested in diversified farming, or in irrigation, or in scientific cultivation; they wanted to make fortunes overnight. The cultivation of wheat, which had been "quietly undertaken but suddenly realized with dramatic abruptness," by one of the largest landowners in the State, Dr. Glenn, "gave a new matter for reflection to the thinking men of the West." And well it might, for the easiest use to which the huge estates could be put was the cultivation of wheat. Wheat growing was consistent with large-scale operations. It involved a minimum of expense, and, relatively speaking, a minimum of labor, and it promised quick returns. As a consequence of these and other factors, the decades from 1860 to 1880 witnessed the rise of the great wheat farms of California. The census of 1850 showed only 1486 farmers in California and listed no farm laborers; ten years later there were 21,687 persons classified as farmers and 10,421 as farm laborers. Production figures for wheat showed a remarkable increase after 1860. In that year the State produced 6,000,000 bushels; in 1870 wheat production had risen to over 16,000,000 bushels; in 1880 to 29,000,000 bushels, and in 1890 to 40,000,000 bushels, giving California in that year second place among the wheat producing States of the union. Many factors contributed to the rapid expansion of wheat acreage: the inflated prices which followed upon the discovery of gold; a rapidly growing population within the State; a remarkably favorable climate; and the fact that California wheat could stand long shipment, by boat, to England. But, apart from these considerations, two basic elements were involved: the immense size of the farms and the scarcity of labor.

It is difficult, today, to get even a working notion of the size of the immense farms that then existed in California. William Godwin Moody, visiting the State at the time, wrote an interesting piece called "Bonanza Farms," which, in the title, aptly describes the great wheat ranches. He refers to a visit made to one farm in Colusa County containing about 57,000 acres, ninety miles in width, "the greatest number of acres under plow by one man." This particular ranch, the Glenn Ranch, in 1880 received $800,000 for wheat shipped to London. The other great farms — the Robinson ranch near Sacramento; the Bidwell ranch near Chico; the Gonzales ranch near Salinas (which employed about five hundred men and had an annual income from wheat alone in excess of $200,000) — were, as someone described them, "estates of baronial magnitude." Charles Loring Brace, who visited the State in 1867, refers to a farm in Livermore Valley which had 10,000 acres of wheat under cultivation in one field. From 1848 to 1862 California, for the most part, got its flour from Chili and the East. But, after 1860, it began to grow wheat. Between 1860 and 1870 the number of improved acres increased 115 per cent. In 1870 the largest wheat farm in the world existed in the San Joaquin Valley (this particular farm had been purchased with greenbacks, when gold, the currency of the State, was at from 150 to 200; that is to say, the land cost from sixty to seventy-five cents an acre). In 1872 Stephen Powers spoke of vast wheat farms in the State where "you may hear for weeks together the chatter of the reapers and the headers." It was estimated that, in 1868, 150,000 acres of new land were planted to wheat.

Visitors frequently commented upon the waste and

extravagance involved in this highly speculative farming. "The lands receive neither rest nor manure," wrote one observer; "and even straw is burned." Again: "The truth is, such is the improvident habit of the people, that these magnificent grain-fields, which might be the granary of the world, are being rapidly reduced to the conditions of the Virginia tobacco fields — many farms are almost ruined." Wrote still another observer: "It is a shameful and deplorable fact, that many of the naturally best grain-producing portions of our State have been cropped every year for from ten to fifteen years in succession, with grain, and in many cases with one single unvaried crop — wheat. The result has proved just what the farmers have time and again been told it would bring about — exhaustion of the soil. In many localities, where once the land yielded from forty to sixty bushels of wheat per acre, it now yields scarcely enough to pay for the labor of sowing and harvesting. What is still worse, many of these improvident grain farmers are disposing of their exhausted lands and moving to other sections to find a virgin soil, which they, in turn, will in like manner exhaust." In other words, within a decade the land barons of the State had seriously undermined the agricultural resources of California. The same feverish frenzy that had characterized mining in California also characterized wheat farming, which was not, strictly speaking, farming at all, but a variety of mining.

With large-scale operations of the type mentioned, there came into existence a wealthy type of land operator. Charles Loring Brace describes a visit to the home of one of these squires. He refers to the type of farmer in question, "the large farmers," as peculiar to California; he had never encountered such opulence on farms before. He mentions the open-handed hospitality of his host who invited him to stay for a month and describes the immense home, with its galleries and verandahs and its beautiful wood paneling. He noted the easy indolence of manner and the atmosphere of wealth and leisure. The Reverend John Sessions likewise described the great ranches where "large country estates are built and building, with large pleasure grounds laid out tastefully by professional gardeners." This was, of course, the heyday of the great wheat ranches, the period so vividly portrayed by Frank Norris in *The Octopus*. Nearly every observer of the period bears witness to the character of these immense "bonanza farms."

When wheat growing on a large scale was first introduced in California, methods of production were essentially primitive. "Single-shared plows, harrows made of limbs, and scythes were used; mustangs stampeding through a corral threshed the grain." Such inefficient methods of production, coupled with the fact that labor was scarce in California, forced the large wheat growers to tap whatever sources of labor were available. The only cheap labor then available in California was Indian labor, and Indians were promptly recruited for the fields. They had formed, of course, the labor base during the colonial period. After the American conquest, they continued to be commonly employed on the large ranches. Brace, visiting one of the large wheat ranches, tells of seeing a camp of Digger Indians on the ranch. He describes them as "perhaps the lowest tribe of the human race — they were all disgustingly dirty, and with but little clothing on them, living, in part, on pine seeds, acorns, and grass seeds; a diminishing race." (It is unfortunate that

Brace could not have lived until 1937, when social investigators, visiting the San Joaquin Valley, reported that
white workers, on these same farms, were living in the
woods like wild animals.) Apart from their appearance,
the California Indians were good workers. J. S. Hittell
refers to them as "very industrious and trustworthy laborers." Back of their degradation was a long history of exploitation under Spanish and Mexican rule. The sorry tale
of Indian degradation is told, of course, in Helen Hunt
Jackson's novel *Ramona* (1884). Even under the mission
rule, it was customary to pay an Indian half the wages of
a white man or Mexican. Indians, Alessandro (a character
in the novel) complains, "worked on the biggest wheat
ranch in Cajon; we've harvested miles and miles of wheat."
The Americans, he continues, "when they buy the Mexican's lands, drive the Indians away as if they were dogs;
they say we have no right to our lands." Under the lax
Mexican rule, the Indians managed to retain a kind of
ownership, or possessory right, over their villages and
communities. Although the Mexicans did not respect these
pueblo rights, which were embraced within their grants,
they did not bother to dispossess the Indians, most of whom
continued to work on the ranchos as more or less vassal
wards of the owner. Once the Americans came into possession of the grants, however, the Indians were ruth-
lessly uprooted. Moving farther back into the mountains,
they continued to be employed at ridiculously low wages,
or no wages at all (a bottle of whisky was one method of
payment) on the ranches. Henryk Sienkiewicz, the Polish
novelist, who lived for a time in Southern California in
1876, observed that most of the orchard labor was performed

by Cahuilla Indians from the San Bernardino mountains. The practice of using Indian labor continued throughout the early period of American occupation; in fact, as late as 1910 references can be found to the fact that they were still being used, to some slight extent, in the fields. It is impossible, today, to give an accurate account of the number of Indians employed or to indicate the extent to which they were used on the great wheat farms, but that they did constitute an important source of farm labor is well established. Chinese were, likewise, employed on the large wheat ranches. Brace, visiting the wheat-growing areas in 1867, observed that most of the labor was being performed by Chinese and Indian workmen. The Chinese, he states, got $1.50 a day and board "and prove excellent workmen," while the Indians got $1.00 a day without board. It should be remembered, moreover, that labor was very scarce in California during these years and that workmen, in San Francisco, were receiving relatively high wages.

It was not long, however, before these primitive methods of wheat growing were discarded in California. Visitors to the State, in the late sixties and seventies, noted that methods of wheat production in California differed radically in many particulars from those in use in the Middle West. Not only was the scale of operation much larger, but mechanized methods of production were being rapidly introduced. The insufficiency of labor, coupled with the immense size of the ranches, brought about a much greater use of machinery in California than was customary in the Middle West. Just as the scarcity of labor had brought about the first large-scale use of modern mining methods and machinery in California, so was agriculture quickly mechanized. "Machine sowing, the multi-shared plow, and mechanical harvesters rapidly diminished the dependence upon hand-labor." The early adoption of the combine harvester on the bonanza wheat farms of California marked, as Lee Rogin has pointed out, "the logical ultimate step in the evolution of large-scale methods of harvesting." It is interesting to note, in this connection, that Karl Marx, in 1880, wrote to Friedrich Sorge, a correspondent in America, "I should be very much pleased if you could find me something good (meaty) on economic conditions in California. California is very important for me because nowhere else has the upheaval most shamelessly caused by capitalist centralization taken place with such speed." It took place with such speed in agriculture that it was not long before the wheat growers had ceased to rely upon hand labor to any considerable extent. The large number of Indians who had been employed on the ranches became, in fact, superfluous. White labor, single men, migratory workers, began to supply the limited demand for labor on the large wheat ranches. It was then that "hobo" or "tramp" labor first became a striking peculiarity of California agriculture, about which a word of explanation is necessary.

The proceedings of the State Agriculture Society, in 1886, after mentioning the great wheat farms, state that, in the wheat-growing areas, there were many vast sections with "not a solitary family living there, and where troops of nomads come and plow and sow and move on with their blankets." The same proceedings state: "Our nomadic herds of farm hands must have all the year employment and an abiding place with their work; they must be fed and housed as civilized men should be fed and housed; the wide gap between employed and unemployed must be closed." One needs to be reminded that this statement was made not in 1937, but in 1886. The same nomadic herds exist today; and the problem of feeding and housing them is more acute than ever. In earlier transactions of the same society, in 1882, one finds this statement: "The labor problem, as relates to the farm, becomes more and more serious with each succeeding year. In its early history our state was isolated from great centers of population. For years the overflowing population from older settlements found profitable employment east of the Rockies. The common laborer was not possessed of sufficient means to pay his expenses to California." Whence, therefore, came these nomadic herds of blanket men? For the most part, the records are silent; but they do contain a few significant hints.

Josiah Royce, in his history of California, states that many settlers who came to California to farm after 1850 left in disgust when they discovered that they had already been excluded from a great many of the best farming sections of the State. They could find no lands to settle upon, although millions of acres were uncultivated and unoccupied. Other settlers, however, refused to accept this condition: they settled on the land and became "squatters." In many cases the squatters knew that the land was claimed by some one as a grantee or assignee of a Spanish land grant, but they also knew that the grant was fraudulent and they refused to respect it. In other cases, they settled upon and improved the land in ignorance of the fact that, when the grant was surveyed, the holder would "float" it in such a manner as to include their farm. "Squatterism" is referred to very guardedly in the histories, but that it reached serious proportions is conceded. Royce states that by 1850 squatterism had assumed the character of a "general predatory conquest," i.e. that the great estates were threatened with seizure and appropriation. In that year, 1850, however, squatterism was crushed and the movement to seize the land was stifled. On August 22, 1850, a serious squatters' riot occurred in Sacramento. Hundreds of squatters banded together to resist eviction from lands claimed by Captain John Sutter under a Mexican grant. They literally took possession of the town of Sacramento, marching through the streets in military formations. The social division underlying the conflict was between small farmers and land barons backed by the armed forces of the State and Federal Governments. The land barons won. The National Guard arrived in Sacramento, and, after a day or two of rioting, order was restored. Those of the squatters who could not, or would not, pay the price demanded by the land grabbers were evicted, and that they constituted a majority of the squatters is clear. What became of them? A few, perhaps, found other land; but not much land was available. Most of them, I take it, took to the road.[1] A writer in 1871, referring to these blanket men, states: "To see one of these men toiling along the dusty highways, penniless, weary, and footsore, begging a ride from the teamsters, begging a meal from the foremen, none would suppose him a denizen of a state advertised over the world for the extent and fertility of a soil to be obtained for nothing" — an ironic statement, indeed. Among these pitiful nomadic

---

[1] See *Casa Grande*, 1906, a novel by Charles Duff Stuart, in which squatterism is described, although somewhat unrealistically.

herds — they appear in the writing of the period as scarecrow figures, dark shadows on the landscape — how many were squatters?

## 2. Fruit Versus Wheat

Beginning with 1870, a great change took place in the character of California agriculture. The years from 1870 to 1878 marked a period of financial stringency within the State, for, in 1870, the eccentric economic structure of the State went to pieces. The period of the seventies — "the terrible seventies" — survives in the recollection of many persons now living as one of the utmost hardship. The speculative mining ventures collapsed; banks failed; and, in the wake of this general debacle, many of the new industries and businesses failed. As part of this recession, came a decline in the profitability of wheat. Complex factors were involved: fluctuation in world prices; drought; competition from the new grain areas of Russia and the Mississippi Valley; and high freight rates. The decline continued throughout the decades so that, by 1880, the average return to the grower was only about four per cent. It was not long before the land barons of California realized that the great bonanza years, based on the cultivation of wheat, were at an end.

For a number of years after 1870 the issue that began to be debated in the proceedings of the State Agricultural Society, and in the farm journals, was that of fruit versus wheat. It was not long before large sections of wheat acreage were converted, by the introduction of irrigation, into orchard lands. Charles Howard Shinn states that "Cali-

fornia made a new start," in the period between 1870 and
1878, "and escaped industrial ruin, chiefly by reason of
vineyards, gardens, orchards, seed farms, and hop-yards."
In the transactions of the State Agricultural Society (1885),
these significant statements appear: "A few years since
nothing was deemed profitable to plant but wheat, rye,
oats, and barley. But the increased demand, and facilities
now opened, enables California to expand her productions
in fruit and wine." In 1871 fruit shipments from the State
amounted to 1,832,310 pounds; in 1884, this figure had
increased to 11,996,000 pounds. The State Agricultural
Society, in 1885, took cognizance of the fact that "dried,
canned, and green fruits, including oranges and lemons, as
products of our orchards, and raisins, wine, and brandy as
products of our vineyards, are rapidly supplanting the
other great farming industries of the state."

Prior to 1849, nearly every mission in California had, at
one time, possessed a flourishing orchard. Most of these,
however, had either been destroyed or had seriously de-
teriorated from neglect after secularization. The farmers
who came to California after 1849 were, for the most part,
unfamiliar with orchard cultivation. There was an irrigated
orchard in Sacramento in 1849, and fruit trees were planted
in Trinity and Siskiyou counties in 1850, but, from a commercial point of view, fruit was not grown extensively in
California until about 1870. In addition to the decline in
the price of wheat, several other factors encouraged the
planting of orchards. Perhaps the most important was the
completion of the transcontinental railroad in 1869. Later,
in 1881, the Southern Pacific opened a new line by way
of El Paso to New Orleans; and, in 1885, the Atchison,

Topeka, and Santa Fe line was completed to Los Angeles. Previously, California had been forced to rely upon water transportation. Fruit crops, because of their perishability, could not be shipped by boat. Wheat, therefore, had remained the only important crop which fostered the growing of livestock and did not represent, at the same time, a transportation problem. With the completion of the various railroad lines, and the development of the refrigerator car (1888), fresh fruit could be shipped to the Eastern markets. For a time, however, the fruit acreage expanded slowly because of the prohibitive freight rates. It cost, for example, one thousand dollars to ship a car of ten tons from San Francisco to Chicago. "The expansion of the area of fruit-growing," it has been stated, "has been in exact proportion to the decrease in freight rates." Another related factor which contributed to the transition from wheat to fruit was the rapid development of the dried-fruit industry which made long distance shipments, even by boat, possible. With the development of the dried-fruit process, and the establishment of large canneries, California fruit was soon being transported throughout the world.

Still another factor, and one which has been frequently ignored, was the extraordinary development of horticulture and viticulture in California. The marked emphasis on mechanical methods was also accompanied by an amazing development in scientific methods and processes based upon novel experimentations. In 1875, Luther Burbank, an amateur New England nurseryman, came to California and purchased an acre of ground near Santa Rosa, and began to experiment with fruit, seeds and slips. By 1893 he had issued *New Creations in Fruit and Flowers*, which had an

important influence on the development of California agriculture. "California plants," he wrote, "have so many different climates, altitudes, moisture conditions, growing
seasons, and so on, to deal with that they show more varia-
tions in themselves than plants almost anywhere in the
world" — a statement which foreshadowed the shift to
diversification, the outstanding feature of present-day California agriculture. Burbank worked for years in the development of types of fruit that would stand up under long
transportation hauls and that would arrive at the point of
destination in a sound and attractive condition. "I could
see," he wrote, "that fruits would be in great demand in
California." The amazing achievements of this rather naive
scientist were appropriated by the California landowners
with typical greediness. Burbank, for example, worked for
years to develop a type of pea that could be grown commercially in California. After he had completed his experimentations, one of the largest growers in the State took
over the seed which he had developed — for nothing —
and made a fortune out of its exploitation. Today the
growing of this same type of pea constitutes one of the
chief commercial crops in a large section of the State.

But no single development in the whole process by
which the transition from wheat to fruit was effected was
of greater importance than the introduction of irrigation.
A major drought occurred in California in 1863–1864. The
drought was so severe in its consequences that it struck a
death blow at the livestock industry of the State which, of
course, was closely related to wheat raising. "The plains
were strewn with carcasses," writes one historian. "In
marshy places and around the *cienegas*, where there was

a vestige of green, the ground was covered with their skeletons, and the traveler for years afterward was often startled by coming suddenly on a veritable Golgotha — a place of skulls — the long horns standing out in defiant attitude, as if protecting the fleshless bones. It is said that 30,000 head of cattle died on the Stearns Ranchos alone." The drought put an end to cattle raising, as a distinctive industry in California, and fixed the attention of the large landowners upon the problem of irrigation. The first important irrigation projects were developed in 1872, with the development becoming very rapid after 1885. California has, today, a remarkably high percentage of the total irrigated farms in the United States. Irrigation, which naturally increased capital costs, brought about intensification of production. Since irrigation was first introduced, the expansion of the total area under cultivation has not greatly increased, but the intensification of the use of the area under cultivation has greatly increased. The value of the intensive crops represented less than 4 per cent of the total value of California agricultural production in 1879; by 1929, the intensive crops represented practically four fifths of the total. In order to finance its vast irrigation projects, California agriculture came more and more under the direct control of banking and financial institutions.

In 1886 the first full train of deciduous fruit was shipped from California and the victory of fruit over wheat was firmly established. Shipments of green and canned fruit steadily mounted after 1871; and shipments of vegetables, grown commercially, also began to increase. From 1886, when fruit was definitely in the ascendancy, until 1893, the fruit acreage was swiftly expanded. The expansion

of orchard acreage was accompanied by the same wasteful-
ness in method, the same reckless disregard of land and
market, the same abounding greediness, as had marked the
development of the great wheat farms.

By 1893 the fruit industry was seriously undermined and
ruin faced the growers. Once again they were saved by
a new development — sugar beets — and, as will be pointed
out later, they promptly proceeded to inaugurate, with
typical recklessness, a new trend which, in turn, was swiftly
exploited.

The transition from wheat to fruit had several important social consequences; each revolution in California
agriculture, in fact, has provoked minor social upheavals.
The development of fruit brought the growers into much
closer relation with the cities than had formerly existed;
it meant irrigation, and irrigation necessarily involved
heavy capitalization. Irrigation costs in California were very
high because of the physical difficulties involved. In some
areas, the maintenance costs alone for irrigation ran as
high as one hundred dollars an acre, and, in most cases, it
involved a staggering sum per acre to bring water to the
land. With fruit cultivation on a large scale came diversification of crop. As a result of this same transition, the
average size of California ranches decreased from 462 acres
in 1880 to 397 acres in 1900 and the number of ranches
more than doubled. But this decrease in the size of the unit
did not involve any essential change in the character of
ownership. To a substantial degree, the large holdings
were maintained and the predominance of the large growers
was at all times apparent. Lastly, fruit cultivation brought
about a sharp change in the labor requirements of the

growers. "If specialized farming [i.e. fruit growing] was to compete with mechanized and extensive farming [i.e. wheat growing], the latter of which could cheapen production by the application of machinery, then specialized farming, which had to rely on labor to so much greater an extent, could do so only by cheapening the labor which it required in its own field." The same point was made in a report of John D. MacKenzie, of the State Department of Labor, in 1909, when he said: "The transition from the cereal growing period to the development of specialized agriculture increased the ratio of temporary help required by the farming districts beyond the normal supply available within the state during periods of largely increasing population." This tendency was, of course, aggravated by the swiftness and intensity with which the transition was effected. What has long been termed "the farm labor problem" in California may be said to date from the introduction of intensive farming with the attendant requirements for an abundance of cheap, skilled, mobile, and temporary labor. The rudiments of the problem as it exists today existed in 1886. From 1886 to the present time, the problem, in so far as the growers were concerned, has simply been to recruit and to maintain this supply of labor. From 1871 to 1886, the growers found an easy solution in the presence of the Chinese; but, as will be shown later, every solution which the growers have achieved has been a temporary solution, for the ultimate solution of the problem necessarily involves a basic change in the type of ownership and a breaking up of the large estates.

## CHAPTER V

## THE CHINESE

"WHEN the growing of fruits, both deciduous and citrus, began to occupy the attention of California, there were present among us many Chinese." This innocent statement, made by a speaker before the State Fruit-Growers' convention in 1902, conceals within its blandness an interesting and significant phase of the social history of California. In order to understand the important role which the Chinese played as farm laborers in California, however, it is necessary to recapitulate some rather turgid history.

In 1860 there were approximately 45,000 Chinese in California. Of this number it is estimated that about 20,000 were working in the gold mines, a large number were still employed on the construction of the transcontinental railroad, and a fairly large number were employed at miscellaneous tasks in San Francisco. At an early date, they began to be employed, in fairly large numbers, on the great farms. Brace, traveling around the State in 1867, frequently saw "Eastern [i.e. Chinese] laborers with their broad hats leisurely working in the fruit-gardens, as if in a tea plantation." Their use as farm laborers began to increase rapidly after 1870. In 1870 they constituted 10 per cent of the farm laborers reported by the Census; by 1886, according to the politically minded anti-Chinese California

Bureau of Labor, they constituted seven eighths of the agricultural laborers of the State. B. Schrieke makes a somewhat different calculation. He states that, in 1870, 90 per cent of the agricultural labor of the State was performed by Chinese and that, in 1880, this figure had decreased to about 75 per cent. These and other estimates show a wide variation, so that it is impossible to calculate with accuracy the extent to which the Chinese were employed on the farms. I am inclined to believe, however, that Chinese labor was more widely used in 1870, and in the decade between 1860 and 1870, than some historians realize; but, with the growth in fruit acreage after 1870, the Chinese soon assumed a dominant role as farm laborers. "Before long Chinese coolies [according to Walter Woehlke] had a monopoly of the so-called 'squat' labor on the large plantations, the vegetable patches and orchards."

In the cultivation of wheat, relatively little labor was required. Not only was this true because of the nature of the operations involved, but, as Cleland and Hardy point out, "The insufficiency of labor in California forced upon the California ranchers a much greater use of machinery than was customary in the Middle West." With the introduction of intensive, specialized farming, however, the situation changed. These operations required a large supply of cheap labor, and, at the time, labor was still extremely scarce in California and commanded the high wages of the gold-rush period. It is quite apparent, therefore, that the transition from wheat to fruit acreage would have been delayed for a quarter of a century, had it not been for the presence of the Chinese in California. They were a vital factor, one is inclined to state *the* vital factor, in making the transition possible. The growers not only needed a large supply of labor at a time when labor was scarce, but, at a time when wages were high, they demanded the cheapest possible type of labor in order to compete with those of their associates who were engaged in large-scale wheat production through the use of mechanized methods.

So far as the growers were concerned, therefore, the "Chinese situation" was made to order. For it so happened that when the growers turned to the Chinese as a source of farm labor on a large scale, i.e. about 1870, the Chinese were already a despised minority. Discriminatory legislation had been passed against the Chinese as early as 1850. By a decision of the Supreme Court of California in 1854, the Chinese had been included within the provisions of a statute which prohibited the testimony of Negroes, mulattos, and Indians, in cases to which white men were parties, Mr. Justice Murray holding, by a remarkable ethnological argument, that a Chinaman was, in California, a variety of Indian. This decision, of course, invited the murder and robbery of the Chinese. Newspapers had stated as early as 1850 that the Chinese were being murdered with impunity and this state of affairs grew rapidly worse after 1854. For example, in 1862, eighty-eight Chinese were murdered in California and there were serious riots in the State in 1877. Anti-coolie clubs existed in the State, as fairly strong political groups, as early as 1862.

The feeling against the Chinese which had, at first, been general in character, rapidly became crystallized into a fixed determination to drive them out of the State. But this campaign was frustrated, from a legislative standpoint, by reason of the adoption of the fourteenth and fifteenth amendments to the Constitution of the United States, under the provisions of which many local ordinances and State statutes passed in California against the Chinese were held invalid. Consequently the anti-Chinese campaign had to resort to low cunning and terrorism in order to achieve its objectives. As the campaign developed, it took the form, first, of driving the Chinese from the mines, and, later, of attempting to drive them from San Francisco.

The business of driving the Chinese from the mines presented no great difficulties. As early as 1850, a statute was passed the effect of which was to force Chinese miners to take out a special license before they could work in the diggings. When this failed to discourage the Chinese, the miners took matters into their own hands. According to Bothwick, "the miners would not allow the Chinese to come among them." In 1858 the miners of Mariposa County passed a resolution to the effect that "any Chinaman who tries to mine must leave on twenty-four hours' notice, otherwise the miners will inflict such punishment as they deem proper." Throughout the mining districts of the State, similar resolutions were adopted in the period from 1858 to 1867. That these resolutions were illegal did not prevent their enforcement. Chinese claims were jumped as fast as they were located, and, if the claimants protested, they were driven out or murdered. For all practical purposes, of course, they were barred from the courts. It is not surprising, therefore, to find that by 1870 the Chinese had been driven from the mines.

Expelled from the mines, many Chinese sought in San Francisco the protection that had been denied them in the mining districts. But San Francisco, with a strongly organized labor movement fighting to preserve the high wages of the gold-rush period, was a hotbed of anti-coolie sentiment. The San Franciscans were, in fact, amazingly ingenious in their attempts to legislate against the Chinese. They passed such ordinances as the following: a "cubic-air" ordinance which, if enforced, would have condemned all Chinatown; an ordinance making it illegal for any person to carry baskets on the sidewalks suspended on poles across the shoulders (aimed, of course, at Chinese laundry-men); and a "queue" ordinance providing that the hair of every male prisoner in the jail should be cut to within an inch of his scalp. These measures failing to discourage the Chinese, the San Franciscans proceeded by riots and the instrumentality of a trade-union boycott to force the employers of Chinese labor to discharge their employees, and to replace them with white laborers. Not only were the Chinese excluded, for all practical purposes, from the mines and from regular employment in San Francisco, but, in 1869, the transcontinental railroad was completed and some ten thousand Chinese who had been employed in its construction were thrown out of work. As a result of this general state of affairs, thousands of Chinese were literally driven into the agricultural districts at a time when the large growers were beginning to demand a large supply of cheap labor.

From the growers' point of view, the situation was not only desirable, it was well-nigh perfect. The Chinese, being a despised minority fighting for the mere right to exist in a hostile territory, could be employed at sub-subsistence wages. In other respects, moreover, they were ideal farm laborers. They had no families and, consequently, were satisfied with "the cheapest, meanest quarters." They boarded themselves in some mysterious manner. When the season was over, they vanished into San Francisco and obligingly re-appeared when required. Lastly, they were extremely efficient workers; on this point, the growers have always been unanimous. I quote from an editorial in the *Pacific Rural Press*, September 16, 1893: "The Chinese are the mainstay of the orchardist and thus far it must be said, form the only supply of labor which he can depend upon. They are expert pickers and packers of fruit. It is difficult to see how our annual fruit crop could be harvested and prepared for market without the Chinaman." There is an abundance of similar evidence. "The Chinese," wrote Shinn, "are expert in garden and orchard work." "The availability of cheap Chinese labor," said the *Pacific Rural Press* (June 10, 1893), "gave the fruit growers hope. They extended their operations and the Chinese proved equal to all that had been expected of them. They became especially clever in the packing of fruit; in fact, the Chinese have become the only considerable body of people who understand how to pack fruit for eastern shipment." Unstinting as this praise sounds, it is nevertheless inadequate. The growers neglect to mention one or two items of their indebtedness to the Chinese. At this date it is difficult to get the full facts, for not only were these facts imperfectly reported at the time, but a mist of prejudice intervenes and obscures the truth. But, by and large, it is correct to state that, in many particulars, the Chinese actually taught their overlords how to plant, cultivate, and harvest orchard and garden crops. Their skill in this work is acknowledged and it is difficult to believe that they be-

came experts overnight. Most of their employers, moreover, were novices. With the Japanese at a later date it is
possible to point out the specific contributions which they
made to California agriculture. Unfortunately, with the
Chinese, one can only guess at the facts. True it is, however, that the growers never criticized the Chinese on a
single score, and, to this day, continue to "sigh for the
good old days" of coolie labor.

During the critical years in the transition from wheat
to fruit, the Chinese constituted a perfect solution to the
growers' labor problem; but difficulties began to develop.
The movement against the Chinese did not abate; on the
contrary, it became more virulent and aggressive. In its
campaign against the Chinese, "organized labor found the
tacit, if not open, support of those small manufacturers
and also farming interests that did not require large amounts
of labor, but who felt the competition from those who
were able profitably to exploit the availability of the
Chinese." General Chipman, long spokesman for the dominant landowning interests of the State, let the cat out of
the bag in a speech delivered on November 7, 1895: "The
large bulk of the men of this State — the men who produce
fruit — small orchardists — could never have counted on
alien labor, which enabled the large orchardists to crowd
out the small ones." As a consequence of this amalgama-
tion of social forces — organized labor, small manufacturers,
small farmers — a strong political bloc was formed in California which forced the adoption, in 1879, of a new State
Constitution. One of the chief items of business at this constitutional convention was that of "starvation by constitutional enactment," i.e. of devising ways and means to

discriminate against the Chinese. Several significant provisions were adopted: No Chinese could be employed on any State, county, or municipal or other public-works project; corporations were prohibited from employing Chinese labor; and incorporated cities and towns were authorized to remove the Chinese without their limits or to prescribe the limits within which they should live. This "Hottentot legislation," as it was called, merely added fuel to the flames; stronger measures were urged; and, finally, in 1882, the first exclusion act was passed by the Federal Government.

The large growers, needless to say, fought many of these measures, and, after 1879, they continued to employ Chinese labor in defiance of the various measures which had been adopted. But large anti-Chinese conventions were held throughout the State in the eighties and, as Miss Eaves points out, "the holding of these large conventions outside of San Francisco is indicative of the more general feeling against the Chinese. The smaller cities and towns of the state were repeating the earlier history of San Francisco, — in a number of the smaller towns where there was great unanimity of feeling, the inhabitants took matters into their own hands; they expelled the Chinese and gave them rough notice not to return." In 1885 hordes of tourists and prospective settlers came to California as a consequence of a rate war then being waged by the railroads. The State Agricultural Society, in its proceedings for the year 1886, commented upon the fact, and said: "They found depression and general dread of inability to harvest crops; they found irresponsible persons leading masses to the ruin of the farmer and fruit grower; they found the boycott." This statement would indicate that, by 1885, the anti-Chinese riots and boycotts of San Francisco had spread to the farming districts and had already begun to cause trouble for the large growers employing Chinese labor. Pressure was doubtless added to the anti-Chinese campaign in the rural districts by the arrival, after 1885, of many settlers from the east looking for work. The tide of anti-Chinese sentiment continued to mount, in any event, and, by 1893, a condition approximating civil war broke out in the great valleys of California.

The immediate cause of the riots of 1893 was the passage by Congress in 1892 of the Geary Act. This act continued in effect the provisions of the exclusion act of 1882 for ten years; it also provided for the deportation of all Chinese illegally within the United States; forced the burden of proving legal residence upon the Chinese; and required that all Chinese laborers register under the act within one year of its passage. It has been stated that nineteen-twentieths of the Chinese in California failed to comply with the registration features of the act and were hence subject to deportation. When even this measure failed to force the growers to relinquish their precious Chinese labor, the people in the rural districts, following the earlier example of their fellow citizens in San Francisco, took matters into their own hands and proceeded to drive the Chinese from the fields.

"White men and women who desire to earn a living," wrote the *Los Angeles Times*, August 14, 1893, "have for some time been entering quiet protests against vineyardists and packers employing Chinese in preference to whites." These protests soon ceased to be quiet. Businessmen in

Fresno, disturbed by the mounting anti-Chinese agitation and the boycott, called a mass meeting and got, from some of the local growers, a tentative promise to discharge "nearly all of their Chinese help." But on August fifteen, riots broke out near Fresno: Chinese were driven from the fields and were "compelled to make lively runs for China-town." Chinese labor camps were raided and fired. In Napa Valley, on August seventeenth, a white laborers' union was formed, and a mass meeting protested the further employ-ment of the Chinese in the prune orchards. The same day three hundred Chinese field workers were driven from their work in Fresno. This type of rioting soon spread through-out the State. In Southern California, at Compton, the Chinese were barricaded in packing sheds where they were forced to sleep for safety, while "hoodlums," in the words of one grower, "raided the fields and drove out the Chinese." In Redlands, heart of the citrus belt of Southern California, night raiders broke into Chinese camps on September first; Chinese were robbed in the streets of the town; and a mass meeting was called to protest further lawlessness. The disturbances soon became so acute in Redlands that, on the following day, the National Guard was summoned to the town and two hundred special deputy sheriffs were sworn in. The large growers protested loudly against the rioters, calling them "hoodlums" and "anarchistic agita-tors," and swore that they only hired Chinese labor because "we cannot pay the wages demanded by the whites." But the rioting continued. On September third anti-Chinese raiders swooped down on Redlands' Chinatown, broke into houses, set fire to several buildings, looted the tills of Chinese merchants, and generally terrorized the Chinese. The

Chinese protested that they were being beaten and robbed and called attention to the fact that although eleven rioters were arrested, not one was convicted. Under the Geary Act, any citizen could file a complaint against a Chinese laborer for non-registration. Hundreds of complaints were filed under this section, and the Chinese fled from the fields, trying to escape arrest and deportation, while the local press, witnessing the exodus, crowed loudly about "the purple-coated celestial-heathens" fleeing from the wrath of an "aroused citizenry." In the San Joaquin Valley the rioting was general: At Tulare, Visalia, and Fresno, hundreds of white men were busy "routing out the Chinese, terrifying them with blows and pistol shots, and driving them to the railroad station and loading them on the train." The rioting spread farther north, with a major disturbance at Ukiah, and, in several instances, local units of the National Guard had to be called out. "The rioters," wrote the *Pacific Rural Press*, "assume to be workingmen, but they are, in fact, a set of low tramps and bummers who, if offered work, will not accept it, or persist in it." This, of course, was not the case; in Compton, for example, the "rioters" were assisted by sailors and longshoremen from San Pedro. In many communities the law-enforcement officials openly sympathized with the rioters; the merchants, in the various towns, frequently supported the anti-Chinese campaign. This type of rioting continued, on a smaller scale, the following year, the *Pacific Rural Press* reporting, on November 17, 1894, that "vandalism" had broken out at Vacaville, where "marauding tramps, 150 in a bunch, organized in squads with captains and lieutenants," had ordered the growers to discharge all Chinese and Japanese help and had entered orchards, driven out all oriental labor, and cut down trees. The magazine stated that all growers must be on their guard to protect their laborers "from these cormorants, the tramps."

The net result of the riots was that the Chinese were driven from the fields. It has been frequently stated that the Chinese ceased to be employed in the fields after the passage of the first exclusion act, in 1882, but, as I have shown, the passage of this act was a mere incident in the campaign. The Chinese closed out their various Chinatowns in the small towns throughout the State and either left the country or moved into the cities for protection. The growers, who had been able to fight the boycott for a time, finally conceded that they were licked. "Indispensable as the Chinese are," said one report, "they must go, as gradually as possible." So serious was the problem created by the exodus of the Chinese from the fields, B. Schrieke estimates, that between the time when the Chinese were driven out and the Japanese came in, "over a half-million acres of farm land had been put out of cultivation in California." This statement is probably exaggerated, but, as late as 1902, the farmers of Pajaro Valley petitioned Congress to let the Chinese return, and complained of crops rotting in the fields. "The tranquillity of California," wrote the *Pacific Rural Press*, "is one of its greatest charms." The tranquillity of rural California is a myth and the bloodshed and rioting of 1893 and 1894 constitutes merely a chapter in the history of farm labor in the State.

In order to see the riots of 1893 and 1894 in proper perspective, it is necessary to recall that the depression of 1893 was acutely felt in California. The *Coast Seamen's*

*Journal* reported that "not for over twenty-five years has San Francisco witnessed such destitution, misery and suffering." By June, 1893, twenty-seven banks had failed in California, and ten of them never resumed operations. Industry was at a standstill. "Sacramento drove its unemployed out of the city limits — free employment bureaus, soup kitchens, public woodyards, street sweeping, and charitable ventures of various sorts were resorted to to help the hungry and desperate population." Carl Browne, who had helped Dennis Kearney organize the anti-Chinese agitation, formed the California contingent of Coxey's Army and directed its march toward Washington. It is amusing to note the agitation which swept the propertied classes at that time. In 1893, for example, word reached Fresno that one thousand unemployed men were en route from Denver, where they had been ejected by the authorities. The local Chief of Police, fearing riots when the "army" reached Fresno, begged the growers to drive out the Chinese and made elaborate preparations to resist the invasion. In many cities in California money was appropriated to feed the unemployed and, in Fresno, the white unemployed were registered for work and given seventy-five cents a day and board if they would work in the fields and take the places made vacant by the Chinese exodus. It is interesting to note that the Chinese, at the time, were getting $1.40 a day.

In the wake of these disturbances, and alarmed by the depression of 1893, the growers began to take stock of the situation and concluded that they could no longer fight the Anti-Chinese Party in the State. The *Los Angeles Times* reflected this change of sentiment in an editorial which appeared August 26, 1893. The editorial was prefaced with a statement that wheat farming was doomed; it did not encourage farm settlement, and, without people, wealth could not be accumulated. The Chinese had "for more than a quarter of a century been an important factor in the economy of California," but they must, apparently, go. "The big vineyardists were the ones who favored Chinese labor, while the small ones favored white labor." There were, however, some valid objections to the Chinese; for example, they shipped an estimated annual revenue of $10,000,000 out of the State, which, if white labor were employed, might be added to local purchasing power. The problem was to get "large bodies of laborers," needed by the orchardists "for a few weeks during the year," and to get these workers, who must be trained workers, as quickly as possible. The editorial then suggests, rather tentatively, the idea of settling white families on small tracts of land. The families could do the picking of fruit during the season, and, adds the *Times*, "They could afford to work at *reasonable rates*, because they would have no rent to pay, and would be in receipt of an income from their tract of land which should be sold to them on very easy terms." The history of this suggestion I trace elsewhere; it is mentioned here to show that it has a long background in California.

With the expulsion, by violence and terror, of the Chinese from the fields, the first chapter in the long history of the growers to maintain "an adequate labor supply" came to a close. The social division reflected in the fight, although confused by the issue raised by the Chinese, was fairly clear. On the one hand was a small clique of large growers, who had prevented a democratic and economically sound settlement and development of the land, pitting their interests against those of the small farmers, manufacturers, and organized labor of the State. The mistake that the latter group made was in not organizing the Chinese laborers and forcing through the reforms in landowner-ship which they thought they had achieved with the adoption of the Constitution of 1879. Into the provisions of this constitution they had written several important declarations: "That land should be granted only to actual settlers and in quantities not exceeding three hundred acres"; also, "the holding of large tracts of land, uncultivated and un-improved, by individuals and corporations, is against the public interest, and should be discouraged by all means not inconsistent with the rights of private property." But, in their excitement, they forgot all about the reform agitation which Henry George had so brilliantly conducted in the early seventies, and went on a witch hunt. Had they substituted Henry Miller, as a symbol, for the prover-bial John Chinaman, conceivably there might have been more point to their rioting.

## CHAPTER VI

## THE FACTORIES APPEAR

IN THE years from 1892 to 1900, the fruit industry, which had assumed the ascendancy in California agriculture, suffered a severe setback. Through reckless overexpansion, a bad drought in 1898, and the labor disturbances of 1893, the extension of fruit acreage was definitely checked and the industry was faced with bankruptcy. So decisively had the wild boom in fruit lands collapsed, that orchard trees were cut down and used for firewood and many orchards were abandoned.[1] Once again the growers had to effect a transition in methods of land use in order to maintain profits and to continue intact their large holdings. With the heavy capitalization costs which had been developed, it was impossible to revert to wheat production. What the industry needed was a new intensive crop, capable of producing quick profits, which would supplement existing crop productions. The crop, fortunately, was already in existence, awaiting a favorable moment for its expansion. "Sugar beets," a California industrialist proclaimed, "worked a revolution in our industrial life." But in order to understand the consequences which followed upon the intro-

---

[1] *Pacific Rural Press*, January 11, 1899.

duction of large-scale sugar-beet production, a word of background is essential.

## 1. Sugar Beets

In 1869 a small sugar-beet factory was constructed by two German settlers at Alvarado, California — one of the first successful commercial ventures in extracting sugar from beets in the United States. Between 1869 and 1889, the Alvarado plant was the only sugar-beet factory in the State. The sugar-beet industry in California, however, only began to develop with the appearance of Claus Spreckles. Spreckles had made a fortune in Hawaii growing cane sugar. With all the resources at his command (and they were considerable), he had opposed the annexation of Hawaii. Fearing that annexation would result in restrictions being imposed against the importation of cheap coolie labor to the islands, he had done everything possible to stymie those who wanted to incorporate Hawaii into the union. Coolie labor was, and is, the backbone of the plantation system; wherever the sugar mill appears, the plantation system comes into existence. Anticipating interference with the plantation system in Hawaii, Spreckles decided to transplant it to California. In 1889, therefore, he constructed a sugar-beet factory at Watsonville, in Monterey County. On the theory that the sugar-beet industry was a feeble infant that needed protection, and State support, he got various concessions from the State of California, in the form of tax exemptions, and whatnot, before the factory was constructed.[2] The "infant" character of the industry

[2] See *Something about Sugar*, 1917, by George M. Rolph.

is indicated by the fact that the Watsonville factory made 80 per cent profit in the second year after it was opened. All the beets grown for the Watsonville factory were, at first, raised by American farmers in the immediate vicinity of the plant. "The Japs," said Claus A. Spreckles (a son), "were not working in the fields at the time." Spreckles, unfortunately, was soon involved in a furious price war with the American Sugar Refining Company (an Eastern trust controlled by Henry O. Havemeyer) which lasted from 1889 to 1901. To meet the fierce competition during this struggle, Spreckles refused to pay the local growers the initial price of four dollars a ton for beets. As a consequence, the growers ceased to grow beets around Watsonville, converted their acreage into apple orchards, and the plant was closed. In 1902, however, the Spreckles interests merged with their eastern competitors and established the Sugar Trust. Thereupon the new combine constructed, at Salinas, California, the largest sugar-beet factory in the world.

The sugar-beet industry in California really dates from the passage of the Dingley Tariff Act of 1897 which imposed a heavy duty (an ad valorem rate of 78.87 per cent) on imported sugar. It is estimated that this duty presented the California sugar-beet growers with an annual bounty of approximately $140,000,000. With this "encouragement," the sugar-beet industry in the State rapidly expanded, with sugar-beet factories being constructed in various parts of the State. Most of these new factories, however, soon sold out to the trust.

To escape the initial cost of converting abandoned orchards and wheat acreage into sugar-beet farms, the sugar-beet factories at first encouraged small farmers to raise sugar beets under contract. At an early date some of the possible dangers implicit in this arrangement were widely sensed. The *Pacific Rural Press*, for example, pointed out (May 1, 1897) that "at present the sugar maker invites the neighboring farmers to grow beets. But with the steady modern progress toward concentration and monopoly of business, the next step will be for the sugar maker to grow beets with a great beet plantation, worked on a large scale, under a thorough system of Asiatic labor, and he will be able to raise beets cheaper than his neighbor, the small farmer." This prediction was swiftly fulfilled. The small grower, wholly at the mercy of the trust which arbitrarily fixed the price paid for sugar beets, was soon forced out of business; in most instances, he became a tenant of the factory. Through direct and indirect means of control, the sugar-beet acreage rapidly became concentrated in a few large holdings. The small growers, however, began to agitate against the Sugar Trust, and, in 1911, the Hardwick Committee, appointed by the House of Representatives, commenced its investigation.

The testimony at the hearings of this committee is of exceptional interest. Prior to the death of Claus Spreckles, in 1907, his sons, Claus A. Spreckles and John D. Spreckles, had become involved in a bitter personal quarrel. John D. Spreckles had stayed with the trust after the merger. The other son, Claus A. Spreckles, had broken with the trust, and had made a huge fortune in the Hawaiian Islands in cane sugar. Prior to the Hardwick investigation, the brothers had not seen or spoken to each other for fifteen years. As a sugar-cane grower, Claus was bitterly opposed to the Dingley Tariff. He had gotten out an interesting pamphlet prior to the hearing which thoroughly exposed the specious contention of the trust that the tariff was necessary in order to protect "the high living standard of the American worker." By the use of a number of illuminating pictures, he had clearly demonstrated that precisely the same labor, that is, cheap coolie labor, was being used in the sugar-beet industry in California as was used in the Philippine Islands and in Hawaii. More: He had gone one step further and had produced photographs of workers in the German sugar-beet fields, showing, by contrast, that their standards were in fact higher than those prevailing in California.

His testimony before the Hardwick Committee has, in view of later developments in California farm labor, a remarkable pertinency. Referring to the Japanese and Hindu labor in the California fields, he said: "It is the avariciousness of the beet people that they employ them. If you want to build up a large Japanese and Asiatic colony in California, continue to give the bounty to the sugar-beet people. They are raising strawberries by the Japanese and Hindu laborers, when they are not raising beets. They use the same labor. In the mill they do use white men very largely, and from what I understand they operate the mill for three months and then let them tramp around over the State for the next nine months. California abounds with tramps. They have the climatic conditions, so they can walk the railroad tracks every day in the year." At this point, Congressman Raker, from California, spoke up: "They live in the summer the year round in California by tramping. It is a good country for tramps [Laughter]."

Continuing his testimony, Spreckles said: "The fact that foreign labor is employed almost exclusively both in the fields and factories is carefully concealed by the sugar-beet people and the excessive profits made possible by our high sugar tariff are obtained by promoters in the refineries and not by farmers in cultivating sugar beets."

An interesting colloquy took place between the members of the Hardwick Committee and John D. Spreckles. "The statement," asked Congressman Raker, "that this tariff is for the purpose of protecting the high-priced laboring man in America does not apply to the sugar industry, does it?" To which Spreckles answered: "No."

Raker: "You have to have the Japs?"

Spreckles: "Oh, yes, you cannot get any other kind of labor. If it had not been for the large number of these East Indians coming in there, whose labor was not so good, we would have had to take all Japs. Otherwise we would not have had the means of harvesting our crop. The East Indians, however, are an emaciated lot of people and they have not the strength to do the work."

Raker: "But it is the same kind of labor that does this work in the Philippines and in Hawaii that does your work in the West?"

Spreckles: "Yes. If we do not have the Japs to do the field labor, we would be in a bad fix, because you know American labor will not go into the fields." (His brother, however, had testified that, at first, when the factory was paying American growers the price which they had demanded, no difficulty was experienced in getting white workers.)

The testimony of other California growers, most of

them puppets of the Sugar Trust, was to the same effect. They admitted that of the total labor required in the industry, 10 per cent was factory labor and chiefly white-American, and 90 per cent was field labor which was practically 100 per cent foreign labor. In the northern California fields, the field labor was almost exclusively Japanese; in Southern California, it was 1/5 Japanese and 4/5 Mexican. Referring to the Mexican field labor, one grower said: "I don't know where they come from. They just keep coming, year after year. When the work is finished, I do not know where they go. That is the condition of our country." All of the field labor was employed on the *padrone* or contract system. "We could not grow beets unless we did have that kind of labor. They do the dirty work on our farms." Henry T. Oxnard, one of the large California growers who had joined the trust, was asked: "Then your business is based more or less upon the protection you receive from the Government?" "Yes, yes, it is," he replied, "you might say entirely."

By 1911 the individual growers had ceased to be a factor in the industry. John D. Spreckles testified, for example, that his company owned outright twenty thousand acres of sugar-beet land. "We had to buy some lands," he testified, "because of the farmers. We had to educate them in the cultivation of beets and they were loath to do it. They were accustomed to handle grain, to scratch the ground up a little bit and put in wheat and go back to town in the back of the saloon and play cards." There were, at the time, three sources of sugar beets for the factory: lands owned and operated by the factory; lands owned by the factory but rented to others; and independent growers. In

all three cases, however, the field labor was Japanese contract labor. In the case of the renters, for example, their
contract with the factory stipulated that certain types of
labor were to be provided directly by the factory. The few
small independent growers likewise employed Japanese
labor (they could not survive unless they met the competition of cheap labor), but they had ceased to be an important factor. The plantation system had been established.
It was more profitable in California, however, than it had
ever been elsewhere, for it was protected by an outrageous
tariff. Hailed as a great boon to the commonwealth of
California, the sugar-beet industry drove American farmers
from lands which they had settled and improved; converted
prosperous farming communities into plantations operated
by coolie labor; moved the factory into the rural sections;
and took most of the profits out of the community
where they had been created. In many respects, California had developed a colonial economy. By 1911 at least
one fourth of the sugar beets were grown on land owned
and operated by the trust. On lands which the trust
rented, it received one fourth of the crop as rental and itself
fixed the price paid for the balance of the crop. The rental
arrangement was, if anything, more profitable to the trust
than outright operation.

The sugar-beet industry, both in the factory and in the
field, created a sharp demand for cheap, seasonal labor.
James Bardin, one of the large shipper-growers in Salinas,
estimated that, for every man who formerly got work in
the wheat fields, 41½ men were needed in the cultivation,
harvesting, and processing of sugar beets. When sugar beets
were first grown in Anaheim (Southern California), only

about 20 or 30 workers were employed; within two years the number employed in sugar-beet fields in that vicinity had increased to 2000. But the season, as such, was short: approximately three months. Sugar beets, moreover, will not keep more than a week after they are taken from the ground; hence every effort is made to rush the harvest, a circumstance which intensified the demand for labor within a short period of time. With the sugar-beet acreage rapidly expanding, as new factories were built throughout the State, the demand for a large supply of migratory labor swiftly increased. Growers in the fruit and vegetable sections complained of an acute labor shortage and they, in turn, were forced to rely more and more upon Japanese labor. In 1899 there was a sharp increase in the demand for farm labor, coincident with the inauguration of sugar-beet production, and, by 1902, the shipper-growers were complaining of an unprecedented labor shortage "with tons of fruit and vegetables rotting in the fields." A labor survey, conducted at the time, closed with the biblical cry: "The harvest truly is great but the laborers are few." The factory system had arrived.

Nowhere in the United States were profits from sugar-beet acreage higher than in California. Not only were climatic and soil conditions favorable, but labor was cheaper. A report of the Department of Labor, in 1917, indicated that the sugar-beet industry in California made the highest net profit per acre and paid the lowest production costs per acre of any sugar-beet area in the United States. With the introduction of sugar beets — a highly intensive crop — production costs increased and the value of land skyrocketed. Sugar-beet production more than doubled the value of the land; in some cases, acreage increased from $100 an acre to $500 an acre, after sugar beets were introduced. While machine methods were later introduced, most of the labor involved was at first hand labor of a particularly arduous variety. It was estimated for example, in 1917, that 70 per cent of the labor involved in the production of sugar beets was hand labor. A survey made by the State Department of Labor in 1897 pointed out that "the beet crop demands large bodies of laborers on brief notice and the work will not admit of delay." The industry itself was never hesitant about voicing its demands for cheap labor: "The sugar-beet industry absolutely needs a labor supply at living wages and, sentiment aside, it must have it or lands and improvements must be idle." [3] Factory labor was not much of a problem; the difficulty involved was to recruit large numbers of workers, on short notice, and for a brief season, in the fields — the "squat" labor, so-called. To do this work cheaply and effectively, foreign labor was utilized. The newspaper files indicate that much foreign labor was imported, i.e. a colony of Greeks was established at Stockton, in 1902, to work in the sugar-beet fields. In 1897 about a third of the field labor was Chinese, but the work was rapidly taken over by the Japanese. In 1909, the Labor Commissioner reported that 6000 Japanese were working in the sugar-beet fields.

The introduction of sugar beets, moreover, had other consequences. It tended, for example, to bridge the gap between the country and the city. To function effectively, sugar-beet factories had to be located near beet fields, so the factories moved into the countryside. The factories, in

[3] *Pacific Rural Press*, January 4, 1902.

turn, demanded excellent communications and brought into existence a well developed network of highways. In this manner, "sugar beets helped to bring into existence the whole system of agricultural, orchard, and gardening industries in California."[4] In those communities where a sugar-beet factory was established, a cluster of small farm industries soon sprang into existence. The large-scale commercial cultivation of strawberries, for example, developed when the new highways began to appear; likewise, apple orchards began to prosper as highway construction improved. Many similar farm industries appeared in the wake of the sugar-beet factory. Under the influence of this development, the farm tended to become a factory and farming became an industry. In 1899 the agricultural products of California were valued at $100,000,000. With the turn of the century, some sixty or more crop industries had been established. It was discovered that the State was admirably adapted to this type of agriculture, as the variety of soils, seasonal conditions, and the fact that rainfall was concentrated in one period, made specialty, or diversified, farming highly profitable.

Sugar-beet production influenced the development of other crop industries, also, by creating a vast army of coolie labor. "Strawberries and sugar beets go together very nicely," Mr. John D. Spreckles had testified. One reason for this correlation was, of course, the fact that the Japanese laborers who had been recruited to work in the sugar-beet fields could be used, in the off-season periods, to work in berry fields. "The lower rates of pay of agricultural laborers," said John D. MacKenzie, Labor Commissioner, in

[4] *Pacific Rural Press*, December, 1897.

1910, "had not a little to do with the agricultural expansion which has been witnessed. The presence of a nomadic labor force, so fluid that some migrated from northern California to the opposite extreme of the state in the course of twelve months, and the ease with which its daily needs could be provided for made it possible to expand by developing beet and other industries in new territory, in advance of a settled population at all commensurate with the enterprises undertaken."

### 2. Fort Romie

When the production of sugar beets first began, California was in the throes of a depression. But, despite this fact, the supply of seasonal farm labor was not as plentiful as the sugar-beet growers desired. As a consequence, they began to experiment with various methods for recruiting additional farm laborers. In collaboration with the *San Francisco Call*, and the San Francisco Chamber of Commerce, Claus Spreckles began to support the program of the Salvation Army to create "a peasant proprietorship," i.e. to settle the unemployed on the land. Commenting on this general proposal, Spreckles said: "All I ask is that the people who are located on the lands shall be industrious and raise beets." An editorial in the *Pacific Rural Press* (March 27, 1897) praised the Salvation Army–Spreckles project; and lauded the idea of creating a "peasant class" to assist the sugar-beet growers in founding their industry. "Relish and contentment," read the editorial, "are essential to enlistment in rural life"; therefore, to anchor the worker to the community, by making him a type of peasant, adds to his "contentment and relish," and, incidentally, forces him to work at a lower wage rate.

Acting on Spreckles' encouragement, the Salvation Army, in 1898, purchased a tract of land near the town of Soledad, in Salinas Valley, close to the Spreckles sugar-beet factory. The tract was cut up into small lots of ten and twenty acres and sold to indigent families, mostly from San Francisco, on long-term payments. The community was known as Fort Romie. At first the colony did not succeed; the settlers lacked experience and the water supply was inadequate. But the Salvation Army came to the rescue and arranged to bring water to the land from the Salinas River, and, from that time on, the colony was moderately successful. By 1912, according to information furnished me by one of the original officials in charge of the project, "practically all of the land was paid for by the colonists and the colonization books were closed; they showed a profit to the Salvation Army, above all expenditures, of some $12,000." A bulletin of the Bureau of Labor, issued in September, 1903, describes the colony settlement and states that "the nearness of the famous sugar-beet factories of Mr. Claus Spreckles at Watsonville and Salinas, renders the success of the colony doubly certain." There were at that time (1903) about seventy colonists, including men, women and children at Fort Romie. H. Rider Haggard, visiting the colony in 1905 as a Commissioner for the British Government, reported that the settlement was a success, and, in general, endorsed the Salvation Army's program of returning the "landless man to the manless land." Mr. Haggard stressed certain factors responsible for the success of the colony: the fact that the land was irrigated and therefore capable of intensive cultivation; the spirit of co-operation that prevailed among the settlers; and the care with which the project was supervised. Most of the colonists worked for the sugar-beet companies, taking contracts for hoeing, thinning and topping sugar beets. That they did not receive exorbitant wages is apparent from the circumstances of their settlement. Mr. Spreckles' contribution to this philanthropy was his employment of the settlers when he needed them.

So far as I have been able to determine, the Fort Romie experiment was the first attempt made in California to settle the unemployed on the land. During periods of depression since 1898, this suggestion has recurred again and again, and one or two attempts have been made to put it into practice on a large scale (these ventures are described later). In 1934 Mr. Upton Sinclair, campaigning for the office of Governor, revived the proposal and promised, if he were elected, to throw the resources of the State behind the movement.

Contrary to popular impressions, Fort Romie, like the several later experiments, was a success. The experiment was so limited in scope, however, that it cannot be given too much significance. Commenting on the experiment, a farmer wrote in the *Pacific Rural Press* (October 30, 1897): "There is scarcely a practical farmer in this country who could feel himself competent to make a living from a patch of five or ten acres." But on irrigated land capable of intensive cultivation, with proper management, adequate financing, and co-operative methods such experiments can be successful. Fort Romie was a demonstration of this fact, but, with the general improvement of conditions after 1898, the experiment was forgotten. The growers were not interested in the demonstration, as it only involved seventy people, and they wanted thousands of workers. Although they have on occasion given lip service to the idea of colonization, they have never regarded it as a solution of their labor problem. To colonize "peasants" takes time and money, and the growers had discovered what seemed to be a quicker and easier solution.

In large part, it was the discovery of the Japanese that made the Fort Romie experiment superfluous. The appearance of the Japanese in the fields permitted the sugar-beet growers and their colleagues to utilize to the full the opportunities presented by favorable soil and climate in advance of a settled population. Some form of colonization would, under the circumstances, have been the only alternative. But colonization was abandoned for coolie labor. Coolie labor was cheaper and more effective. Colonization, moreover, would have been a threat to the large holdings; it involved a subdivision of the land and the establishment of small units. "The real problem," wrote H. A. Millis,[5] "is found in the development of a capitalistic agriculture with high land values, retarding the natural subdivision of the land and its settlement by families producing a number of crops and doing most of their own work." The growers that Mr. Millis interviewed in 1915 stated to him that they thought it was better to hold their property and have the land cultivated by camps of tenants than to subdivide it and sell it as small farms. The reason for this preference was, of course, that the small owners could not afford to pay the high prices which intensive, industrialized production had created for land values. It is significant that when the Japa-

[5] *The Japanese Problem in the United States,* 1915.

nese, in the course of a few years, began to settle on the land, as renters and owners, they were promptly excluded. Every threat to the integrity of the large holdings has received similar treatment. The exclusive use of the Japanese in the fields would have brought about a gradual subdivision of the land; but this tendency was quickly detected and as quickly scotched. The details of this particular operation, however, are reserved for a later chapter.

### 3.  The Development Associations

At an early date, California industry began to interest itself in the problem of encouraging immigration. The agitation seems to have been related, at the outset, to the Chinese question. It was thought that the Chinese eventually would have to go and that it was necessary, in advance of the fact, to recruit workers to take their place. A pamphlet issued in 1869, *Common Sense Applied to the Immigration Question,* by C. T. Hopkins, stressed this consideration and announced that an Immigration Association had been formed to encourage Eastern families to migrate to California. Formed at a later date, the California Development Association for many years carried on a systematic campaign to encourage immigration. Back of it, and similar associations, were the farm industrialists. In fact these "farmers" are largely responsible for having set in motion the tides of immigration which, of recent years, have threatened to engulf the State. It is, indeed, rather ironic to discover that the industrialists who lately have been decrying the "influx of transients" and posting illegal border patrols at the boundaries of the State to turn back immigrants are themselves largely responsible for the condition of which they complain.

In the transactions of the State Fruit-Growers' Convention for 1902 appears a report by H. P. Stabler on the labor problem. According to this report, the growers, in 1900, when they first experienced an acute labor shortage, had organized a committee to encourage Eastern immigration. This committee boasted that it had been responsible for bringing 30,000 people to California on special "colony" railroad rates which had been negotiated with the railroads; but, the report adds, the plan had not worked satisfactorily, for, "when it came to the guarantee or the giving of work to people, no one would stand behind us." With respect to this large initial influx of workers, it is also pointed out that "We have made no effort to take care of these people and they will not go into a twenty acre field and live with hogs." The report continues: "We have so degraded a certain class of labor, that there is not a man who lives in any agricultural locality who wants to get in and do this work." Throughout the first quarter of the century, the farm-industrialists actively engaged in the business of recruiting, by advertisements and solicitation, Eastern and Middle Western families to "migrate," i.e. to come West and work during the harvest. No work was guaranteed; the conditions of employment were grossly misrepresented; and no provision whatever was made to house or to care for the thousands of immigrants recruited in this manner. Needless to say, the farmers disclaimed all responsibility for the hordes of transients that came to California, and they have never been able to understand the phenomenon of the tramp or to regard with anything other than disdain the homeless and destitute people who gather in the cities during the winter months. As typical of this attitude, I quote from an editorial in the *Pacific Rural Press* (March 20, 1897): "These tramps drift to San Francisco as a haven of rest for the winter, relying upon charity to save them from the penalties of idleness and improvidence."

In 1901 the railroads were again induced to make special rates during the harvest season for Eastern "immigrants," i.e. seasonal workers, as "thousands are needed and there is great difficulty in securing help to harvest the crops." In 1902, the fruit growers established a permanent committee to conduct regular campaigns in the East for immigrant labor, stating that the "desirable workers of the East" must be induced to come to California for the season. In 1904, the growers sent a committee of ten men to the Eastern states to recruit farm laborers.⁶ One of the committeemen stated: "We prepared a special pamphlet setting forth the needs of the California fruit growers in the way of labor." Entitled *Grasp This, Your Opportunity*, over a hundred thousand copies of the pamphlet were distributed in the East. Although some 9301 workers signed applications, as a result of this campaign, and came to California to work during the season, the growers still complained that they did not have enough help. The report outlining this campaign and its results is truly eloquent in its smugness. The entire campaign only cost $3,500 — to move ten thousand people across a continent, work them a few months, and then turn them loose to find their way back or starve. A later report boasts that it cost the growers only four dollars or less, per head, to bring workers to California from the

⁶ *Pacific Rural Press,* February 13, 1904.

Eastern states. Immigration, apart from some program for colonization or settlement, was, of course, merely aggravating an already aggravated situation. The immigrants, for the most part, had the option of joining the migratory army of workers or of returning East. They could not purchase, except in rare instances, the high-priced California farm land. But the activities of the development associations were successful in setting in motion a steady current of transient labor Westward. In April, 1935, the Federal Government was supporting 77,118 transients who were stranded in California — 13.8 per cent of the total number of transients in the country who were being assisted by the Federal Government.

### 4. First Organization Efforts

As the California farm factories continued to expand production and to demand an ever larger supply of seasonal labor, there was a slight tendency for farm wages to increase. With the demand for labor increasing and wages rising, an initial attempt was made to organize farm labor. In 1901 a draymen's strike in San Francisco attracted the attention of the farm workers and pointed strikingly to future developments in California. "If this strike," wrote the *Pacific Rural Press*, "should continue, and if the stevedores should be drawn in, there would be a serious reduction of the output of the canneries." This collaboration, however, did not develop; but the statement clearly indicates that the growers have long been aware of the power which labor might exert if and when farm workers, teamsters, and longshoremen unite. Even so, the draymen's strike caused considerable alarm; it created, according to the farm journals, such "hateful conditions" that the farmers began to consider, even in 1901, the necessity for a "general law prescribing a closed season for strikers during the gathering and movement of staple crops." [7]

The draymen's strike seems to have given the labor leaders an idea, for preparations were made, during the strike, to organize farm labor. On March 28, 1903, after "two years of preparation," a farm laborers' union was formed at San Jose, with one H. Ryan elected president. The union proceeded to set up locals throughout the State and to elect delegates to the various federated trades councils. Among the activities organized by the new union was a labor bureau designed to secure some measure of regularity of employment and to formulate some accurate notion of the actual demand for farm labor. *Pacific Rural Press* (February 28, 1903) stated that the "farm laborers' union is becoming something more than an apprehension; it is moving toward realization. It is now proposed to send walking delegates through the state to form farm-hand unions." Later, on May sixteenth, the same journal observed that the residents of Santa Clara Valley were becoming "excited" about the union — "Fruit Workers Union No. 10,770." Unlike some present-day unions, the farm laborers had but one demand: they demanded a wage of two dollars a day. The president of the union, Ryan, quickly disclaimed any more ambitious program. "I am at liberty," he said, "to state that not a member has ever ventured such a radical suggestion as an eight-hour day for every worker in the fruit industry." In June, a local of the union was organized at Gilroy, Cali-

[7] *Pacific Rural Press*, August 24, 1901.

fornia, and demanded $1.50 a day without board, with hours from 7 A.M. to 12, and from 1 P.M. to 6 P.M. with overtime to be compensated at the rate of twenty cents an hour.

Although the union continued to function for some years, it never developed into an effective organization. It seems to have won some concessions, however, and it did make an impression on one or two of the growers. One grower, C. W. Thomas, called the attention of his associates to the fact that "the conditions which are forced on white migratory workers have a tendency to degenerate the man," and that unionization would inescapably follow if conditions were not improved. "Labor agitation," he pointed out, "is already in the hands of men inimical to the farmer." He advocated colonizing white farm labor and improving housing and working conditions, and providing schools for the children of migratory workers. The workers should be colonized so that they would be docile; they could, moreover, supplement their meager earnings by doing gardening on "waste" lands. He also warned his colleagues against permitting farm workers to have direct contact with city workers. City workers, he said, do not at present respect farm workers; and thus one group can be played off against the other to the advantage of the farmer. To this end, "some effort should be made to protect unorganized farm labor against organized skilled labor," a statement which indicates that organized labor in San Francisco was beginning to toy with the idea of organizing farm workers.

Several later attempts were made to organize farm labor in the years from 1900 to 1913, but, in most instances, the unions seem to have been disbanded shortly after their

formation. The type of organization used was the familiar
American Federation of Labor setup, with locals being
established in the towns. It was soon discovered that agricultural labor, at least at that time, could not be organized
in this manner. In most cases, the workers migrate; consequently the union ceases to exist at the close of the season.
Nor could the workers afford to pay the dues, small as they
were, which the American Federation of Labor required.
Little is known concerning the number of locals established
or their membership. That the unions were not particularly
effective is indicated by the fact that the growers, aside
from a few snarling editorials, ignored their existence.

Quite apart from the foregoing considerations, the extent
to which the Japanese had monopolized field labor in the
years from 1900 to 1913 made organization difficult, if not
impossible. The Japanese, as I will show later, had their own
organizations. They were not interested in American trade
unions. The dichotomy, moreover, which the growers had
developed between field labor and factory or shed labor,
with the foreign groups being assigned to the former and
the white workers to the latter, created a barrier which
made unionization extremely difficult. This barrier had to
be broken down, and the position of the Japanese shaken,
before genuine organization could make any headway. It
should be observed, however, that unions sprang into existence with the first appearance of factories in the fields. It
was not until 1913, with the Wheatland Riot, that farm
labor struck its first blow in California and it was, inter-
estingly enough, in 1913 that the first measure was enacted
by the California legislature in its campaign to exclude the
Japanese from the land.

## CHAPTER VII

# "OUR ORIENTAL AGRICULTURE"

In order to understand the present-day industrialized agriculture of California, with its heavy labor requirements, it is necessary to keep in mind the interacting effect of two factors: land monopolization and the availability of large units of cheap labor. If the large holdings had not been monopolized from the outset, it is quite likely that many small-acreage units would have developed. In a study of land-grabbing in California which appeared many years ago [1] it was pointed out that "this grabbing of large tracts has discouraged immigration to California more than any other single factor." There were at all times settlers galore, but no free land. Conversely, if the owners of the large estates had been unable to tap huge reserves of cheap labor after wheat cultivation had ceased to be profitable, it is quite likely that the development of large-scale intensive agriculture would have been retarded, perhaps never undertaken. The existence of large ownership units made possible the exploitation of cheap, coolie labor; while the availability of great reserves of cheap labor delayed the subdivision of the land and prevented land settlement by small individual owners. The availability of large reserves of

[1] "The West Coast Land Grabbers" by Bailey Millard, *Everybody's Magazine*, May, 1905.

cheap labor unquestionably accelerated the pace at which agriculture was industrialized in California.

At the outset it was not easy to secure an adequate, i.e. readily exploitable, reserve of cheap and efficient labor. For a time, the Chinese were admirably suited to the needs of the growers, but, when the Chinese were driven out, it became necessary to recruit the large army of farm laborers which the industry required from other sources. Immigration from Europe tended to stop in the Eastern industrial sections; it did not, for the most part, move westward. At one time, the farm industrialists thought that the completion of the Panama Canal would bring thousands of immigrant laborers to California; but the anticipated influx of cheap immigrant labor never materialized. Consequently the growers, at an early date, began to look Eastward, to the Orient, and south, to Mexico, for coolie and peon labor. From 1882, when the first Chinese Exclusion Act was passed, until about 1930, the history of farm labor in California has revolved around the cleverly manipulated exploitation, by the large growers, of a number of suppressed racial minority groups which were imported to work in the fields. A volume might well be written on each of these groups; the following sections merely summarize, in a general way, the circumstances under which each group has been recruited, exploited and excluded.

### 1. The Japanese

It is commonly believed that, with the passage of the Chinese Exclusion Act in 1882, the Japanese were immediately recruited to take the place of the Chinese in the economy of California. The facts, however, do not support this theory. So great was the temporary havoc worked by the exclusion of the Chinese, and by the campaign which drove them from the fields, that "over a half-million acres of farmland in California" were put out of cultivation. In 1882 there were 132,300 Chinese in California, but only about 86 Japanese resided in the state at that time. It was not so much the Exclusion Act of 1882 and the anti-Chinese riots of 1893 that resulted in the importation of the Japanese, as it was the development of sugar-beet production. Here was a new farm industry, requiring an extremely arduous variety of hand labor, in connection with which the Japanese could be quietly and inobtrusively imported. Anti-oriental sentiment was still strong throughout the State, and any immediate and general importation of Japanese would have been violently opposed.

Beginning in 1890, the Japanese were quietly imported. That they were induced to come to California is established beyond question. An official state document, strongly biased against the Japanese, concedes that "the Japanese were regarded as very valuable immigrants and efforts were made to entice them to come." [2] It was "during the nineties," according to Ichihashi, that "the Japanese appeared, although in small numbers, in all the important horticultural and agricultural districts of northern and central California where they were employed as seasonal hand workers." It was primarily in field, garden and orchard that the Japanese first appeared. The earliest recorded reference to their employment as farm laborers is a statement to the effect that "in the summer of 1888 about sixty Japanese were *invited*

[2] *California and the Oriental*, 1920.

to Vacaville to gather fruit." Japanese farm laborers appeared in Fresno in 1890, in Pajaro Valley in 1893 (in the sugar-beet fields), and in 1900 in Southern California (now their stronghold). By 1904 they were to be found in every part of the State. There were 2039 Japanese in California in 1890; by 1900, this figure had increased to 24,326, and, by 1910, when the Chinese and the Japanese populations were approximately equal, there were 72,156 Japanese in the State.

A report of the Industrial Commission on Immigration (Vol. XV, 1901), states that "in the State of California alone there is today a great army of Japanese coolies, numbering upwards of 20,000. They do not colonize as do the Chinese; they are scattered about the state, doing work in the orchards, vineyards, gardens, and hop and sugar-beet fields." The same report indicates that by 1898 the Japanese were doing most of the work in sugar beets and hops, and that they were rapidly monopolizing the work involved in berry cultivation (an industry closely related to sugar-beet production). By 1909, 30,000 Japanese were employed in California as farm laborers. "As laborers, they occupied a dominant position in most of the intensive, specialized agriculture, which at that time produced about half of the entire amount of agricultural products marketed. Their position thus was substantially the same as that of the Chinese except that the sector of agriculture which they occupied had grown to be very much more important than it had been at the time of the Chinese." [3] They were used chiefly during cultivation and harvest and found practically no employment on general, that is, non-specialized,

[3] *Migratory Labor in California*, 1936.

farms. "The presence of oriental labor in California cannot be considered of much value to the American farmer who actually farms his own land. The oriental farm laboring class is valuable principally to land speculators or developers who do not farm their own lands." [4]

It is important to note several characteristics of Japanese farm labor in California. In the first place, most of the Japanese who came to California were experienced farmers. They went directly to the fields to work; they were farmers, or farm laborers, from the outset. The soil and climate of California, moreover, were admirably adapted to the type of agriculture in which they had been trained. As farm laborers they were, if anything, more efficient than the Chinese and more industrious. They were, by the circumstances of their importation, perfectly suited to the requirements of farm labor in California. "The first requisite of seasonal laborers," writes Ichihashi, "is ability to move about quickly without incurring much transportation expense." The Japanese, at first, did not colonize; they moved throughout the State, at their own expense, working as migratory farm laborers. They were not even "bunkhouse labor"; no one knew just where they lived. "The Japs and Chinks," said J. L. Nagle, of the California Fruit Growers Exchange, "just drift — we don't have to look out for them. White laborers with families, if we could get them, would be liabilities." The second requirement of California farm labor is its ability to hibernate, i.e. the seasonal worker is expected to disappear when the crops are harvested. The Japanese were extremely accommodating on this score. They vanished at the end of the season. Moreover they

---

[4] *California and the Oriental*, supra.

quickly organized themselves in a manner calculated to enhance their efficiency as farm laborers, forming "clubs" and "associations" of Japanese workers, and designating a "secretary" who located work for them and directed and co-ordinated their work in the fields. It has been estimated, for example, that at one time there were as many as three hundred such employment agencies or associations. That they rationalized methods of employment and facilitated the quick movement of the Japanese from crop to crop is incontestable.[5] Being mostly men of middle age with no settled homes, or families, they were highly mobile. They provided their own camping facilities, such as they were, and asked no favors.

So perfectly did the Japanese fit into the pattern of industrialized agriculture in California that, at first, there was no opposition to them from any source. They performed a function which seemed almost indispensable in the operation of the horticultural and agricultural industries in California. There was no prejudice against them; in fact, they were enthusiastically welcomed. They were a godsend to the large farm industrialists of the State, and, at first, there was no popular resentment against them. Writing in retrospect on the Japanese problem, Robert Welles Ritchie correctly states: "Let us be very blunt and say that the Japanese never displaced white men."[6] They drove no one out of employment, for, in truth, there was a shortage of labor. Not only did they perform the most menial and undesirable

---

[5] See *Japan and the California Problem*, 1921, by T. Iyenaga and Kenoske Sato.

[6] *Country Gentleman*, March 1, 1924.

varieties of field labor, but they created new crop industries and expanded the demand for farm labor.

Because of their skill and industry, the Japanese brought about great changes in California agriculture. It is impossible to appraise adequately the full extent of their remarkable contributions. At an early date, the Japanese began to experiment with rice cultivation in Sutter, Yuba, Colusa, Glenn, and Butte counties. The land which they leased for this purpose was "waste land," covered with a layer of "hardpan" and, as a consequence, not under cultivation at the time and generally regarded as worthless. It was a Japanese, K. Ikuta, who, in fact, first demonstrated that rice could be grown successfully in California. By 1918, the Japanese had some 25,000 acres in rice in California. Today the industry has a gross annual income in excess of $20,-000,000. The great delta section of the Sacramento River, today perhaps the most valuable agricultural land in the State, was largely reclaimed by Japanese workers. It was in this area that a Japanese, George Shima, became famous as the "Potato King" of the world. The Japanese towns of Florin and Livingstone, which figured so largely in the anti-Japanese hysteria of 1919 and 1920, were waste lands, famous for their sands and winds, until the Japanese reclaimed them and began to grow berries. "The most striking feature of Japanese farming in California has been this development of successful orchards, vineyards, or gardens on land that was either completely out of use or else employed for far less profitable purposes." In the Sacramento, San Joaquin, Santa Clara, and Imperial Valleys, it was the Japanese who, for the most part, were responsible for the reclamation of waste lands. The hardships they experienced in the course of this pioneer activity requires no emphasis. In many cases, they worked under exceedingly unhealthy conditions, in swamps, river deltas, and marshes. In Fresno County alone, when water and sanitary conditions were bad, the Japanese lost an estimated three thousand lives. It is impossible even to approximate the enormous contribution which the Japanese made, in the course of a quarter of a century, to California agriculture.

It was not long, however, before anti-Japanese prejudice began to be organized and exploited in California. A number of complex factors must be considered in tracing the rise of anti-Japanese sentiment. Despite the eloquent arguments to the contrary which their defenders have advanced, it is a fact that the Japanese at first underbid all other farm-labor groups. When they first entered the fields, they worked for thirty-five and forty cents a day, and less, and provided their own transportation and boarded themselves. They not only underbid white laborers, but, at the outset, they even worked for less than the Chinese and the Hindus.[7] To the extent that they at first depressed farm wages in California, the Japanese were, of course, highly regarded by the large farm industrialists. To the same extent, however, they tended to antagonize the small farmers who found it increasingly difficult to compete with the large-scale farms; and, also, they began to incur the ill will of other farm-laboring groups. The problem is even more complex than I have indicated. For example, when the Japanese began to own land themselves, they employed members of their race

[7] See *The Japanese Problem in the United States*, 1915, by H. A. Millis, by all odds the best work in this highly controversial field.

to the exclusion of all other groups. Millis refers to a study made of 1773 Japanese-owned farms in 1915. These farms employed 17,784 workmen, of whom 96 per cent were Japanese. But, as the Japanese began to monopolize farm labor, they demanded higher wages. Wages of Japanese farm laborers increased 50 per cent in fifteen years. By 1907 their labor enjoyed a scarcity value and they were the highest paid farm-labor group in the State. As they came to demand higher wages, however, they incurred the animus of the large growers and the chief group support which they had theretofore received was removed. "The patient little slant-eyed people" began to alienate middle-class groups which had previously been indifferent to their presence. As indicative of how sentiment was changed in California, I quote from an editorial in the *Los Angeles Times:* "Japanese labor is not cheap labor. The little brown traders know how to get as much for their product as the traffic will bear." (January 17, 1920.)

The real prejudice against the Japanese, however, dates from the time when they began to be small owners, rather than farm laborers. In a report on Japanese landownership issued in 1909, John D. Mackenzie, Commissioner of Labor Statistics, pointed out that "the moment this ambition [land-ownership] is exercised, that moment the Japanese ceases to be an ideal laborer." Through their thrift and enterprise, the Japanese soon began to exercise their ambition to own land. "Land," to quote Millis again, "tends to fall into possession of the race occupying the pivotal place in the labor supply." Occupying, as they certainly did, the pivotal place in the labor supply [they supplied 80 per cent of the celery labor, 90 per cent of the berry labor, 70 per cent of

the asparagus labor, 65 per cent of the cantaloupe labor,
90 per cent of the garden labor, 70 per cent of the deciduous fruit labor, 85 per cent of the lettuce labor, and practically all of the sugar-beet labor], the Japanese rapidly moved
forward into the landowning classification. The moment
this change in status became apparent, the Japanese ceased
to be desirable aliens. Testifying before a Congressional
Committee in 1925, S. Parker Friselle (manager of the
5000-acre Kearney Ranch near Fresno, owned by the
Regents of the University of California) admitted that the
Japanese were model citizens and excellent farm workers.
"But," he said, "they do not want to work for anybody else.
The Japanese wants to work his own farm." "If he could
have been kept as a laborer," writes Eliot Grinnel Mears of
the Japanese (*Survey*, May, 1926), "it would have been a
great benefit [*sic*] to California." It was this ambition —
land hunger — that resulted in the hysterical campaign
against the Japanese, which, tapping the current of feeling
that had been developed against the Chinese, culminated in
the enactment of an Alien Land Act in 1913 (re-enacted in
1919); and the Federal restriction on further Japanese immigration in 1924.

The Japanese, by acquiring land, antagonized both the
large shipper-growers and the small farmers in California.
The large farm industrialists opposed Japanese ownership
for two reasons: It threatened the continued existence of
large units of production and it decreased the supply of
farm labor. Most of them were in favor of the Alien Land
Act because, as one of them put it, the act prevented the
"Asiatics from getting a firm foothold and permanent position in the community." Having permitted the Japanese to

convert large tracts of waste land into immensely valuable farming properties, the large industrialists were quite willing to use the Alien Land Act as a club to force the Japanese to sell to them. From this point of view, the Alien Land Act was designed to consolidate and to safeguard large ownership units in California. Whether so designed or not, it clearly had this effect.

The small owners, on the other hand, favored the Alien Land Act for other reasons. As farmers, the Japanese "carried on the process already begun in California; they intensified cultivation even further than it had been done before them, raising the productivity of the land and its yield, and raising land values correspondingly. This process, which was general throughout California and was the natural historic direction intended and carried on by the bulk of California agriculturists, was resented when the Japanese became a partner to it. It implied difficulties for the small farmers who wished to buy or lease land: the higher prices stood in their way."[8] In 1904, the Japanese owned 2442 acres of land and leased 54,830 acres. After the Gentleman's Agreement of 1905, which was interpreted as a stabilization of Japanese-American relations, the ownership figures mounted: by 1909 the Japanese owned 16,449 acres and leased 137,233 acres; but these figures, standing alone, do not account for the widespread resentment against the Japanese in the rural sections. To understand this resentment, it must be kept in mind that the Japanese were clustered in the irrigated sections, the areas of intensive cultivation. In these sections, the small farmers and tenants found it difficult to compete with the Japanese

[8] *Migratory Labor in California*, supra.

who consistently overbid them for leases. In 1917 the value of the crops produced on Japanese-owned or controlled acreage in California was three and a half times as much as that obtained by California farms in general. The Japanese were naturally able, not only to bid more for leases, but to pay more for land, than their competitors. As a consequence, land values rapidly rose in the areas where they had concentrated.

Another factor, of great importance in so far as the large growers were concerned, was the circumstance that the Japanese, as farm laborers, developed "a sort of spontaneous organization that made them not quite as tractable as the Chinese. The consensus of opinion of growers on this subject is almost unanimous in the early years of the century." From the proceedings of the California Fruit Growers Convention of 1907, this quotation is taken: "The Chinese when they were here were ideal. They were patient, plodding, and uncomplaining in the performance of the most menial service. They submitted to anything, never violating a contract. The Japanese now coming in are a tricky and cunning lot, who break contracts and become quite independent. They are not organized into unions, but their clannishness seems to operate as a union would. One trick is to contract work at a certain price and then in the rush of the harvest threaten to strike unless wages are raised." A farmer, in 1902, commented upon the Japanese as follows: "He is like the Irishman's flea; you think you have him but you haven't." "The Japanese," he said, "have a deficiency in their mental make-up, for they cannot or do not understand that honor should obligate them to stay with their employer when he needs them most." Caught between the small farmer and the large grower, the Japanese, although putting up a stubborn fight, were to a large extent squeezed out of California agriculture and robbed of the full fruits of their contribution.

The feeling against the Japanese in California is outlined in a highly prejudiced, but nevertheless illuminating, novel: *Seed of the Sun* by Wallace Irwin (1921). Mr. Irwin tells the story of an American gentlewoman who, returning to her California estate, finds that she has to depend upon Japanese laborers. When she wants them at harvest time, they are not to be found. The inference is left that they, the Japanese, wanted to see the crop destroyed so that they might buy the farm or make a favorable lease. Actually, the more likely explanation is that they simply demanded higher wages. The hysterical tone of the novel is amusing. Bad as the Japanese were, it seems that the I.W.W. were worse. The lady owner thus voices her intense California indignation: "I've never told you the things I went through in Sacramento and Stockton, begging and imploring white men to work at any price. Right in the midst of the harvest season great muscular louts stood with their hands in their pockets, gathered in knots to talk about world revolution and to insult women as they passed. Out round Lodi the I.W.W. delegates were nailing up signs demanding five dollars a day for an eight-hour day and seventy-five cents an hour for overtime. Work seems to have gone out of fashion. What's happening to our country?" When some of these wobblies appeared to work, Mr. Irwin's heroine — vociferous in her self-righteous Americanism — hires them but with misgivings. "At sunset they went on strike and demanded five dollars apiece, a full day's wage. Anna paid

Japanese laborer near Palo Alto, California.

Potato diggers near Sacramento, California.

"Imported" California field workers.

Hindu workers in California fields.

the bribe to get rid of them, because they were dangerous men, with cruel, weak and criminal faces." The description is illuminating; at a later date scores of I.W.W.'s actually served long sentences in San Quentin Prison for the offense of making such demands.

The Japanese in California are, today, no longer an important element as farm laborers. The Immigration Act of 1924, excluding Japanese from entry, has prevented the replenishment of the pool of first generation Japanese, who much more than the second generation supplied agricultural wage labor in the desired quantities. The enforcement of the Alien Land Act, moreover, had a tendency to drive the Japanese into the cities. After 1920, the large growers, who of course employ the bulk of farm labor in California, began to use Filipino and Mexican labor, as it was unorganized and cheaper. The Japanese who remain in agriculture have moved into the ownership category, notably in Southern California, through various methods and devices whereby they have been able to escape the provisions of the Alien Land Law. For practical purposes, this law is today, in many communities, a dead letter. But it should not be forgotten that the statute, when first adopted, had the effect of appropriating large values created and owned by the Japanese. An examination of court records in California would clearly indicate the manner and extent to which the act has been used to rob the Japanese. The Japanese have made their peace with the Californians but at a heavy price.

### 2. "Rag Heads"

Boasting vociferously at all times of their intense Americanism, the farm industrialists of California have always been indifferent as to the sources they have tapped for cheap labor. Any labor will do, providing only that it is cheap and docile. In the years 1907, 1908, 1909, and 1910, "the tide of turbans" began, as Hindustani workers appeared in the fields. Entering the United States for the most part by way of Canada, they gradually drifted south to the great farm valleys of California. For a time they worked as railroad section hands, but it was not long before they became an important source of farm labor. Most of them were trained agricultural workers, with experience in the cultivation of corn, sugar cane, cotton and melons. In 1907 the first "rag head" — as the Hindus are referred to in California — workers appeared in the San Joaquin Valley, and, in 1910, they were to be found in the fields near Sacramento and in the Imperial Valley. According to Paul Taylor (*Mexican Labor in the United States*, 1928) Hindu workers helped "pick cotton in 1910 in the first cotton harvest of any great commercial importance in Imperial Valley." It was soon discovered that the Hindus were well adapted to laboring conditions in the areas of intense heat, notably in the Imperial Valley, and in harvesting crops that require a monotonous and arduous variety of labor, such as asparagus cutting. For many years these picturesque "rag heads" were to be seen in California, "continually on the wing, coming from the melon and cotton crops in the Imperial Valley en route to the fig orchards and vineyards of Fresno or the rice fields near Sacramento."

From the growers' point of view, the Hindus fitted nicely into the pattern of farm labor in California. Not only were they good workers, but they could be used as one additional racial group in competition with other racial groups, and thereby wages could be lowered. A notable fact about farm labor in California is the practice of employers to pay wage scales on the basis of race, i.e. to establish different wage rates for each racial group, thus fostering racial antagonism and, incidentally, keeping wages at the lowest possible point. As part of this general strategy, "it is a common custom of the ranches to entrust a particular work to a group of laborers of the same nationality." In this manner, of course, the races are kept segregated and are pitted one against the other. Because of their difference in custom, language, and appearance, the Hindus were a particularly valuable intermediary group. They were used, and still are to some extent, as a wedge to separate the Mexican and Oriental groups. How general the custom is of pitting one race against the other is indicated by the fact that, in 1937, the bookkeeper of the Hotchkiss Ranch (one of the large farm-factories in the San Joaquin Valley) had to be a trained linguist, as he was dealing with four or five racial groups. The foreman of the Giffen Ranch, in the same area, stated to a reporter that: "Last year our Hindu workers struck. So this year we mixed half Mexicans in with them, and we aren't having any labor trouble." The diversity of races, of course, also increases the difficulty of union organization.

Regarded as excellent farm laborers, the Hindus no longer figure as an important racial group in California. Like the Japanese, they moved rapidly into the landownership class. By 1918, they operated, as owners or lessees, some 45,000 acres of rice land in California. The census of 1930 gives the number of Hindu residents in the State as 1873, and the number of residents seems to be decreasing. The number of Hindu workers in the State, however, is in excess of this figure. Prior to the war, there were approximately 10,000 Hindu workers in the fields. As California farmers, they soon faced the same restrictions that were imposed against the Japanese. By the Immigration Act of 1917, which excluded immigration from certain "barred zones," further Hindu immigration was prohibited. Since further immigration has been prohibited and since most of the Hindus in California are men, many of them have returned to India in quest of wives. It should also be pointed out that the Alien Land Act operates against Hindus as well as Japanese, and its enactment naturally tended to discourage further Hindu immigration.

In *Caste and Outcast* (1923) Dhan Gopal Mukerji tells of his adventures as a Hindu farm laborer in California. Speaking of his fellow countrymen, he writes: "I found them very hard working people, living almost wholly on vegetables, and having in general such a low standard of living that the native Americans were agitating against Hindu immigration on the ground that my countrymen were pulling down the wages and getting all the jobs." He discovered men "drinking up their wages in order to forget they were alive, all the old Indian bringing up was being swept away by a few months of inhumanly cruel work." Mukerji states that he went to work, in the asparagus fields, at half past three in the morning and worked until after dark at night, picking asparagus at a few cents a box.[9]

[9] For further details on the harsh adventures of the "rag heads" in California see *Hindustani Workers on the Pacific Coast* (1923) by Rajani Kanta Das.

### 3. The Armenians and Others

According to an immigration study made in 1894, there were Armenian colonies at Fresno, Reedley, Fowler and other communities in California. During the last quarter century, however, the Armenians have concentrated at one point: Fresno. Today, Fresno, California, has the largest Armenian colony in the United States; it is estimated that one fifth, or possibly one fourth, of the entire population of Fresno, is made up of Armenians. There are, in fact, more Armenians in California than in the rest of the United States. By and large, the Armenians came to Fresno from the Eastern industrial sections and, in California, they have concentrated upon one industry, raisin growing. Amazingly successful in this field, they moved rapidly into the land-owning classification being, as a race, free from the restrictions of the Alien Land Act. While the local residents hate to confess their indebtedness to the Armenians, it is quite apparent that the Armenians are largely responsible for the development of the raisin industry in California. They brought with them, as one farmer observed, "a familiarity with the vine." Being a thrifty people, they contributed no small part of the capital necessary to develop the great vineyards of the San Joaquin Valley. "The Armenians," writes their historian M. Vartan Malcom,[10] "have shown a desire for land not less strong than that of the Japanese." And, in their desire for land, "The Armenians have paid a higher price per acre for the farms purchased by them than any other race." As a consequence, they have

[10] *The Armenians in America*, 1919.

been pretty thoroughly fleeced by land companies and by the banks. Of 3000 farms operated by them in Fresno in 1921, 20 per cent were rented. "All members of the Armenian family work on the ranch. Some add to their earnings by working in packing houses or nearby ranches."

That their occupation of the land near Fresno has not been an altogether pleasant experience is indicated in a revealing and highly significant court action.[11] This decision arose out of a dispute in Fresno in 1923. The local growers, in order to stabilize price conditions in the raisin industry, had organized the Sun-Maid Raisin Growers Association. But, at that time, they did not have the support of the State in organizing the farmers. Today, for example, under the pro-rate laws, they can, in effect, compel farmers to join. At that time, however, they had to rely upon "persuasion." The defendant, Papazian, an Armenian farmer who had lived in Fresno for fifteen years, refused to join the association, sensing that the association had been organized for the protection of the large, not the small, grower. The answer of Papazian in the suit alleged, and it was not denied at the trial, that he had been forced to sign an agreement with the association. His banker had threatened to foreclose the mortgage on his farm if he refused to sign; and, when he still persisted in his refusal, "night riders" descended upon his home and threatened him and his family. He was so concerned for his safety that he moved his family into another county and commuted to his farm. Still bent upon obtaining his "consent" the night riders finally burned his home to the ground. Papazian, naturally, signed the agreement. He testified that such methods were gen-

[11] *Sun-Maid Raisin Growers* v. *Papazian,* 74 Cal. App. 231.

erally used in Fresno by the association to force the small farmers to "sign up."

Many other racial groups began to appear in California after 1890, and, as tenant farmers, they soon acquired a foothold in subsidiary lines, such as dairy farming, or in certain crops such as artichokes. Charles Howard Shinn observed in 1891 that "The Portuguese are already the peasantry of the rich valleys." In 1921 some 8000 Portuguese were mentioned as operating farms in California, of whom 70 per cent, incidentally, were tenant farmers. Most of the Portuguese came to California from the Azores and Canary Islands, about 1890, as sailors and fishermen, and then drifted into the farming communities along the coast, notably San Luis Obispo, Watsonville, and Humboldt. Certain communities, such as Crow's Landing, are 90 per cent Portuguese communities. Dairy farming in northern and central California is approximately 75 per cent Portuguese operated. It is apparent that the foreign groups, notably the Swiss, Portuguese, and Italians, moved into the backward areas and occupied, as tenant farmers, the position made vacant by the exodus of the original settlers. A report of the Industrial Commission on Immigration (Vol. XV, at p. 500, 1901), states that "the list of vine growers of California in the year 1881, when viticulture was yet in an incipient state, gives 141 Italians." In 1897, some 45,625 Italians were living in California, of which a large group were engaged in farming as small owners and tenants, operating some 2726 farms in the State. In certain crops, such as artichokes, the Italians have a predominant position. The famous Italian–Swiss wineries and vineyards in Sonoma County were established in 1881 as co-operative ventures. Today, these former co-operatives are controlled by Mr. Joseph Di Giorgio, about whom a word of comment might be illuminating.

In 1921, Mr. Di Giorgio owned some 20,482 acres of the best fruit lands in California. An immigrant from Sicily, he began as a fruit commission broker and gradually began to operate fruit farms. In the San Joaquin Valley, he operates two large farm-factories, one at Arvin, or Weed Patch, of 6000 acres; another, of 6000 acres, at Delano. His company, Di Giorgio Fruit Corporation, is today the world's largest shipper of fresh fruit, with some 40,000 acres of fruit land in the United States, principally in California, in addition to large acreage in Mexico, Central America, and South America. The company has an estimated net worth of $30,-000,000. At the Weed Patch, or Arvin, "factory," about 1000 employees are hired the year round, with an additional 2500 employees during the picking and packing season. The so-called "permanent" employees live on the ranch, in a company town, operated much as a mining company town or a steel town, with the usual paternalistic devices, such as hospital, dormitories, tennis courts, and so forth. In an interesting interview in the *Los Angeles Times*, August 15, 1937, which appeared under the title "I Work; You Work; the Land Works," Mr. Di Giorgio set forth his views on labor organization. It seems that some organizers appeared at his factory and said, "Mr. Di Giorgio, we're going to unionize your farm." "You're going to what?" he demanded. "My men are free men. You aren't going to do anything here they don't want done!" So concerned was Mr. Di Giorgio about the "freedom" of his employees, that he promptly called a meeting and addressed his men on the subject of unionization. "You know that one day the fruit is green," he orated, "and the next it's ready, and the third and it's rotting. We're in the shipping business and it's gotta move. How can you have a union? If you think you can, go ahead and try it. If this farm goes to hell your jobs do, too." The employees then "voted" and, after the vote was taken, announced the result. "Mr. Di Giorgio, we have voted." "That's a good American way," Di Giorgio replied. "Do you give your pay to those fellows in the city, or not?" To quote from the interview: "A smile flashed across the man's sunburned face. 'The men say nothin' doing.' 'Good,' said Di Giorgio, 'on the Di Giorgio farms we grow crops — and men!'"

### 4. *The Mexicans*

Mexican labor, to some extent, was used in California agriculture prior to the World War. It was during the war, however, that the great influx of Mexican labor began. The newspapers and farm journals in 1917 contain many references to large groups of Mexicans, in units of 1500 and 2500, being brought into Imperial Valley by truck from San Felipe and Guaymas "to relieve the labor situation." The Immigration Law of 1924, which practically stopped immigration from Europe, gave an added impetus to Mexican immigration. Governor C. C. Young, in 1930, appointed a Fact-Finding Committee which, in that year, made its report on *Mexicans in California*. At that time, the Mexican population in the State was estimated at 250,000. The farm journals refer to the year 1920 as a "Mexican harvest," indicating that at least fifty per cent of the migratory labor employed that year was Mexican. In February, 1926, the growers in the San Joaquin Valley, over the protest of the Central Labor Council, began to import Mexicans on a large scale and to agitate in Congress for the "importation of Mexicans under federal supervision." In that year, Mr. S. Parker Frisselle was sent to Congress "to get us Mexicans and keep them out of our schools and out of our social problems." [12] In the same magazine for March 2, 1927, it was announced that 15,000 Mexicans had been imported to the San Joaquin Valley for the harvest of that year. Over a hundred trucks, loaded with Mexicans, were counted passing over the Ridge Route in a single day. It was stated in the *Pacific Rural Press*, March 8, 1930, that, during the period 1924 to 1930, an average of 58,000 Mexicans were brought into the State to work in the fields each year. In the decade 1920 to 1930 the Mexicans were unquestionably the largest single element in the 200,000 agricultural laborers in the State.

During this decade, 1920 to 1930, the farm industrialists were enchanted with the Mexican. The Mexicans were available in large numbers (at least 150,000 worked in the fields during these years); they were good workers; unorganized; and, at the end of the season, "hibernated." Time and again, in their deliberations, the growers have emphasized the fact that the Mexican, unlike the Filipino, can be deported. It has been estimated, for example, that 80 per cent of the Mexicans in California have entered illegally, due to technical violations, and are subject to deportation. The Mexican, moreover, is easily exploited not only by the growers, but by the small merchants in the rural towns. "The Mexican," writes Ralph H. Taylor, dean of the Cali-

[12] *Pacific Rural Press*, February 13, 1926.

fornia farm-capitalist publicists, "has no political ambitions; he does not aspire to dominate the political affairs of the community in which he lives." "The Mexican," writes A. C. Hardison, a California building-and-loan-company official, "gives less trouble with collections than the whites." "The Mexican laborer," writes Dr. George Clements of the Los Angeles Chamber of Commerce, "if he only realized it, has California agriculture and industry in the hollow of his hand. We cannot get along without the Mexican laborer." In 1927, Simon J. Lubin, in an address in Sacramento, charged that the farm industrialists were importing peon Mexican labor and stated that, in certain cases, Mexicans were being guarded in barbed-wire stockades on the ranches. Commenting on this address, the *Pacific Rural Press* (December 17, 1927) entered a pious, if somewhat equivocal, protest. "Peon? Isn't the word peon a little out of character when applied to a Mexican family which buzzes around in its own battered flivver, going from crop to crop, seeing Beautiful California, breathing its air, eating its food, and finally doing the homing pigeon stunt back to Mexico with more money than their neighbors dreamed existed?" The article closes with an interesting admission: If Mexican immigration were barred, it would mean that industry and agriculture would compete for labor, and the price of farm labor would mount. But, if agriculture is permitted to exploit its own exclusive labor sources, then no competition exists and agricultural wages can be kept at a subsistence level. The general attitude of the growers towards the Mexicans is summarized in a remark made by a ranch foreman to a Mexican: "When we want you, we'll call you; when we don't — git."

The first jarring note in the beautiful accord between the growers and their 150,000 peons occurred when, in 1925 and 1926, Congress began to consider the Box Bill and the Harris Bill, both of which measures were designed to place Mexican immigration on a quota basis (the quota allotment would have been 1575). These measures "created a first-class panic in California." The farm industrialists immediately dispatched their cleverest lobbyists to Washington to fight the measures. S. Parker Frisselle, appearing before the Congressional committee which had the bills under consideration, described the Mexican. "The Mexican," he said, "is a 'homer.' Like the pigeon he goes back to roost." "We in California would greatly prefer some setup in which our peak labor demands might be met and upon completion of our harvest these laborers would be returned to their country." Reporting back to the Fruit Growers' Convention in 1927, Mr. Frisselle stated: "As you know, the Mexican likes the sunshine against an adobe wall with a few tortillas and in the off time he drifts across the border where he may have these things." Referring to the protests of the State social-welfare agencies that the Mexican was a heavy burden on these services, he said: "If charity spends one dollar on the Mexican in California, the State profits two dollars by having him here. The Mexican can be deported if he becomes a county charge, but the others are here to stay." In the congressional hearings, he was asked if the Mexican ever becomes a land-owner. "No," was the reply, "the Mexican is not aggressive. He is amenable to suggestions and does his work. He does not take the Chinese or the Japanese attitudes. He is a fellow easy to handle and very quiet in his living, a man who gives us no trouble. He takes his orders and follows them." The employment of this agreeable fellow, the Mexican, thousands of whose countrymen were imported annually to work in the fields, steadily depressed wage rates for farm labor in California. In 1928, when wages were at the peak, Mexican labor was earning 35 cents an hour, but, with the depression, this rate sank to 15 cents and 14 cents an hour. Nor do these rates adequately reflect the miserable condition of Mexican labor in California, as the work in the fields is seasonal, and the Mexicans are supposed to support themselves in the off seasons and to pay their own transportation expenses.

Throughout the years from 1914 to 1930 the large farms used Mexican labor as their main source of cheap, easily exploitable farm labor in the State, beating down wage rates and forcing the cities to assume the burden of supporting the Mexicans during the period of "hibernation." But the agitation over the Box Bill and the Harris Bill frightened Mexican labor. Despite the fact that both measures were defeated (largely because of the powerful opposition of the California growers) many Mexicans left the State. An "increasing exodus" was reported in 1931 as a result of "intimidating propaganda." [13] Another factor tending to discourage the entry of Mexicans was the fact that the State Department began to change its entrance requirements. "The State Department," wrote Mr. R. V. Garrod, February 5, 1930, "has reduced the rate of legal entrants from Mexico from a six year average of 58,000 per annum to approximately 16,000. This has been done by strictly enforcing the present immigration requirements. The new deportation law, effective July 1, 1929, has permanently

[13] *California Cultivator,* June 20, 1931.

stopped the illegal entries from Mexico, estimated to have been around 40,000 per annum in recent years. Thus total entrants from Mexico have been reduced from around 100,000 per annum to approximately 16,000." Dr. Clements has estimated that 150,000 Mexicans were "either frightened or repatriated back to Mexico."

An added factor was the circumstance that, during the depression, the cities began to rebel. The burden of the Mexican in the winter months became oppressive, and thousands of Mexicans were "repatriated." Beginning in February, 1931,[14] thousands of Mexicans, many of whom were citizens of the United States, were herded together by the authorities and shipped back to Mexico, to get them off the relief rolls. The last figures which I had on the "repatriations" indicated that in excess of 75,000 Mexicans had been shipped out of Los Angeles alone, at the expense, not of the growers, but of the taxpayers of the city of Los Angeles; but, when the harvest season once again came around, the growers dispatched their "emissaries" to Mexico, and again recruited thousands of Mexicans. Many Mexicans have been "repatriated" two and three times, going through this same curious cycle of entry, work, repatriation. The threat which the authorities held over the Mexicans was, of course, that either they must "agree" to repatriation or relief allotments would cease. The net result of these developments – the agitation for a limitation on Mexican immigration and the repatriation shipments – has been a marked curtailment in the use of Mexican labor.

Another factor should, however, be noted. In November,

[14] See an article which I wrote for the *American Mercury*, March, 1933.

1927, a Confederation of Mexican Labor Unions was organized in Los Angeles, and, on April 22, 1928, the Mexican Labor Union of Imperial Valley was set up in an attempt to organize a strike among the cantaloupe pickers. The growers promptly cracked down a swift reign of terror. The local sheriff announced in the press that if the strike was not called off, "a general deportation movement of all Mexican laborers employed in the valley would begin." Approximately a hundred arrests were made; large numbers of Mexicans were turned over to the immigration officials for deportation; scab farm labor was recruited in Texas and Oklahoma; and the strike was broken. While organized on a nationalistic basis, the Mexican unions showed I.W.W. and syndicalist influences in their methods of organization. While this first strike was broken, Mexican field labor grew more and more restive in the years 1930, 1931, 1932, 1933 and 1934, and, to a like degree, became less satisfactory to the growers. Still an important factor in the farm-labor groups in California, the Mexican, like his predecessors, was used for a purpose, and, when other developments intervened, was, like the Chinese and Japanese, discarded. The period of the Mexican was, roughly, between 1914 and 1934.

## 5. The Filipino

The last racial group to be imported into the California fields was the Filipino. Filipino immigration became important, for the first time, in 1923, when 2426 Filipinos entered the State. The occasion for their importation was, primarily, that the growers feared the Mexican would be placed on a

quota basis under the Immigration Act of 1924. "The Filipinos," said the *Pacific Rural Press*, "are being rushed in as
the Mexicans are being rushed out." In 1923 there was no
restriction on Filipinos, as they were nationals, and, consequently, entitled to enter continental United States as a matter of right. From 1923 to 1930, the number of Filipino immigrants constantly increased, 5795 entering in 1929 alone.

There are, today, approximately 35,000 Filipinos in California, most of whom were brought here to work in the
fields, and a great majority of whom are still so employed.
At the outset, they, too, were model workers. Young, male,
single, they could be herded about as occasion demanded.
They worked as a racial group, under a variant of the *padrone* system, with a labor contractor supplying the men at
a fee. For the most part, they were used on the large ranches,
particularly in asparagus cutting, in which some six thousand are still employed. When they were first recruited,
they were paid the lowest rate which migratory labor received. Like the other racial groups, their isolation was exploited to beat down wage rates. In certain lines, as for
example in the asparagus fields, the growers were enabled to
use, when Filipino labor was introduced, more men per
acre, which made it possible to have the asparagus fields
gone over more thoroughly. As might have been expected,
the use of more men per acre had the effect of decreasing
the average daily earnings of the men employed while it increased the return, per acre, to the grower. The Filipinos
travel around in groups of seven or eight, in battered cars,
following the crops. A State Relief Administration worker
reported recently that, in the Imperial Valley, he had found
a group of fifty Filipinos "bunked in an old schoolhouse

from November to the following April and during that time they received less than $50 in wages, subsisting for weeks on a handful of rice and a little bread."

The history of the Filipino in California follows the pattern established with the Chinese, the Japanese, and the Hindus. Strong anti-Filipino sentiment began to be manifest in California at an early date. In 1927 Congressman Welch of California, and Senator Hiram Johnson, introduced a bill in Congress which had as its aim the exclusion of the Filipino. This bill was defeated when it was established that the Filipino, being a national, could probably not be excluded. When the Philippine Island Independence Act was passed, March 24, 1934, the avenue was open for excluding Filipino immigration, and on July 11, 1935, a measure was passed by Congress to provide "free transportation" to the Islands for those Filipinos in California who cared to take advantage of the offer. The measure provided, however, that "no Filipino who receives the benefits of this act shall be entitled to return to the continental United States." Thus the bill is, in effect, both a deportation and exclusion measure. Great pressure has been brought to bear upon the Filipinos in California to induce them to "take advantage" of the offer and many Filipinos have, in this manner, been deported.

Although highly regarded as a field worker when he arrived, the Filipino is no longer persona grata to the growers. The reason for this change of attitude is simply that the Filipino, like his predecessors, soon demanded higher wages. "It costs a $100 a head," to quote Mr. Frisselle, "to bring the Filipino in. And we cannot handle him like we can the Mexican: the Mexican can be deported." Dr. Clements, again referring to the Filipino, recently stated that the Filipinos have "proved to be more disturbing and more dangerous than any other Asiatic group that has ever been brought into this state." Filipinos no longer scab on their fellow workers, and they no longer underbid for work. Prior to 1934, they formed the Filipino Labor Union, restricted to agricultural workers, and soon had established seven locals of the union in the State with a membership of about 2000. The Filipino is a real fighter and his strikes have been dangerous. In August, 1934, about 3000 Filipino workers went on strike in the lettuce fields near Salinas, California. An army of special deputies descended on the Filipino picket line and herded a group of about 700 Filipinos together and drove them from the community. As part of this campaign, a Filipino labor camp was raided and burned to the ground. Many Filipinos were corralled and held incommunicado; and, of course, the strike was broken. Once the Filipino attempted to organize, he ceased to be a desirable worker.

## CHAPTER VIII

## SOCIAL CONSEQUENCES

CALIFORNIA agriculture has been, as I have pointed out, to a large degree "Oriental agriculture." Its mammoth farm factories have been built by cheap Oriental and peon labor, imported for a particular purpose and discarded as soon as that purpose has been achieved. For over half a century this sordid business of race exploitation has been going on in the State and it would be difficult to find a meaner record of exploitation in the history of American industry. In the Eastern industrial districts, the theory of the "melting pot" has had at least limited application and to a certain extent assimilation has been achieved. But, in California, the idea of the "melting pot" has never prevailed. Here the practice has been to use a race for a purpose and then to kick it out, in preference for some weaker racial unit. In each instance the shift in racial units has been accompanied by a determined effort to drive the offending race from the scene. Up to a certain point, therefore, it can be said that California has solved the difficult social problems involved in the use of alien labor by the simple expedient of driving the alien groups, one after the other, from the State. But important vestiges of the problem remain and the experience undergone with each group has definitely, and perhaps permanently, affected the social structure of the State. In this chapter, I want to touch upon some aspects of this larger problem.

## 1. The Roots of Vigilantism

California is the home of vigilantism. The first vigilante committee was inspired by a "crime wave" which swept early-day San Francisco. But, even in this first manifestation of mob spirit, an "anti-foreign" motivation may be found. The criminals of the period, who had excited the self-righteousness of the Californians, belonged to two groups: Australian touts — "The Hounds," as they were called, from Sydney and Van Diemen's Land — who had come to California and, instead of mining for gold, had robbed the San Franciscans; and the Mexicans. One Mexican bandit, Joaquin Murieta, has, of course, a legendary fame in California.[1] Regardless of how much literal truth there may be in the Murieta legend, it is quite likely that the general outline of the story is founded in fact. The Mexicans were, of course, violently rousted about by the Americans after the conquest of California. Murieta is supposed to have been cheated and robbed by American settlers, driven from his home, and his wife, according to the legend, was raped while he was chained to a post. "Mexican crime" in California, about which I will say more a little later, dates from the resentment which most Mexicans experienced at the treatment accorded them after 1849. Not only did the first vigilante committee have this underlying racial bias — i.e. it was aimed at Greasers and Australians — but later manifestations of the same vigilantism spirit had even

[1] See *Villains and Vigilantes*, 1936, Stanton A. Coblentz.

more definite roots in race hatred. In the Sand-Lot Riots, led by Dennis Kearney in the seventies, a major factor back of the movement was, of course, anti-Chinese sentiment. Violence against the Chinese was general in California, particularly in the mines, as early as 1850.

How deep-seated the hatred of the foreigner is in California may be indicated by the fact that, on two occasions, it has swept the entire State. During the agitation, first against the Chinese, and later against the Japanese, both political parties were swept into the current of race hatred. Not a single outstanding California politician, regardless of personal convictions, was able to stand out against the flood of feeling that was released on both occasions. Both campaigns, that is, against the Chinese and the Japanese, were accompanied by mob violence, wholesale destruction of property, and general intimidation. When they invoke the "vigilante" spirit, therefore, the California industrialists are appealing to the hatred of the alien, which is, as I have indicated, of long standing throughout the State. In the farm communities, where violence has been intense and general during so-called "labor disturbances," a major factor in the strategy of the large shipper-growers has been the fact that most of the workers involved were "foreigners." It is easier to whip up a frenzy of mob feeling against Mexicans and Filipinos, for example, than against native white Americans. Because of this general background, it has been comparatively easy for the California industrialists to go one step further, and to identify, in the popular mind, the "Red" or "Communist" with the "foreigner." The hatred of the foreigner is thereby transferred to the radical, and the phenomenon of 1856 and 1877 is repeated.

The vigilante problem has many phases. Not only is it easier to arouse feeling against aliens than against natives, but the fact that aliens can be abused with impunity tends to encourage violence. Most so-called vigilantism in California has had, as I have indicated, an anti-foreign bias, and it has gone unpunished in most instances precisely for this reason, namely, that it has been directed against those who have been without legal rights, or who, for other reasons, have been powerless to protect themselves. The viciousness of the vigilante tradition to date has been that it feeds itself; it is self-perpetuating. From the outset, racial feeling has been at the root of the phenomenon of mob violence. Nowadays, of course, vigilantism is sophisticated by self-conscious artistry, and it is not always colored by race feeling. But historically, vigilantism is intimately related to the prejudice against the foreigner of a different color.

## 2. Race Riots

Race riots, aimed at the various alien groups which the farm industrialists have imported to California, have been of frequent occurrence. A few sample cases indicate the pattern which may be found underlying all these manifestations of mob violence.

On October 24, 1929, a carnival was being celebrated in Exeter, California, at the conclusion of the harvest season. Throughout the day, Filipino field workers, parading the streets, were molested by white transient laborers. Filipinos were crowded off the sidewalks, denied entrance to places of amusement, and generally abused. One of the Filipinos thus molested stabbed a white man with a bolo knife. A mob was immediately organized and Filipino workers were driven from near-by labor camps, rousted out of the fields, their camps burned to the ground, and the Filipinos themselves beaten and assaulted. Similar anti-Filipino riots occurred in Tulare, and Watsonville, in 1930. An investigation, made by the State Department of Industrial Relations, showed that in each instance the feeling against the Filipino had its origin in economic competition between Filipino and white workers. Certain growers had employed Filipino workers, in preference to white workers, "because they were not averse to working ten hours a day." Most of the riots were set off by some incident — the appearance of white girls in Filipino dance halls, or a quarrel between a white worker and a Filipino — but the incident by itself failed to account for the general feeling against the Filipino which rapidly crystallized in mob action.

Of recent years, the feeling against the Filipino has been intensified by reason of the desire of the large growers to get rid of him as a worker. In one outbreak of mob violence against Filipinos at Watsonville, it was found that, a few days before the riot occurred, the local Chamber of Commerce had gone on record urging that the Filipinos be excluded and a local judge had publicly inveighed against them. In San Francisco, Judge Sylvain Lazarus recently denounced the Filipinos from the bench as "a race scarcely more than savages" and later ordered the police department to arrest any Filipino seen with a white girl. The Chief of Police in El Centro, California, in December, 1935, issued a bulletin to "arrest all white girls and Filipinos seen together at or near Main Street," while, at the same time, a local judge, in Imperial County, delivered a series of harangues to service clubs denouncing the Filipino as a miscreant and criminal. Dr. George Clements, publicist for the large shipper-growers, has referred to the Filipino in the *Pacific Rural Press* (May 9, 1936), as "the most worthless, unscrupulous, shiftless, diseased, semi-barbarian that has ever come to our shores." This Filipino-baiting has, as its motive, the desire on the part of the growers to get the Filipino out of California.

The Filipinos have been, by and large, powerless to protect themselves. Most of the 30,000 or so Filipinos in California are ineligible to citizenship. They cannot vote or hold public office. As "aliens" they are subject to a maze of discriminatory legislation; and, when they run foul of the law, as frequently happens, they are usually asked to accept "deportation" as a condition of receiving a suspended sentence or being placed on probation. Local officials do not need to respect them, because they do not vote. The same situation, in general, has always existed with respect to the various alien groups that the growers have imported. Violence, in other words, has been encouraged not only because of race feeling against the victim, but because of the powerlessness of the victim to retaliate.

Riots similar to those directed against the Filipino have been aimed at other groups. On January 26, 1908, a riot broke out in Live Oak, California, against Hindu workers. A mob marched to a camp of Hindu workers, burned it to the ground, beat and terrorized a hundred or more Hindus in the camp, drove them out of the community, and, in doing so, robbed them of about $2,500. When the Governor of California ordered an investigation, the local district attorney countered with a defense of the rioters, ad-

vancing the unique argument that the Hindus had been robbing hen roosts and, moreover, had been guilty of indecent
exposure. The men arrested for robbing the Hindus were
swiftly exonerated. In his report to the Governor, the district attorney said that he did not anticipate further trouble, as the Hindus who had returned had promised not to
expose themselves and to "obey the laws of decency as well
as the cubic area regulation," and that all was well. "The
cubic area regulation" is an old California ordinance aimed
at the Chinese. It had been invoked in this case against the
Hindus because they were living in huts.

For years the Mexicans have suffered the same kind of
discrimination. They have been victimized, by robberies and
assaults, and, when they retaliate, they are quickly convicted. The prejudice against all foreign "color" groups
is ingrained, and their testimony in the courts is generally
disbelieved. Most of them, of course, suffer in silence. They
have no political weapon of retaliation. This is the kind of
situation upon which California vigilantism fattens itself
and grows strong.

It is amusing to find that race prejudices have been for-
mulated as social doctrines in California and are taught in
the schools of the State. In 1921, R. L. Adams, of the University of California, published a text, *Farm Management*.
In the chapters on farm labor, nearly every dogma of the
growers is accepted and set forth as scientifically determined fact. Dr. Adams favors the segregation of workers
according to race. He believes that Mexicans are "childish,
lazy, unambitious"; that the Japanese are "tricky" and that
their standards of sexual morality are deplorable; the Hindu
is "lean, lanky and enervated," lacking in "will power and
energy"; while Negroes are "notorious prevaricators, and

constantly annex to themselves such minor things as chickens, lines from harnesses, axes and shovels." On the whole, Dr. Adams feels that migratory labor in California has been "careless and even downright unappreciative of attempts to provide more livable surroundings." Hoboes are "best cared for with some cheap shelter where they can flop. These men should be provided with a reasonably warm, dry place to sleep, but as a rule no special housing is needed for them. They are satisfied to furnish their own bedding and sleep on a pile of hay." He advises the farmer to check up on "left-overs" in food and to watch the "refuse barrel." The type of food, and shelter, for each farm labor group is carefully described, showing that, even in the matter of treatment, discrimination is sedulously cultivated on the wholly gratuitous assumption that there are fundamental differences between the groups involved. Dr. Adams differentiates, for example, between the "hobo" and the "migratory worker," providing a different standard of treatment for, and even attitude toward, each. One must never joke with one's workers, he admonishes; but, on the contrary, a "respectful distance must be maintained." Lastly, he warns against permitting poker playing: "One cannot afford to allow poker playing or gambling of any kind, or tolerate radical talk or preaching by discontented individuals." Thus poker playing and unionization activities are placed in the same category by this employer-minded pundit.

### 3. Social Maladjustment

It is scarcely necessary to point out that the various racial farm-labor groups in California have not led particularly well-adjusted lives while laboring in the fields. Occasionally committing crimes of violence, they have catered to the popular prejudice against them in California. Most of the early Chinese, and later the Japanese, immigrants were, as is well known, single men. For years the Californians have reveled in sensational stories about the importation of "picture brides" — that is, the arrival of unmarried girls from the Orient in California. Lurid stories, sensationally headlined, about "the slave traffic," described for the rabid anti-oriental natives the procedure whereby a Japanese farmer or a Chinese laundryman arranged, in the days prior to the exclusion laws, for the importation of a wife. Obviously the procedure was not born of any innate desire on the part of orientals to choose bed companions on sight unseen, but rather because of the inherent nature of the situation of male isolation in California. Nevertheless, the California press, during the "yellow peril" hysteria, published long lists of "picture brides" and the State of California made an official tabulation of "picture-bride" marriages, the statistical information being compiled under heads such as follows: "Surname: Kawashima; wife, Soi; Age, 24; husband, Nisabano; address, P.O. Box 46, Orwood" — and, by so doing, convinced everyone that the Japanese were an immoral people, essentially unassimilable, practising customs wholly at variance with the high ideals of Anglo-Saxon-Hispano California culture. All this tommyrot to the contrary notwithstanding, sane Californians will today, twenty years after the "yellow peril" agitation, concede that the Chinese and the Japanese residents of California are model citizens and that they have, to a very large degree, become assimilated.

The same prejudice, however, was visited upon the

Hindu and the Filipino. "The Hindu," to quote from an official California report of 1920, "has no morals. His lack of personal cleanliness, his low morals and his blind adherence to theories and teachings so entirely repugnant to American principles make him unfit for association with American people." Because of the fact that Hindus did not import "picture brides," lacking the rationality of the oriental, the Californians jumped to the conclusion, in which there may possibly have been some measure of fact, that many of the Hindus were homosexuals. The official report referred to above hints luridly of certain practices and customs of Hindu workers which cannot be set forth in an official State paper. So deep-seated is this notion, that the historian of the Hindus, Rajani Kanta Das, devoted a section of his book to a consideration of whether or not Hindu workers in California were, in fact, largely homosexuals.

The same popular conception exists with reference to the Filipino. Not more than 10 per cent of the Filipinos in California are married, and the ratio of resident Filipino males to females in the State is about 14 to 1. Naturally this is a situation which from the Filipino's point of view borders upon the tragic. Some years ago in the case of *Roldan* v. *Los Angeles County*, 129 Cal. App. 267, it was held that a Filipino was not a "Mongolian" within the meaning of a miscegenation statute, and therefore could contract a legal marriage with a white woman. But the legislature of California was not to be subverted by any such errant legal liberalism, so they promptly amended the law to make it apply to "members of the Malay" race. Consequently Filipinos cannot marry white girls in California and there are no Filipino girls to marry. What might be expected to happen under these circumstances has in fact actually happened. Filipinos haunt taxi-dance halls, frequently enjoy the society and charms of prostitutes, and the State of California luxuriates in a feeling of general moral uprightness and continues to speculate darkly about the homosexual proclivities of the Filipino. Taxi-dance halls are not always notable for an atmosphere of tranquillity, and, whenever a fight occurs, or a murder, or a general brawl, the Californians merely put it down as another evidence of the ingrained criminality of the Filipino. In some investigations, however, it has been pointed out that the dance halls, dives and amusement joints operated near the great asparagus fields in the Stockton delta are owned by ranch foremen and labor contractors, who thus manage to fleece the Filipinos out of the meager earnings which are paid them.

Feeling a definite sense of social ostracism which is all too real, most racial groups in California tend to become exceedingly clannish. The fact that they are usually employed as a racial group, or unit, and that they work by themselves, has intensified this clannishness. The isolation of the Hindu, for example, his enforced racial solidarity, has brought about a condition of race neurosis. Hindus, frequently engaging in business with members of their own race as partners, are celebrated court litigants. They are perennially in the courts, fighting and squabbling among themselves. The number of Hindu murders in Sacramento County, that is, cases where Hindus have been murdered by other Hindus, is amazing. I saved clippings a few years ago which indicated that some forty-nine such murders had occurred in Sacramento County alone.

From an early date, a large percentage of California's

huge army of migratory farm workers have been aliens. Although it is difficult, because of the lack of reliable figures, to approximate the exact percentage of aliens, it is nevertheless permissible to assume that, at various times, foreign groups have comprised 75 per cent or more of the total number of migratory workers. At certain periods, the percentage has unquestionably been higher; at present, due to the influx of drought area refugees, it is doubtless lower. But over a period of fifty years, or perhaps even longer, say from 1860 to 1930, a majority of the migratory army has been made up of foreign workers, most of them ineligible to citizenship. In 1914 a careful student of the problem estimated that there were at least 150,000 migratory farm workers in the State; and by 1930 this figure had risen well above 200,000. When one considers, therefore, that over a period of half a century the State has had this huge, rootless, ambulatory alien army moving about, living in shacks and sheds, without homes, without roots of any kind in the community, it is easy to see that they have injected into the State a considerable measure of social disequilibrium. It is no slander against these workers to assume that much miscellaneous crime can be traced to the circumstances of their unsettled existences. Mexicans, cooped up in the cities during the winter months, have, for example, frequently run foul of the law. Under the circumstances, this situation is what one might well expect. Without going too far afield, I should like to point out that much "California crime," so-called, has its origin in a misdirected form of social protest.[2]

[2] See, for example, *Bandits and the Southern Pacific*, 1929, by C. B. Glasscock.

### 4. *Foreign Tenancy*

Even among those foreign groups that have acquired a foothold in the agricultural districts, it is significant that land tenancy has risen with their presence. The Commonwealth Club of California in a report prepared in 1922 [3] found that "wherever tenancy is concentrated foreigners outnumber Americans." To quote further from the report: "Our investigations show that preference for certain types of farming, aided by the ability more successfully to compete along selected lines of activity, has resulted in a parceling out of our agriculture to certain races." Rice growing, for the year 1922, when the report was prepared, was 75 per cent tenant-farmed, chiefly by foreigners. In an article which appeared in the *Pacific Rural Press* [4] it is stated that of 100,000 farms in California, some 35,000 were operated by foreigners. The same article states that 25 per cent of the farms in the State were being operated by tenants and that the incidence of tenant farming among foreigners was particularly high.

The Commonwealth Club report, carrying the investigation a step further, indicated that where tenancy existed, absentee ownership predominated and that, in certain sections, such as Imperial Valley, 85 per cent of the ownership was absentee in character. "One familiar with the irksomeness of much hard work, the isolation and monotony of some of our California farming sections, the discomforts of heat, mosquitoes, malaria and kindred irritations, knows

---

[3] *Land Tenancy in California*, Vol. XVII, No. 10.
[4] January 1, 1921.

full well why Americans have given way to Japanese, Chinese, Portuguese, Italians, and others in the following of fruit picking and packing, truck growing, sugar beet production, dairying, rice raising and similar exacting types of agriculture."

No mention is made in the report, unfortunately, of the relation between tenancy and large ownership concentration. Since 1922 when the report was prepared, it has been demonstrated many times that it is the character of ownership, rather than the type of labor involved, that has resulted in the employment of aliens. Dr. Elwood Mead, who was chairman of the State Land Settlement Board in California, found, for example, that "Americans will do any kind of farm or garden work if there is back of it sufficient stimulus to their pride, interest, and ambition." Settlement of American farmers on the land, he believed, was the best method of "ending the menace of alien land ownership and of creating communities that do not amalgamate and of subjecting this state to the menace of racial antagonism."

Tenancy, as such, is not the problem of California agriculture. It is the growth of the employer-employee relationship in California, and the percentage of paid agricultural workers, that carries real significance. More than 36 per cent of all large-scale farms in the United States are located in California; and the growth of large-scale farming, industrialized agriculture, is inseparably connected with the availability of large numbers of migratory workers. In 1930, the percentage of paid farm laborers in the United States was 26 per cent; while in California, paid farm laborers made up 57 per cent of all persons gainfully employed in agriculture.

The employment of aliens to reduce wage rates and to lower standards of living has tended to make it extremely difficult for American workers to compete. One of the largest California farm operators has stated that "in many instances the housing provided for farm help in California would be scorned by an up-to-date hog raiser as unfit for his hogs. It is such conditions that produced the typical California hobo. How could any but the most debased of American humanity be induced to regard their labor under such conditions as white man's work?" Most observers emphasize the same conclusions: "From the outset of agricultural cultivation in California," writes Tom Ireland,[5] "Chinese, Japanese, and later Mexican labor has been used to depress production costs, with a resulting standard of living far lower than the average for American agricultural laborers."

## 5. Homing Pigeons

California farm industrialists have always justified their employment of alien labor on the ground that, with particular reference to the Mexican, migratory labor left the State after the harvest season and, therefore, presented no social problem. The fable of the Mexican as a "homing pigeon" has, however, been eloquently refuted by the records.

In 1927, Los Angeles, with a Mexican population of approximately 7 per cent of the total population, reported that 27.44 per cent of its charitable expenditures was devoted to Mexican cases; 25 per cent of the budget of the general hospital was used for Mexicans; the city maternity service

[5] *Child Labor*, 1937.

reported that 62 ½ per cent of its cases were Mexicans and that these cases consumed 73 per cent of its budget; the bureau of municipal nursing reported that 40 per cent of its clients were Mexicans; and, in the children's hospital, 25 per cent of the children were Mexicans. When these and similar statistics were cited to Mr. S. Parker Frisselle, spokesman for California agriculture before the Congressional Committee holding hearings on the Box and Harris Bills, his only comment was that the Mexican should be "kept moving." Almost 90 per cent of the charitable expenditures of the city of Riverside, California, were devoted to Mexican cases in 1925, and a large incidence of sickness and disease was found among migratory Mexican workers.[6] Later investigations have shown a large percentage of Mexicans listed in the tabulations of the various health departments of the California cities and counties.

The Mexicans, by and large, have never returned to Mexico at the end of the harvest season. They have, on the contrary, "hibernated" in the cities and towns. Known to social workers and public officials, their presence is not generally suspected by the urban taxpayers who, by supporting these people in the winter months, are carrying, of course, a portion of the expense of operating the farm factories of California. Curious persons have frequently asked me, "Where are all these migratory workers that you are talking about? We have never seen them." These same people simply do not use their eyes. Within two miles of the pleasant California college town of Whittier, for example, is an amazing Mexican community which has existed for years. Removed a short distance from the main highway,

6 *Survey*, June, 1925.

and crowded into a few blocks made up of shacks and hovels, some 2500 Mexicans make their homes, most of them farm workers. Similar "Little Mexicos" can be found throughout Southern California. The segregation which exists, throughout the State, of alien farm-labor groups into special communities, has been carried over into the school system. Although the charge is vociferously denied, Mexican and Negro are segregated in the rural schools. Arthur Gleason interviewed the principal of one rural school in 1924. "Mexican children," she said, "will not be admitted to this school. The reason is public sentiment. The trustees will never put those children in here. This school is a white school, in the language of the district." Foreign groups, therefore, develop their own centers: the crowded hillside squatter Mexican camps in Los Angeles; the dingy Japanese residential district; the Filipino flophouses.

Because of the influx of drought-bowl refugees, public attention, in the last year, has been fixed upon the social consequences of migratory labor, the evils of which have, of course, long been pointed out. In 1924, when interviewed by Arthur Gleason, Dr. Dickie, then secretary of the California State Board of Health, graphically described the situation confronting California: "This migratory stream," he said, "has swollen to a swift current, and the State does not yet realize its own future is involved. All kinds of people are swept in. There are hoboes in Fords, and I saw a group of gypsies the other day riding through Berkeley to the next crop in a Cadillac. These people can communicate disease from one end of the State to the other in forty-eight hours. The tremendous growth in population in California has bred problems so fast that we don't yet know we have a situation new on the earth. In the delta lands of the San Joaquin Valley, among Japanese asparagus workers, we have had a spread of typhoid fever. There is practically no drainage, and the water becomes contaminated. These migrants would naturally like to ride around the same circles, the same as a commercial traveler. It is the employment agencies that throw them long distances and scatter them, sometimes three or four hundred miles, when there is not a crop near by; and they often send more people than are wanted. Control of the labor supply is needed to reduce the area of migration. The migration as it sweeps on makes a vacuum and a suction like an express train. It draws in thousands of people from the colder States. After they have been snowed in through the Dakotas for half a lifetime, they pack their harvest and motor into California for a warm winter. We add a large population for six months of every year. These people are hard workers and have money. Don't be deceived because they dress plainly. They are just the people a growing State wants. Give them good housing and hold them."

## CHAPTER IX

## *THE WHEATLAND RIOT*

THE ERRATIC and violent development of agriculture in California has been paralleled by the sporadic turbulence which has characterized the history of farm labor in the State. The story of migratory labor is one of violence: harsh repression interrupted by occasional outbursts of indignation and protest. Nor is there much probability that the future will be one of peaceful adjustment to new social conditions; no one familiar with the dominant interests in California agriculture can have any illusions on this score. Violence, and more violence, is clearly indicated. It is indicated not only by the established patterns of industrialized agriculture, but, more explicitly, by the past record of violence in the industry. This record, it should be observed, stems from the early social behavior of the Californians. The history of the Vigilance Committees of 1850 and 1856 is well known and requires no repetition. While it is true that these early committees were organized to cope with crime, it is indisputable that they were largely representative of the "merchants and propertied" classes and that, at least in 1856, their activities were directed in part against organized labor. During the period when the vigilantes were in action, they completely usurped the functions of governmental officials, defied the Governor of the State, conducted their own trials, equipped and drilled an armed force, and operated in effect as an insurrectionary junta. The story of the vigilantes entered deeply into the consciousness of the merchants, businessmen, and industrialists of California. They never forgot the experience and their successors have never hesitated to constitute themselves "vigilantes" whenever the occasion has demanded "action." In 1934 "vigilante committees" appeared in practically every city, town, and rural district in California during the "Red" hysteria of that year. The significance of this deeply rooted tradition of violence must constantly be kept in mind. Insurrection was once sanctioned — violence was once glorified in the historical annals of the State — these facts have been remembered. Hence present-day industrialists are quick to drape themselves in the cloak of the vigilante tradition. Mining camps throughout the West, in Montana, Idaho, and Nevada, quickly improvised Vigilance Committees, on the San Francisco pattern, when they were first faced with a strong labor movement. Vigilantism, as such, had its origin in California.

The eruptions of farm labor have been at infrequent intervals and, in every instance, they have been violently suppressed, each incident provoking a long chain of prosecutions in the courts. No tearful glorification of the occasional protests of farm labor, however, is to be found in the official histories. Whatever theoretical considerations may be entertained concerning the use of violence in labor disputes, it is evident that, from a historical point of view, migratory labor has made gains in California when it has been militant. It has been potentially militant for a great many years, but, when strong protest movements have occurred, they have, in each instance, been directed by a clearly class-conscious leadership. One of the earliest instances of the stirring of deep-seated unrest in migratory labor was the Wheatland Riot, which occurred on the ranch of a large hop grower named Durst, near Wheatland, California, on August 3, 1913. Wheatland, clearly marked as one of the most significant episodes in the history of migratory labor in the West, also forms an important chapter in the social history of California. In the lurid illumination which the fires of the riot cast forth, the ugly facts about the condition of farm labor in California were, for the first time, thoroughly exposed. The riot and the subsequent trial attracted national attention.[1] It resulted in two important public documents bearing on the subject of farm labor (Report on the Wheatland Riot, issued June 1, 1914, and the Section titled "The Seasonal Labor Problem in Agriculture," Vol. V, Reports of the United States Commission on Industrial Relations), and one of the first serious studies of migratory labor (*The Casual Laborer*, 1920, by Carleton H. Parker).

The Wheatland affair marked the culmination of several years of agitational and organizational work on the part of the Industrial Workers of the World. To see the affair in proper perspective, therefore, it is necessary to indicate something of the background of these activities.

In the years between the Chicago convention at which the I.W.W. was formed in 1905, and 1913, the wobblies had been active in the fields, along the highways, on the

[1] See *Harper's Weekly*, April 4, June 20, 1914; *The Outlook*, May 16, 1914; *Technical World*, August, 1914.

trains, and in the jungle camps, with their spectacular propaganda and vivid agitation. The roots of the I.W.W. — if the organization may be said to have had any roots — were to be found among the migratory workers of the West. Not only were these workers unmercifully exploited — the conditions under which they worked making them highly susceptible to the inflammatory agitation of the wobblies — but they followed, in general, the routes pursued by the I.W.W. organizers. Organizers, coming from the timber camps of the Northwest, drifted south into the agricultural fields. Always on the move, the wobblies, themselves essentially migratory, moved naturally into the currents of farm labor. Their organizational techniques — job action, organizing on the job, low dues or no dues at all — were well adapted to the circumstances under which farm labor was employed. They moved with the workers and organized them, so to speak, in transit.

During the years 1905–1913, the wobblies had demonstrated considerable strength in California. They had, for example, conducted two sensational "free-speech" fights: in San Diego and in Fresno. The fight in Fresno was of particular importance, as Fresno has long been the nerve center of agricultural labor in California, located as it is in the heart of the San Joaquin Valley. In Fresno the wobblies fought for the right to maintain a headquarters, to distribute literature, and to hold public meetings. For six months, through one fall and winter in 1910, they battled the Fresno authorities. As often as they were crushed, they launched new campaigns, finally succeeding in winning a kind of tolerance for their activities. The courage and tenacity of the wobblies in Fresno attracted the attention of many migratory workers and made a deep impression throughout the State.

The San Diego fight was, if anything, even more sensational. Beginning in January, 1912, the San Diego authorities began to suppress wobbly meetings, the campaign culminating in a remarkable ordinance which outlawed free speech throughout the city (San Diego then had a population of about 40,000). The wobblies promptly sent out word for a "concentration" on San Diego, the idea being to crowd the jails and to raise such a fracas that the city fathers would despair of making arrests. Newspapers, at the time, carried scare headlines about "thousands" of workers converging on San Diego; in fact, only about 150 wobblies were involved. To cope with the situation, the authorities sponsored a local vigilance committee which established camps and posted armed guards along the highways leading to San Diego (one of the first California "border patrols"), turning back all transients. In San Diego itself the vigilantes rounded up all persons even remotely suspected of being wobblies and marched them, one night, to Sorrento. There the wobblies were made to mount an improvised platform, kiss the American flag and sing the national anthem, while hundreds of vigilantes stood about armed with revolvers, knives, clubs, blackjacks, and black snake whips. Then they were marched to San Onofre and driven into a cattle pen and systematically slugged and beaten. After a time, they were taken out of the pen and beaten with clubs and whips as, one at a time, they were made "to run the gantlet." One wobbly subsequently died in jail; scores received serious injuries. Not only was this performance sanctioned by the authorities, but the Merchants Association and the Chamber of Commerce passed resolutions praising the vigilantes. Speaking on behalf of San Diego, the *San Diego Tribune*, in its issue of March 4, 1912, spoke of the wobblies as follows: "Hanging is none too good for them and they would be much better dead; for they are absolutely useless in the human economy; they are the waste material of creation and should be drained off into the sewer of oblivion there to rot in cold obstruction like any other excrement." When one local editor protested, the vigilantes attempted to lynch him. The facts, as I have given them, merely summarize the findings of Mr. Harris Weinstock who was appointed by Governor Hiram Johnson to investigate the incident.

After the San Diego free-speech fight, wobbly locals were established throughout California: in Fresno, Bakersfield, Los Angeles, San Diego, San Francisco and Sacramento. From these locals, camp delegates were sent into the fields to organize workers "on the job." Many "job strikes" were called and, frequently, they were successful. Largely because of the sensational character of their propaganda and the militancy of their free-speech fights, the wobblies built up a reputation in California out of all relation to their actual numerical strength. The I.W.W. had less than 5000 members in the State in 1913 and less than 8 per cent of the migratory farm workers were members. Nevertheless, the wobblies were a great influence. Whenever "labor trouble" occurred in the fields or in the construction camps, it was usually discovered that a "camp delegate" had been on the ground. The songs of the I.W.W. were frequently heard in the fields and in the jungle camps under the railroad bridges. To such an extent had this agitation permeated the mass of farm laborers that when the Wheatland incident occurred the I.W.W. was able to assume complete leadership of the workers. Conditions similar to those which existed on the Durst ranch in 1913 had existed in California for twenty years or longer, but militant action awaited the arrival of the wobblies.

### 1. The Riot

Immediately prior to August 3, 1913, some 2800 men, women and children were camped on a low, unshaded hill near the Durst hop ranch at Wheatland. Of this number, approximately 1500 were women and children. Over half the total number of workers in this miserable camp were aliens; at one of the subsequent mass meetings seven interpreters had to be used; and a field boss made note of twenty-seven nationalities represented in one working gang of 235 men on the ranch. Following the established practice of his fellow growers, Durst had advertised in newspapers throughout California and Nevada for workers. He had asked for 2700 workers when, as he subsequently admitted, he could only supply employment for about 1500. Within four days after his fanciful advertisements had appeared, this strange aggregation of workers had assembled. They came by every conceivable means of transportation; many of them had walked from near-by towns and cities. A great number had no blankets and slept on piles of straw thrown on tent floors. The tents, incidentally, were rented from Durst at seventy-five cents a week. Many slept in the fields. One group of 45 men, women and children slept packed closely together on a

single pile of straw. There were nine outdoor toilets for
2800 people. The stench around the camp was nauseat-
ing, with children and women vomiting; dysentery was
prevalent to an alarming degree. Between 200 and 300 children worked in the fields; and hundreds of children were
seen around the camp "in an unspeakably filthy condition."
The workers entered the fields at four o'clock in the morning, and by noon the heat was terrific, remaining, as it
did, around 105 degrees. The water wells were "absolutely
insufficient for the camp," with no means provided of
bringing water to the fields. "Numerous instances of sickness and partial prostration among children from 5 to 10
years of age were mentioned in the testimony." One reason
for Durst's chariness about providing water was that his
cousin, Jim Durst, had a lemonade concession, selling
lemonade to the workers at a nickel a glass. There was no
organization for sanitation, no garbage disposal. Local
Wheatland stores were forbidden to send delivery wagons
to the camp, so that the workers were forced to buy what
supplies they could afford from a "concession" store on the
ranch.

The commission of inquiry which investigated the incident found that Durst had intentionally advertised for
more workers than he needed in order to force wages down
and that he purposely permitted the camp to remain in a
filthy condition so that some of the workers would leave
before the season was over, thereby forfeiting 10 per cent
of their wages which he insisted on holding back. Carleton
Parker stated that the amount paid, per hundred pounds
of hops picked, fluctuated daily in relation to the number
of workers on hand. Earnings varied between $1.00 and

$.78 a day. Over half the workers were destitute and were forced to cash their checks each night. Throughout the season, at least a thousand workers, unable to secure employment, remained idle in the camp.

The foregoing is a very meager and abbreviated statement of the conditions which were found to have existed at the camp, on and prior to August third. Of the workers assembled, about a third came from California towns and cities; another third were "quasi-gypsies" from the Sierra foothills, with ramshackle wagons and carts; the remaining third were "hoboes," or their "California exemplars, the fruit tramps," with many foreigners among this group, including Japanese, Hindus, and Puerto Ricans. Of this strange assortment, about 100 men were I.W.W. "card men," i.e. they had, at one time or another, carried a wobbly card. Some of the wobblies had organized a loosely formed local in the camp in which some thirty workers had been enrolled. "It is a deeply suggestive fact," reads the official report, "that these thirty men, through their energy, technique and skill in organization, unified and dominated an unhomogeneous mass of 2,800 unskilled laborers" within two days. It was subsequently estimated that about 400 workers of those assembled knew, in a rough way, something of the philosophy of the I.W.W., and could sing some of its songs. Of the hundred card men, some had been in the San Diego fight, some had been soapboxers in Fresno. Among these men were Blackie Ford — an experienced I.W.W. organizer — and Herman Suhr.

Resentment had been steadily mounting in the camp for several days prior to August third. For the most part, the workers were indignant over living conditions; they were not primarily interested in wages. On August third, the wobblies called a mass meeting, Blackie Ford (he was unarmed) addressed the workers, and, among other remarks, told them to "knock the blocks off the scissor bills." He took a sick baby from its mother's arms and, holding it before the eyes of about 2000 workers, shouted: "It's for the kids we are doing this." The meeting had come to a close with the singing of "Mr. Block" — a wobbly song — when the sheriff and his posse arrived with the district attorney (who was, also, Durst's private attorney). The sheriff and a few of his men started through the crowd to arrest Ford. One deputy, on the fringe of the crowd, fired a shot in the air "to sober the mob," and, as he fired, the fighting started. The district attorney, a deputy sheriff, and two workers, a Puerto Rican and an English boy, were killed, and many more persons were injured, in the riot which followed. The posse, apparently astonished at the resistance they had encountered, fled the scene. Shocked beyond measure by reports of the riot, the State was immediately up in arms. The Governor dispatched four companies of the National Guard to Wheatland. The guardsmen marched to the workers' camp, surrounded it, and assisted the local officers in arresting about a hundred workers. Most of the workers had left the camp the night of August third, the "roads out of Wheatland being filled all that night with pickers leaving camp." The townspeople of Wheatland were so badly frightened by the incident that the National Guard remained on the scene for over a week.

Feeling that they had a revolutionary situation to cope with, the authorities were panicstricken and promptly launched a campaign of wild and irresponsible persecution. The Burns Detective Agency was called in and a hundred or more of its operatives were deputized. There followed one of the most amazing reigns of terror that California has ever witnessed. Wobblies were arrested literally in every part of the State. No one was ever able to make an accurate estimate of the number of arrests; many cases were subsequently reported of men being arrested and held by local authorities incommunicado for seventy and eighty days. The total number of arrests ran well into the hundreds. Private detectives seized Suhr in Arizona (he was not even present when the riot occurred) and, without legal formalities, loaded him into a box car and brought him back to California. En route to Marysville, California, where the trial was held, Suhr was kept from consulting his attorney, being taken from hotel to hotel by night. Stool pigeons were placed with him to elicit confessions and he was beaten on an average of once a night with rubber bludgeons. It was several weeks after his "arrest" before his attorneys could even discover his whereabouts. Many other defendants were arrested and hurried from county to county in order to elude defense attorneys who were scurrying about trying to find their clients. So terrible was the treatment of these prisoners that one committed suicide and another went insane. An operative of the Burns Agency was, in fact, later convicted in Contra Costa County for a violent assault upon one of the men who was arrested but never tried. Eight months after the Wheatland riot occurred, Ford and Suhr were convicted of murder and sentenced to life imprisonment and this conviction was sustained on appeal,[2] the first California labor *cause célèbre.*

[2] *People* v. *Ford,* 25 Cal. App. 388.

During the trial sixty or more wobblies rented a house in Marysville, which they used as headquarters. Every day of the trial, they marched from this house to the courtroom. When Austin Lewis, the defense attorney, needed a witness, he merely scribbled the name and address of the witness on a card and handed it to one of these men. Sympathetic brakemen and conductors on the trains invariably honored the cards as passenger tickets and allowed wobblies to travel about the State hunting witnesses.

Wheatland was not a strike, but a spontaneous revolt. It stands out as one of the significant episodes in the long and turgid history of migratory labor in California. For the first time, the people of California were made to realize, even if vaguely, the plight of its thousands of migratory workers. It had been customary to assume the existence of these laborers, but never to recognize the fact of their existence. The deplorable conditions under which they lived and worked were, also, brought to light for the first time. Although the immediate public reaction was one of horror over the I.W.W. menace, so-called, the incident made an impression. It created an opportunity for effective investigation by the Commission on Immigration and Housing in California which, under the distinguished chairmanship of Simon J. Lubin, did much to improve living and housing conditions among migratory workers in the State. As the annual reports of this commission began to appear after 1914, the Californians were given some interesting facts about labor conditions in the State's most important industry. It was discovered, for example, that, in 1914, there were about 75,000 migratory farm laborers in the State; and that, when employed, these people worked on ranches "devoid of the accommodations given horses." Sample studies indicated that about a fourth of them were suffering from one type of sickness or another and that about an equal percentage were feebleminded.

### 2. Kelley's Army

Following the Wheatland affair, and during the winter of 1914, an incident occurred which, for the first time, threw considerable light on the question of what happened to 75,000 migratory farm laborers during the winter months. The number of unemployed in San Francisco that winter was unusually large and the city authorities soon discovered that "General Kelley," a gentleman of mysterious antecedents, had organized an army of the unemployed. About two thousand men had enrolled in the army and were living in abandoned warehouses and store buildings; quite a number were camped in tents in the Mission district. Kelley had his men organized into companies and squads and put them through regular military maneuvers. As the size of the army increased, Kelley became more outspoken in his demands upon the authorities for relief, or "charitable assistance," as it was then called. The officials, and the business interests of the city, soon became alarmed over the situation, and, seizing upon Kelley's desire to stage a "march on the capitol," they escorted his army to the ferries and sent them across the bay to Oakland. The Mayor of Oakland, not at all delighted by this visitation of "rainsoaked, sick, and coughing" men, hurriedly arranged for their transportation to Sacramento. In

Sacramento, they organized a "camp" and were preparing to march on the capitol building, 1500 strong, when a rival "army," of eight hundred special deputy sheriffs, arrived with pick handles and drove them across the river, burned their blankets and equipment, and mounted an armed guard along the bridge to keep them out. In the process of ousting the army, the deputies were none too gentle. E. Guy Talbott, a local clergyman, states that many of Kelley's men "were beaten into insensibility and the most atrocious and barbarous methods were used." Within three weeks the Army, "rained on and starved out," melted away. For years afterwards, however, the story of Kelley's Army lingered in the social consciousness of the Californian as a grim portent of the days to come.

When the Industrial Relations Commission arrived in California in August, 1914, they took testimony both on the Wheatland affair and on the strange rise and fall of General Kelley's Army, and the connection between the two incidents was clearly indicated. "You can't analyze the Wheatland affair and the riot that took place," testified Carleton Parker, "or the problem of the unemployed in San Francisco last winter without bringing into the analysis the seasonal character of employment in California." Testifying further, he said: "The fact that San Francisco is said to have in winter thirty-five to forty thousand men lying up until the earlier season when the first agricultural demand for labor occurs, is explained by the fact that along in November and December, especially in November, agricultural work practically ceases. The State being fundamentally an agricultural State, the industrial life of the

State not being of tremendous importance, and the fact that the State is geographically isolated, means that we have to nurse our own casual labor class through the winter." Witness after witness testified as to the instability of employment, the lack of co-ordination, and the refusal of the agricultural interests of the State to assume any measure of responsibility for the situation which they had created. It is interesting to note that one witness did suggest that if the growers continued to shirk their responsibility, it might be well for the State to condemn some of their holdings and settle the unemployed on the land so that they could earn a living. At about the same time, San Diego, faced with a serious unemployment problem, took over four thousand acres of "waste" land, and gave food and lodging to hundreds of unemployed, and paid them fifty cents a day, while they worked in improving and cultivating the tract. The experiment was quite successful and was continued until 1916, when, the demand for labor increasing, it was abandoned. August Vollmer, describing the operation of the plan in the *Christian Science Monitor*, advocated its extension throughout the State and claimed that there were approximately 11,000,000 acres of "waste" lands in the State that might be put to constructive social use in this manner.

The recognition of an acute social problem in migratory farm labor, a problem so serious as to shake the foundations of the State, which the Wheatland Riot and the appearance of General Kelley's Army had forced upon the people of California, was, unfortunately, destroyed by the World War. Both incidents passed into history. Even the beginning toward a solution of the problem, as indicated by the creation of the State Commission on Immigration and Housing, was soon nullified. Reactionary postwar administrations proceeded to undermine the work of the commission (Simon J. Lubin resigned in protest), and the blind chaos of former years once more prevailed.

## CHAPTER X

## THE WAR SPEED-UP

WITH a war in Europe, agricultural production in California was stepped up to keep pace with an expanding market. Prices began to rise and with each rise in prices the area and quantity of production increased. Beginning in 1914, agricultural production rapidly increased throughout the war years, with a sharp acceleration after the United States entered the war. A marked increase was noticed in all lines of agricultural production,[1] as a result of wartime demands and inflation. The boom in production was, of course, immediately reflected in a frenzied demand for a larger supply of farm labor. Not only had production increased enormously, but the supply of farm labor had decreased. Immigration was at a standstill and the draft took thousands of men from the agricultural areas. Making more money than they had ever made before, enjoying an almost unlimited market and fabulous prices, the land industrialists went beserk in their demand for labor. They howled for laborers, and more laborers. Reading over the transactions of the farm organizations during this period, one is impressed with the obscenity of the

[1] See *March of Industry* by Cleland and Hardy, pp. 115, 118, 123.

large growers' greed, the brutality of their demands. They were literally wild with a frenzy of profit-patriotism.

## 1. The Wobblies Again

During the war, of course, labor organization in the fields was practically dormant. But, at the outset of the period, there was one rather spectacular labor protest which merits description. Following the Ford and Suhr prosecution, the I.W.W. had created a fairly effective organization of agricultural workers. The agricultural section of the I.W.W. was chartered on April 21, 1915. Known as Agricultural Union No. 400 (later changed to Local No. 110), it built up considerable strength in California and in the Middle West. It sent organizers directly into the fields to unionize farm workers. Its field organizers had authority to establish locals at any camp or ranch. It gave form to spontaneous uprisings and organized labor, so to speak, in the act of fighting. In a report prepared for the government during the war, Thorstein Veblen pointed out that the Agricultural Workers Industrial Union had some fifty thousand members, most of its strength being concentrated, however, in the Middle West. In the year 1917, the membership of the union doubled. But its efforts were soon stalemated. On September 7, 1917 — a fatal day in the history of the I.W.W. — the federal prosecutions were launched in Wichita, Sacramento, and Chicago; over five hundred persons were arrested of whom a hundred and sixty were later convicted. In Sacramento, the federal prosecutions came on for trial in December, 1918, five defendants having died in jail of influenza before trial. The remaining forty-two defendants, famous in labor history as "the Silent Defenders," refused to enter any kind of plea and remained silent throughout the trial after issuing a statement in which they said that they knew they would be convicted no matter what they said or did. Their silence was broken, however, when the verdict was returned: They then stood up, in court, and sang the International.

The year 1917 marked the last active appearance of the I.W.W. in the fields in California. "Early in the year, the propaganda of the I.W.W. organized and incited an up-rising in Fresno County, which proceeded to the fields in all the surrounding country and compelled the men working there to leave their work by threats of bodily injury and by the showing of arms and deadly weapons," is the summarization of the disturbances of that year by the *Pacific Rural Press*.[2] "Incidents" occurred throughout the spring and summer. In August, the Toilers of the World — an I.W.W. group — conducted a large cannery strike at San Jose, in connection with which the National Guard was dispatched to the strike area. On September 2, 1917, the *Fresno Morning Republican* carried a story describing the sabotage inflicted by the I.W.W. on local growers. Haystacks had been burned and many trays of raisins were dumped on the ground and covered with dirt. Similar items had appeared in the press during the year. As a result of these and other incidents reported at the time, and to check the organizational activities of the wobblies, a great round-up of the I.W.W. in the fields was launched in September, 1917. On September 6, 1917, the

[2] November 2, 1917.

I.W.W. hall in Fresno was raided, over a hundred men
seized, and some nineteen arrested. The story states that
since the opening of a state labor bureau for farm labor
in Fresno the wobblies had been congregating around the
hall and urging men not to accept jobs and to strike for
better conditions. Similar raids and arrests were made in
Stockton (September fifth), Hanford and elsewhere in the
State. The raids were made by federal officers and the individuals arrested were charged with violation of federal
wartime statutes. The raiding officers seized all books and
papers, and, in most instances, also seized the funds of the
wobblies. This general round-up continued throughout the
fall of 1917 in California. Unquestionably the I.W.W. was
organizing or attempting to organize farm labor, but it is
extremely doubtful if its members were responsible for all of
the acts of destruction attributed to them. In any case, the
farmers took advantage of the situation to use the federal
agents as a force by which to browbeat all farm labor. The
*Los Angeles Times* of September 11, 1917, carried a story
from Fresno, which clearly indicates what was being accomplished. "Because of the hotbed of the I.W.W. discovered in Central California and the fact that crops have
been maliciously destroyed, the U.S. Dept. of Justice has
opened an office in Fresno, with William Freeman, special
investigator, in charge. Farmers having labor trouble and
whose crops are threatened will report directly to the
local office. The bureau was opened this morning and one
of the first reports was from W. Flanders Setchel, a grape
grower, who said that grape pickers had thrown the grapes
on the ground and then trampled on them. Twenty-six
I.W.W.'s were arrested in the government raid last week

and are still held in jail. The 800-ton raisin crop on the Kearney farm is now being harvested by large crews and a special effort is being made to gather the crop before the fall rains. There has been a great shortage of labor, but the situation is somewhat improved this week." It is apparent that the raids were designed to check organizational activities and to force down the wages of farm labor. On September 2, 1917, the Twelfth Federal Reserve Bank had issued a bulletin in San Francisco, stating that the rising cost of farm labor "hampers the effectiveness of this country's efforts." Almost at the day this bulletin was released, the raids started. As a consequence, wages were kept at a minimum throughout the war years (at a time when the farm industrialists were making unheard-of profits) and no further "labor disturbances" were reported. The farmers had federal agents in their communities, running "labor bureaus," to whom they could report any "labor trouble." Under the circumstances, it was a rather ideal setup for the growers. Earlier in the year, in June, farm laborers had struck at Turlock, California, where one thousand carloads of cantaloupes were lost because of a strike. In that case, the local growers had enlisted the townspeople, and had driven the "agitators" from the community.

## 2. The Fun of the Thing

Labor conditions in the fields were so wretched during the war years that even some of the growers confessed that possibly some improvements should be made. One farmer, C. W. Kesner,[3] stated that conditions "were terrible" and that the workers on his farm — he was charging

[3] *Pacific Rural Press*, June 2, 1917.

the condition to their ignorance — "did not have a blanket or a wash tub." At a meeting of the State Council of Defense in Sacramento, May, 1917, migratory workers testified that no provision whatever was made for them on the large ranches. One man said that he had "slept in a piano box in a cow shed and a not too sweet smelling cow shed at that." One of the large growers let the cat out of the bag, at this hearing, when he said that the "Labor Hog" was responsible for conditions in the field. "The Labor Hog," he said, "is an employer who has a crop maturing and necessitating the employment of a large number of hands," so he tries to get twice as many men as he actually needs, "in order to have a surplus of men stranded on the job from whom he may draw at will, as the necessity arises." This method of employment was, of course, the established practice in California; in fact, it still obtains, only on an ever-increasing scale.

Despite these occasional evidences of candor, the majority of the farm industrialists, drunk with profits, remained as impenitent as ever and alternated, in their attitude, between facetiousness and brutality. One grower stated that baths were not necessary for farm laborers. He urged his colleagues to spend five dollars and "run a pipe to the side of the tank house and cap it with a tin spray," as an improvised shower; "it will make them more efficient and they will stay longer." [4] Baths, as such, were "ridiculously inexpensive," but, even so, the pipe-shower arrangement was cheaper and one should not spoil these tramps. One grower, impressed with his benevolence, suggested that, indeed, migratory workers should be treated better. He personally, for example, favored giving them "plenty of clean hay

[4] *Pacific Rural Press*, June 2, 1917.

to sleep on." Still another grower, feeling touched with the poetry of the lives of the migratory workers, described their existence: "The fun of the thing," he said, "comes at night when the day's picking is over and supper is done. All the camp gathers together then and the pickers sing and play banjos, and they make love and gossip — and turn in at all hours of the night, always good-natured and jolly and care-free for a season at least."

At about this same time, Davis Morgan, of the University of California, describing the farm-labor problem in California, summarized with accuracy and much insight the fundamental issues involved. "The existence," he wrote, "of "this large class of uneducated, underpaid, under-housed, and under-fed labor has made possible the operation of our California farms on an unstable basis. It has been possible for farmers to sell their crops for less than actual cost of production." In this manner, they have continued for years to expand their holdings and increase production, at the expense of labor. "As a consequence, the small American farmer is in a predicament for his labor is in competition with the underpaid labor on the larger farms." Mr. Morgan closed his article with a denunciation of the "wild cry for unassimilative peon labor" which was then being raised in California.[5]

### 3. The Deaf Mutes Enlist

Although they were able, in the manner I have indicated, to lower farm wages, the industrialists were not able to get as many workers as they wanted. One of them cried:

[5] *Pacific Rural Press*, May 26, 1917.

"The way to get farm labor is to get it. Get it where it is to be had. Get it just as you would any other commodity."[6] And get it, the farmers proceeded to do. Looking about for native sources of labor, they first raided the schools. Children have long worked, of course, in the California fields. A farmer, in 1892, praised "boy power" on the large farms, stating that he paid, by way of wages, "as many dollars per month as the boy-power was years old," an extraordinary wage standard, to say the least. During the war, through the assistance of state agencies, the Boy Scouts and the Y.M.C.A. youngsters were recruited on a large scale for work in the fields. Detention schools for boys, by way of example, made contracts with the growers to supply labor, the school keeping two fifths of the earnings, the boys keeping three fifths. These youngsters were organized in military units; they marched to and from work. At one camp, the boys got up at five o'clock in the morning; and, after "God's blessing was offered on the food," they sang hymns and patriotic songs, and then marched into the fields, as "Old Glory floats on the breeze"; and, on Sundays, they listened to "the finest kind of Sunday talks," before reporting for work. The boys were organized in squads, with captains and other officers. One detention school reported that it had been furnishing child labor on contract, in this manner, since 1905.[7] The Preston School of Industry at Ione, California (a state reformatory), reported[8] that it had been furnishing boys to the near-by growers for some years, on the

[6] *Pacific Rural Press,* November 3, 1917.
[7] *Pacific Rural Press,* May 7, 1917.
[8] *Pacific Rural Press,* June 9, 1917.

following arrangement: the farmer paying piece rates for work, the school furnishing the board (which redounded, of course, to the advantage of the growers), and the boys, out of their earnings, paying for transportation to and from work. Some of these boys, wards of the State of California, were able to earn, in the proud words of the superintendent, from $20 to $59 for a *season's work*. "From time to time," reported the superintendent, "our boys have been sent out to assist various farm communities when they were unable to secure help in the harvest." In 1918, the school authorities in Napa, California, closed the schools, and sent the youngsters into the fields to work. In this manner, boasted the growers, they had harvested a $2,000,000 prune-and-grape crop, at a labor cost of $20,000 — and a labor cost of one per cent is, indeed, something to gladden the heart of a grower.[9] This practice of closing the schools, and forcing the youngsters into the fields during harvest, was quite common. The State Superintendent of Schools in California gave his wholehearted support to this program. Various organizations were formed for this purpose, such as the Boys Working Reserves; the Boys and Girls Aid Society; and similar organizations.[10] In Berkeley, the deaf mutes were taken from their school and sent into the fields in Yolo County, to harvest the crops, at a time — 1918 — when the fruit crop in California alone was valued at $235,000,000.

After raiding the schools, the growers began to look about for other sources of cheap, unorganized labor. It

[9] *Pacific Rural Press*, January 5, 1918.
[10] *Pacific Rural Press*, August 9, 1919.

was not long, of course, before they hit upon the idea of enlisting women. "Why not draw an unlimited supply of earnest and clear-sighted women?" asked one grower,[11] and the campaign to enlist women was immediately launched. A Woman's Land Army of America, California Division, was organized and hundreds of women were enrolled, in military fashion, "for the duration of the war." Women enlisting were organized in battalions; they wore uniforms; they marched in formation under the flag to the fields and canneries; and they went through military setting-up exercises in the various camps to which they were assigned. "If you can't fight, farm," was the slogan unfurled over their camps. "Sisters all," as one enthusiast described them, they did almost every variety of farm work but were particularly active in the orchards and canneries. The farmers were, at first, delighted. "Looking over their rolling miles of cherries, apricots, peaches and the like, they took counsel. They saw the labor shortage growing yet shorter — and all they could see on the horizon was The Girl." [12] "The girls are all right seven days in the week," said one grower who boasted, in the same breath, of the spectacular profits he had made.[13] The Woman's Land Army worked throughout the California fields in 1917, 1918 and 1919. Its gallant girls were paid twenty-five cents an hour, out of which they defrayed their own expenses and board. "But," added one grower, "it is not the amount of money they can earn that brings these girls to

[11] *Pacific Rural Press*, June 15, 1917.
[12] *Sunset*, November, 1918.
[13] *Pacific Rural Press*, July 20, 1918.

the field — it is the fact that they are doing their bit." "We feel assured," commented another farm philanthropist, "that our bright American energetic girls will organize their own musicales." Joining the chorus of praise, another grower said: "These women and girls will help curb the rapacity of certain foreign alien elements in their demands for higher wages."

Some of the units of the Woman's Land Army numbered, in particular camps, such as those at Lodi and Vacaville, as many as five hundred women. So acute was the demand of the growers for help to assist them in becoming millionaires overnight, at the expense of their nation, that the Chinese women housed in a Presbyterian missionary home in San Francisco were likewise drafted for duty in the fields. The girls from this Christian haven worked in the fields throughout the war, "when the plea went forth to every rancher and every house-wife to save the fruit rotting on the ground for lack of men to pick it." This statement is, of course, so far as the evidence goes, wholly unsupported. Fruit never rots in California: the growers always find someone to pick it. In the camp of the Chinese girls, who, incidentally, had been "rescued" from the "slave" traffic by the Presbyterians, the labor recruits were taught "patriotism" and "how to be self-supporting." They were also given an opportunity, as their leader put it, "to enjoy the summer sunshine of the Santa Clara Valley" — those who have experienced this sunshine can appreciate the irony — "without any expense to the mission." Life among the itinerant laborers, White, Mexican, and nondescript, wrote the historian of the mission, "was heroic in its way. The girls toasted marshmallows, and in spite of weary limbs and sun-burned shoulders, were paid in fellowship as well as in coin." [14]

It was generally thought at the time that the practice of enlisting women for labor in the fields would carry over into the postwar years. One reason why the practice was largely discontinued after 1919, however, is indicated in the files. The leader of the California Division of the Woman's Land Army began to insist upon certain safeguards. The growers, for example, were made to sign contracts with the Woman's Land Army, wherein they agreed to employ a definite number of women for a fixed period of employment; and, toward the close of the war, these contracts contained provisions for an eight-hour day, overtime, camp inspection, and other requirements. Here, at least, was the suggestion of collective bargaining, and, once the emergency was over, the growers naturally dispensed with the girls.

### 4. Oriental Nostalgia

One would think that these sources would have supplied all the labor necessary for the purposes of the growers. But, not satisfied with drafting women, girls, and deaf mutes, they clamored for more workers. Throughout the war, the growers carried on an insistent campaign to have the immigration laws relaxed so as to permit the importation of coolie labor "for the duration of the war." There are times, said one grower, when it becomes necessary to have the "Oriental. These whites feel abused if you look cross-eyed at them." [15] The farm journals continually echoed

[14] *Chinatown Quest*, 1931, by Carol Green Wilson.
[15] *Pacific Rural Press*, May 19, 1917.

with the cry for Chinese labor.[16] The Commonwealth Club of San Francisco set aside a meeting, April 10, 1918, to consider farm labor.[17] At this symposium, the growers' representative pleaded eloquently for the importation of 40,000 Chinese laborers. Every possible type of pressure was brought to bear upon the administration in Washington to permit the entry of Chinese labor; the California Development Association memorialized President Wilson to this effect, and resolutions were sent from many California organizations to Congress, asking that coolie labor enter California. At the symposium to which I have referred, a professor of the University of California stated: "I know of one firm who are making a group of their imported Mexicans work for ten and twelve hours a day, handcuffing them at night to prevent their escape." Mexico, the only source of immigration available at the time, was tapped for labor, and the large-scale importation of Mexican labor started during this period. In June, 1918, the growers sent a representative to Mexico, who arranged for the importation of "several thousand Mexican laborers." [18] The growers advocated that the government supply armed guards to make these Mexicans work in the fields. They also advocated conscription of labor for farm work and, in many communities, men were drafted for service in the army, and then granted exemption, provided they worked in the fields. At the Commonwealth Club symposium, referred to above, university professors joined with farmers in urging the passage of stringent vagrancy laws under which men could

[16] *Pacific Rural Press*, June 22, 1918.
[17] *Farm Labor*, Vol. XIII, No. 3, Transactions of Commonwealth Club.
[18] *Pacific Rural Press*, June 22, 1918.

be forced to work in the fields, and, in the same volume, it is stated that men were arrested for vagrancy, taken before justices of the peace, and sentenced. The sentence, curiously enough, was for the period of the harvest, and the defendants were then turned over to the constable who took them to the fields. The State Council of Defense, considering farm labor on November 16, 1918, "urged the passage of a more drastic law against vagrants as a means to compel men who are offered employment in orchards and farms to accept such work under penalty of prosecution."

The sociological insight of these farm industrialists, and their complacent stooges, the university professors, is, indeed, a matter to incite amazement. At the Commonwealth Club symposium, Professor R. L. Adams, of the University of California, joined with the farmers in urging the suppression of the saloons, as a means of recruiting farm laborers and improving their efficiency. Dr. Adams wanted a prohibition not only against whisky, rum and gin, but against beer and wine, as the saloon "as a place of conviviality" had a bad effect on the men. Conviviality, in other words, is not permissible. It was seriously contended that "these floaters, tramps, hoboes, blanket stiffs, and bohunks" drank because they were "worthless." The closing of the saloons, said a farm journal, "will reduce roadside attractions and facilitate transit as well as insure the greater efficiency of labor upon arrival." [19] At the symposium, one farmer rated the saloon "as a disturbing element," only next to the I.W.W. "propaganda and the walking delegate." As to the I.W.W., he regarded them as a "most contemptible and dangerous element. When located they

[19] *Pacific Rural Press*, April 10, 1920.

should be arrested at once, thrown into prison, and kept at hard labor during the period of the war. If at that time no satisfactory signs of reformation are apparent the commitment should be extended to life." Only one speaker at the symposium called attention to the fact that wages did not increase when prices were increased. The prices of berries, he stated, had doubled, with no increase in the rate for picking; and the same condition prevailed with reference to other crops. As to the type of laborer, the farmers agreed that only "John Chinaman" was desirable. The Hindu, said one speaker, "is a vile caricature of humanity. As for Mexicans in our country, we have to have constables watching them. They also are vile." Itinerant labor was "worthless and inefficient"; only the Chinese were praiseworthy. "The importation of the Chinese would be the easiest, most effective and permanent solution of the vexing farm labor problem." [20]

Toward the end of this hectic period, there was a flare-up of minor proportions. In January, 1919, orange pickers struck in Southern California, with men out at San Dimas, Covina, Monrovia and Duarte. The newspapers promptly launched a story about a "Russian strike" to cripple the citrus industry, and the usual round-up and wholesale arrests took place, the papers then unctuously announcing that the "Bolshevik" conspiracy had been crushed.[21] In April, strikes occurred among farm laborers at Pomona, La Verne, and Ventura; with more arrests. On April 8, 1919, the Standard Oil Company, in its advertisements for Nujol Laboratories, carried the interesting and significant blurb: "Are you a

[20] *Sunset,* July, 1917.
[21] *Los Angeles Times,* January 24, 29, 31, 1919.

Bolshevik? Bolshevism is based upon violence, relies upon force, is deaf to right or reason. To force the bowels to move by taking castor oil, pills, salts, mineral waters, etc., is to outrage nature and bolshevik the body." It is an apt commentary on the period. At the same time, Hulett C. Merritt, member of one of the families that has figured prominently among the large land industrial interests of California for two generations, and a man of great wealth, was convicted in the Federal courts, April 2, 1919, for hoarding food supplies. Patriotism runs high among the landed gentry of California who, during this period, were out to win the war and lower wages.

The years 1919 to 1920 witnessed a significant development in California agriculture. The "unstable basis" of the farm industry, which has been previously commented upon, was made still more unstable by the reckless expansion of the period. The industry, long founded on an irrational and unscientific basis, became more irrational with every year of the war. Urged on by profits which were beyond anything of which they had dreamed, the farm industrialists expanded production, rationalized methods, speeded up labor, consolidated their control, imported thousands of alien laborers, built up their labor reserves, disregarded all thought of permanent social planning, and created a situation ripe for collapse and disaster. By the end of the war, a kind of industrial feudalism had been established in California agriculture,[22] with the great lords of the land more firmly in control than they had ever been and more conscious of their power. The bases for this power, in the main, consisted of two factors: the type of

[22] See *Survey*, May 24, 1919.

ownership involved and the existence of an army — a vast army augmented during the period by Chinese ex-prostitutes, deaf mutes, orphaned children, women and conscripted labor — by the utilization of which great profits were made. The profits went, of course, to the same small clique to which they had always gone. One farmer, with an eye to the future, said: "It is possible that in fifty years or more from now California may be subdivided into a million small farms, and largely feeding a resident farm population of twenty millions." [23] But this vision was far from the reality of the period; and it is still merely a concept.

[23] *Pacific Rural Press*, June 16, 1917.

## CHAPTER XI

# THE POSTWAR DECADE

## (1920–1930)

THE postwar decade in California farm labor was primarily a period of rationalization. The growers, to fight the deflation, were forced to adopt new methods of control. Struggling to retain the huge profits to which they had become accustomed during the war years, they began to impose various types of control upon production and prices, and to rationalize methods of operation, notably in regulating the flow of farm labor to the fields. The developments which took place during these years were implicit in the patterns of operation previously established in the industry, but the emphasis throughout the period was upon rationalization. The industrialized character of California agriculture had been established; it now remained for the growers to create those methods of control which mark the maturity of an industry. Previous to the war, California agriculture had assumed many of the characteristics of a fully developed mechanized industry; but the expansion of production during the war had destroyed the controls which the growers had begun to impose upon the industry. A new status quo, therefore, had to be achieved.

### *1. Deflation*

The inflation of the war period had resulted in a marked expansion of California agriculture, both in area and in intensification of production. Nor did the wartime prosperity immediately cease; it continued well into the decade. Deflation did not strike the industry until about 1925. When the effects of deflation began to make themselves manifest, notably in the decline of prices for agricultural products, the growers swiftly countered with a move to stabilize production. They began to strengthen the position of the co-operative exchanges by extending their control over the various crops. Most of the exchanges had been in existence for many years, but their position had been threatened by the wild and uncontrolled expansion of the wartime period. The postwar decade witnessed an attempt to rebuild the exchanges, so to speak; to extend and to tighten their control over farm products. In large part this campaign was made feasible by reason of the fact that the deflation had liquidated many of the small growers, and the small growers had never been friendly to the exchanges. The elimination of many small growers had naturally enhanced the position of the large growers in each crop industry and greatly facilitated the process of stabilization.

The raisin industry may be taken as illustrative of the methods by which control was achieved. Wartime prices had resulted in an unprecedented boom in the raisin industry. The number of vineyards in the Fresno area rapidly multiplied as small businessmen and townspeople abandoned their occupations and bought vineyard acreage at greatly inflated prices. When deflation hit the industry in

1925, a serious panic developed. Hundreds of small "sucker" farmers were wiped out in the avalanche of foreclosures which followed. The California Raisin Growers Association had been established as early as 1898, but it had never been able to control the industry. Faced with the deflation crisis, the large growers realized that a measure of control had to be imposed. Consequently, in order to restore prices through monopolistic control, they created a new organization, the Sun-Maid Raisin Growers Association, and launched a campaign to extend its control over the entire industry. Some of the small growers, notably the Armenian growers, were able to survive for a time. They were, for the most part, not members of the association. Resorting to a not very subtle variety of race baiting, the Sun-Maid officials began to stir up feeling against the Armenians. When this whispering campaign failed to drive the Armenians into the exchange, the large growers started a campaign of violence and intimidation. To indicate the nature of this campaign, it is perhaps sufficient to say that the growers have never bothered to deny that the small farmers were browbeaten, intimidated and threatened by squads of "nightraiders" and "vigilantes." "The tactics which were resorted to in order to force reluctant growers to sign up," to quote from one observer, "would have done credit to the carpet-baggers of the post-Civil War South. The story of those months will never be told; all that can be said is that desperation resulted in the worst mob violence which Fresno County has ever seen." [1] Needless to say, "order" was soon restored in the

[1] *The Armenian Colony in Fresno County*, 1930, by Richard Tracy La Piere.

industry. Today the dominance of the Sun-Maid Raisin
Growers Association over the raisin industry is complete.
Similar methods, varying of course in intensity, were used
in the other crop industries to recapture wartime profits
through the rigid control of prices. An important factor in
this general campaign throughout the industry was, of
course, the weapon of financial power. The large growers
and the exchanges are, in a sense, the creatures of the banks
and the banks, through the control of credit, have at all
times held a whip over the non-member growers. That
they have not hesitated to use the whip is a matter of public record in California. An examination of each crop
industry in California today would disclose that the dominance of the particular exchange is practically complete.
The degree of control will vary in some industries from,
say, 75 per cent to 90 per cent, but the fact of control
is obvious. Likewise an examination of each individual
exchange will show that it is the large grower who profits
most through the mechanism of exchange control.

Even before the decline in prices and profits had been
arrested through the medium of price control, the growers
had been able to offset their losses by the sharp decline in
farm wages. Although wartime prices continued until about
1925, wartime wages suffered an abrupt decline after 1919.
Farm wages continued steadily to decline from 1920 to
1933; in fact, they continued to decline long after the de-
flationary tendency had been checked. In 1922 the farm
journals gleefully noted that wages were much less than
in 1920 and that "workmen are admirably more efficient
than they were a year ago," i.e. workmen were more willing to accept wage cuts. Throughout the postwar decade
the reports on farm labor issued by the growers are all

to the same effect: an abundance of labor, no strikes, a steady decline in wage rates; and these same reports continued after 1925 when production had been increased in response to a steadily increasing price level. On June 24, 1924, the *Pacific Rural Press* noted that "for the first time since the War we find a superabundance of labor and a *natural* decline in wages." A study made at the time indicated that between 1910 and 1920, farm production had increased 13 per cent while farm wages, in the same period, had declined 4 per cent; [2] and this estimate does not purport to reflect the increased productivity of farm labor during the same period achieved through the introduction of various types of machinery. From 30 cents an hour, wages steadily declined throughout the decade until, in 1933, the growers were paying 12½ and 15 cents an hour for field labor. During the same period, profits had increased and production had been multiplied many times through the stabilization of prices and rationalized methods of operation. The Industrial Welfare Commission, created to enforce the minimum-wage law for women, consented in 1931 to a reduction in the wages of women employed in the canneries from 33½ cents an hour to 30 cents an hour, and, later, to 27 cents an hour. In 1932, farm labor agents advertised for field labor at 15 cents an hour. Any losses which the deflation had occasioned were thus more than offset by the sharp and protracted depression of wages.

## 2. The Padre of the Workers

It was not only in the realm of prices that the growers began to develop new controls during the postwar decade.

[2] *Pacific Rural Press*, June 6, 1924.

They also began to "co-operate to keep wages down." The control of wage rates was largely achieved through the medium of creating "labor exchanges" and "labor bureaus" and "labor pools." Under this new type of control, the growers in a given area, involved in the production of a particular crop, would create an employment agency or exchange. This agency would estimate the labor requirements for the coming harvest season, fix a prevailing wage rate, and then proceed to recruit the necessary workers. The expenses of the labor exchange were met by an assessment levied against the individual growers. Under this practice, the workers more and more began to be employed by the industry rather than by the individual grower on whose farm they worked. As a consequence, the bargaining power of the growers, through their collective action, was greatly increased at the same time that the workers were wholly without organization for their own protection. From 1909 to 1914, the American Federation of Labor had continued its feeble and sporadic attempts to organize farm labor; but, after 1914, alarmed by the Wheatland Riot, it had abandoned all organizational activity among farm workers. From 1919 to 1934 there is no mention of the subject of farm labor in the proceedings of the State Federation of Labor. Throughout the postwar decade, in other words, farm labor was wholly unorganized at a time when the growers were perfecting mechanisms for the control of prices, production and wages. Consequently farm wages continued to decline after 1925, when prices and production had started to increase.

The Los Angeles Chamber of Commerce, through its agricultural department, has advocated the "labor clearinghouse" idea for thirty years. But it was not until the post-war deflation that the growers began to put the idea into practice. After 1920 practically every crop industry in the State began to employ farm labor through a central agency which it controlled. One of the most important agencies of this character is the San Joaquin Valley Labor Bureau, formed April 13, 1926. The manager of this agency, Mr. F. J. Palomares, was employed during the war by the State of California to recruit labor for the wartime indus-tries; later he performed similar services for the Spreckles Sugar Company. A favorite of the large growers, Mr. Palomares is referred to in their publicity as "the padre of the workers," whose duty it is "to shepherd" the workers to the fields during the harvest seasons. Operating as an employment agency, the San Joaquin Labor Bureau has always escaped State regulation on the theory that, since it does not charge the workers a fee, it is not an employ-ment agency. No single agency has done more to depress farm wages in California than this bureau. The wage rates which it announces at the opening of each crop harvest constitute the prevailing rates. No bargaining whatever en-ters into the establishment of these rates. Approximately 50,000 workers are recruited each season through the bu-reau, and it also provides labor for non-agricultural indus-tries, such as the Holly Sugar Corporation. The shipper-growers reserve their warmest words of praise for Palo-mares, the Shepherd-Padre. He knows the Mexicans, they boast, "like an open book and delivers Fourth of July ora-tions to them." Whenever a "labor shortage" arises, Palo-mares is dispatched to Los Angeles, or if need be to Mex-ico, and soon the long caravan of cars begins to trail over the Ridge Route into the San Joaquin Valley, with the Shepherd herding thousands of workers into the fields. Agencies similar to the San Joaquin Valley Labor Bureau exist for practically every crop industry in the State at the present time.

The employment of farm labor through a central agency has resulted in an enormous saving to the growers. From reports of the various labor exchanges which have appeared in the farm journals, it would appear that labor costs have been reduced from 10 per cent to 30 per cent since this manner of employment has been inaugurated. Employment through a central agency minimizes the expense of recruiting labor; it enhances the bargaining power of the growers at the expense of the workers; it divorces the individual grower from all sense of responsibility for the workers; it creates an ever-increasing army of surplus laborers; it speeds up the flow of labor to the fields and quickens the movement of migratory labor from one crop to the next; and, lastly, it gets the migratory workers out of the farm counties at the end of the season. Nor has the process of rationalization stopped at this point. On January 24, 1924, the first Statewide meeting of large growers was called for the specific purpose of discussing farm labor. Many subsequent meetings have been held for the same purpose. Through these Statewide meetings, the growers have worked out estimates of the total number of migratory workers required for a given season in California. Then these "big broad-minded men," to use the phrase of the *Pacific Rural Press*, have fixed wage rates for the various types of labor involved. Thus uniformly low rates are established, not only for each crop, but for the entire in-

dustry in the State. They have also set up the machinery
by which labor can be swiftly moved from one crop area
to the other as the crops mature. To be sure, these arrangements have not worked perfectly and individual growers
occasionally break away from the prearranged plan, but,
in general, it can be said that farm labor in California must
now bargain not with the single grower or group of growers but with the organized farm industry of the State considered as a single entity.

### 3. Cotton Goes West

In the postwar decade California witnessed another
revolutionary change in farm production comparable in
importance to the transition from wheat to fruit and to
the introduction of sugar-beet production. "As suddenly
as the coming of gold diggers," cotton development began
in the San Joaquin Valley. A few growers had experimented
with cotton growing for years; but the real development
of cotton production came in the decade 1920–1930. In
general it was the declining prices of other agricultural
products that encouraged many growers to make the transition to cotton production. It was soon discovered, moreover, that California farms grew a superior brand of cotton and that the production of cotton was potentially
heavier in California than elsewhere, with an average production of 370 pounds per acre as compared with a national
average of 116.5 pounds. Production swiftly rose from
77,000 bales in 1925 to 130,000 bales in 1926, with 170,000
acres being devoted to cotton production. In 1921 there
were only 1500 acres in cotton; by 1937 the cotton acreage

was close to 600,000 acres. With the introduction of cotton production came all the incidents associated with its production elsewhere: tenant farming; cotton-gin companies, such as Anderson-Clayton & Co., with their usurious cropping contracts; and the increasing importance of finance.

From the point of view of farm labor, the introduction of large-scale cotton operations in California had several far-reaching consequences. "Heretofore there has been a hiatus between the grape harvest in September and the early February sugar beet thinning and asparagus cutting. With the cotton harvest beginning in October and continuing through January, the gap will be filled and the cycle of seasonal occupation complete." [3] While this statement somewhat exaggerates the extent of the cotton season, it does properly emphasize the fact that cotton production has tended to stabilize employment and to increase the demand for farm labor. But there were other consequences. Cotton production requires a particular type of labor, i.e. labor trained and skilled in cotton picking. A novice, paid by the pound, can earn practically nothing picking cotton. Picking cotton requires skill and experience and great powers of endurance. Cotton production in the San Joaquin Valley, therefore, gave a definite impetus to the importation of Mexican labor and, at the same time, it set in motion an influx of migratory workers from Texas and Oklahoma. The use of child labor also increased. The cotton growers praised the Mexican as "patient, obedient, religious, and free from bolshevist tendencies." At the same time, the *California Cotton Journal* pleaded for child labor. "At this moment, 1926, the labor shortage is the most seri-

[3] *The Nation*, July 14, 1926.

ous confronting California's cotton industry. The Journal believes that there are thousands of boys and girls in California's public schools who are without the range of the child labor laws and who are not only willing but eager to help harvest the crop. Is it common sense to save an industry from damage? Ways must be found to so interpret the laws that when a growing industry is threatened its provisions may be legally brought to the rescue." This type of blackmail is fairly typical of the social attitude which the cotton interests in the State have at all times adopted.

The Hotchkiss ranch near Los Banos may be taken as a fairly typical California cotton "plantation" or factory. The corporation which controls this property (most of the large California ranches are incorporated) has approximately 10,000 acres devoted to cotton. For the last few years, the corporation has cleared $80,000 or better from its cotton acreage alone. In 1937 it imported some 250 Negroes from Louisiana, under contract, to pick cotton. The corporation maintains a store where food and other supplies are sold to the Negroes at fancy prices. Lunch wagons are rolled into the fields so that the workers may eat while they work. The neighboring town of Firebaugh, which is located on company property, boasts of sixteen saloons. When organizers appear in Firebaugh, the sheriff is notified and the organizers are rounded up and swiftly escorted out of the county. The business of cowing farm labor in California is as simple as that.

The increase in cotton acreage continues at an amazing pace. From 1936 to 1937 the acreage increased from 400,000 acres to 600,000 acres; between 1935 and 1937 the cotton acreage doubled. The increase in cotton acreage has naturally augmented the demand for transient labor. It is estimated, for example, that 30,000 workers were required to harvest the 1936 cotton crop; but, with the increase in acreage, this figure had jumped to 50,000 by 1937. Considering that most transients in the cotton area bring their families with them, it is therefore reasonable to conclude that the increased cotton acreage attracted approximately 125,000 people to the San Joaquin Valley in 1937. Those who were fortunate enough to obtain work were lucky to make from 75 cents to $1.25 a day; family earnings, in some cases, were as low as $3.00 a week in 1937.

## 4. *Who Says White Folks Won't Work?*

An acute labor shortage had existed in California during the war, with the growers demanding the importation of coolie labor to work in the fields. But, with thousands of workers returning to the fields from the army, the growers began to feel secure again. Ardent patriots, they devoted much space in their farm journals to unctuous editorials about replacing alien labor with "the boys returning from France" and about "giving the preference in employment to red-blooded Americans." [4] In actual practice the importation of Mexican labor increased throughout the decade. It is doubtless true, however, that the demobilization increased the supply of farm labor. After 1920, in any case, an increasing number of white laborers began to appear in the fields.

It was immediately apparent, in the early years of the decade, that farm labor was more mobile than it had ever

[4] *Pacific Rural Press*, March, 1920.

been before. Labor seemed to be on the move. The migratory fruit workers now moved about in dilapidated flivvers and the auto camps along the highways came to be regarded as likely sources of farm labor. "Auto campers," wrote the *Pacific Rural Press*, October 10, 1921, "have done much this year to replace Orientals in the raisin district; given a place to camp, they may prove the means of making over foothill orchard districts as real American sections." "The automobile," said the said journal (August 4, 1923), "has developed a new class of fruit workers."

In tapping these new sources of labor it is apparent that the growers did so consciously and that, for a time, they made a few half-hearted efforts to improve working conditions in the realization that "a white gang will not stand for what the foreigners will, either in food or accommodation." [5] Some of the improvements assumed a fanciful unreality. "Many orchardists," wrote the *Pacific Rural Press*, "have erected dance pavilions, and laid out croquet grounds, and many other incidental conveniences that go to add to the pleasure of the tired help after a long day's work under the rays of the torrid sun." [6] Despite the croquet grounds, however, conditions remained as bad as ever; if anything, they became worse. The growers themselves confessed as much. One grower set forth to inspect conditions among the workers. His observations are illuminating. "They camped along the roadside, and lived in tents under which a family, invariably a large one, slept. They cooked in the open exposed to all manner of dust and filth and drew water from a creek, many times from a creek that ceased

---

[5] *Pacific Rural Press*, November 12, 1921.
[6] March 13, 1920.

to flow but leaving enough in the holes for them to drink." [7] This same grower pointed out that there was a difference between the prewar and postwar migratory workers. The former migrants were professional fruit tramps who visited the orchards every season; the horde of postwar migrants were, however, simply homeless transients, many of whom had never worked in the fields before.

The growers were soon lyrical over the discovery of these new "gasoline gypsies." An article appeared at the time which clearly reveals what was happening. "Who Says White Folks Won't Work?" asked Georgia Graves Bordwell in *Sunset Magazine*, December, 1920. She then proceeds to tell the story of a self-righteous California farmer who was having difficulty with his Japanese workmen: They wanted more money. The farmer replies: "That's all right George, never mind about getting me any men — *Americans* are going to harvest this crop." He then dispatches a labor agent to make the rounds of the auto camps to recruit a group of postwar migrants to scab on the Japanese. The experiment proves highly successful, for, "despite the temperamental vagaries of plain cussedness, the crop was harvested by American families." The article is typical for it shows how the growers attempted to invest their drive against the Japanese with romantic and patriotic embellishments. The business of uprooting the Japanese was described as the Re-Americanization of the Fields, the Homecoming of the Americans, and so forth. "New friendships," wrote Mrs. Bordwell, "budded in the warmth of the summer evenings and the grove rang with laughter and music. Even the ear-splitting din of the charivari welcomed a home-

[7] *Pacific Rural Press*, March 13, 1920.

coming camp bride." An idyllic scene, indeed. The growers, she wrote, planned to build camps for the workers in each locality in order to create "a stable yet moving reservoir of dependable labor." The contradiction is interesting: *stable yet moving*. The camps, she wrote, would give a new vision of life to the postwar migrants. "It is for those who, at the end of a few rainbow tinted years in the orchards of California, see at the end a pot of gold in the shape of their own ranch where no one can 'snoop,' where they can pile the boxes to suit themselves and in the fall of the year go up into the hills to hunt for the buck." She is careful to point out, however, that the new white workers must be "dependable" and that they must be prepared to work for "prevailing wages." Instead of finding the pot of gold and the delicious buck, most of these white workers have found disease, starvation and disaster.

By the end of the decade, the industrial character of California agriculture was firmly established. The industry was organized from top to bottom; methods of operation had been thoroughly rationalized; control tended more and more to be vested in the hands of the large growers; and the dominance of finance was greater than ever. Like Eastern industrial enterprises, the California farm factories began to witness the cessation in the influx of new alien racial groups as white workers began to enter the farm factories in greater numbers. With the end of the easy business of exploiting competing racial groups in sight, the farm industrialists shifted the area of exploitation and began to manipulate the flow of labor to their own advantage. The entry of white workers into the fields symbolized the industrial maturity of California agriculture.

## CHAPTER XII

# THE LAND SETTLEMENTS: DELHI
## AND DURHAM

THE FOLLY of attempting to consider the problem of farm labor apart from the question of landownership has long been recognized in California. The two problems are interdependent. It is impossible to attempt a solution of the farm-labor problem without considering the basic issue of landownership. The close interrelation between the two problems has been indicated time and again in the voluminous writing and discussion which has been devoted to both issues. Even farm industrialists, in those rare moments when they have endeavored to think objectively, have toyed with the idea of establishing some type of land-colonization program as a means of stabilizing the supply of farm labor. The land-colonization project, as a means of solving the farm-labor problem, dates from a very early period. Again and again, in the official proceedings of the farm groups and in their journals, references can be found to the theory of colonizing farm labor on the land. Individual growers have, in fact, experimented with the idea; and, as I have indicated, it was tried on a small scale in the Fort Romie experiment of 1905.

Land colonization, on a collective basis, has a definite background in California. Most of the early land settlements in the State were based upon group colonization; a large number of the rural communities, which later developed into cities, were settled by groups of settlers rather than by individual pioneers. For many years the practice was for a promoter to purchase a large tract of land, subdivide it into small acreage lots, endow the subdivision with a euphonious name and then proceed to interest some group in the community as a community. Many of the suburban semi-rural areas of South California came into existence in this manner; and a large number of the settlements in Central and Northern California were planned in similar fashion.[1] Many co-operative and semi-experimental "new life" colonies were established in California. There is a messianic atmosphere in California which has always encouraged various types of utopian experimentation. It is unquestionably true that land-settlement promoters exploited to the full the social idealism of prospective immigrants who wanted to found new communities in California. Some of these early land colonies were advertised as co-operative or semi-co-operative ventures. In fact, some elements of co-operation were to be found in many of the colony settlements, such as co-operative marketing, and so forth. The older colony settlements were, by and large, successful, but as the State grew the colony idea was appropriated by unscrupulous promoters who worked great havoc with their pretentious swindles. In fact the problem became so acute that it received official cognizance and was the subject of several investigations.

[1] See, for example, an article entitled "Colony Life in Southern California" by George H. Fitch, *Cosmopolitan*, November, 1886; likewise an article by John Cowan, on the San Ysidro Colony, *World's Work*, November, 1911.

In 1915 the Legislature authorized an inquiry into the subject of land settlement in California, the report of the commission being published the following year.[2] The initial finding of the commission was that the available farm land was not being utilized: out of 28,000,000 acres of available farm land in California, only some 11,000,000 acres were under cultivation at that time. The reason for this withholding of land from social use was found to be its monopolization by a small group of landowners. The committee found, for example, that 310 proprietors owned over 4,000,000 acres of the best farm lands in the State, i.e. the land best suited to intensive cultivation. They found that in Kern County, four companies owned over a million acres; and that in Merced County, to take one case, Miller and Lux owned 245,000 acres of land. The commission then made a report covering the history of some thirty-two land-colony settlements in the State. It found that these colonies, almost without exception, had been swindles. Most of the colonies had been created during the period from 1900 to 1915. In most instances, the original owner of the land had not sold directly to the developer, but had, instead, sold to an intermediary. Agent commissions, in the re-sale of the land, amounted on an average to more than the original cost of the land, the commissions running as high as forty per cent of the sales price. As a consequence, the price of land had multiplied out of all relation to its earning power. The rapid increase in the price of the land had accelerated the concentration in ownership, and had greatly increased land tenancy. It had also given rise to other evils; it had, reads the report,

[2] *Report on Land Colonization and Rural Credits*, November 29, 1916.

"worked infinite harm to many honest, industrious, but over-sanguine and credulous homeseekers." It had taken millions of dollars out of the State, it had retarded the development of the land and it had led to wasteful and socially profitless speculation. The commission roundly scored the lack of planning which characterized the whole period. The colony promoters had boosted the price of farm lands so high that the lands could only be farmed intensively if they were to be farmed at all. The original owners, therefore, had abandoned direct operations and had leased their lands to foreign tenants, chiefly to orientals. The commission found that the price of the land was about 100 per cent higher than it should be. In the amazing Delta region, near Sacramento, consisting of 500,000 acres of the greatest fertility, the Commission found that in 1915 75 per cent of the land was operated by tenants and, of the tenants, 76 per cent were orientals. The Delta lands had, in large part, been reclaimed by development corporations at great expense; these corporations, in turn, discovered that the land could only be operated at a profit, in view of the staggering improvement costs, by Oriental tenants. The commission also found that the colonization suckers — the visionary home-seekers and community founders — had been frozen out of most of the land colonies. Unfamiliar with climatic conditions in California and also lacking familiarity with farming methods in the West, they had been grossly deceived both as to the earning power of the land and the cost involved in its improvement. The report describes the disintegration that increased land costs had worked in rural areas. Many formerly prosperous rural communities had been literally laid waste. The commission also pointed to the growth of "tenant communities made up almost entirely of Asiatics." (See also a novel, *The Interlopers*, 1917, by Griffing Bancroft.) Some of the rents demanded by landlords in the Delta region of their Asiatic tenants were higher, states the report, than the worst examples of rack-rentals paid by tenants in medieval Europe. Lastly the report points to the fact that the chronic shortage of farm labor could be traced in part to this general situation, in that the supply of native labor which formerly existed in the rural regions had been driven out and that the remaining sources would tend to decrease unless the trends indicated in the report were corrected.

On the basis of this report, the State of California decided to experiment with planned State land settlements, somewhat after the type of experimentation which had been developed previously in Europe and Australia. The State accordingly appropriated in 1917 the sum of $260,000 for experimental purposes, and placed Dr. Elwood Mead in charge of the State Land Settlement. The first planned community selected was that of Durham, in Butte County, where, in 1918, the land-settlement agency purchased 6239 acres of "very good land." The land was divided into 110 farms, varying in size from eight to three hundred acres, and thirty lots of two acres each known as "farm-labor allotments." These farm-labor allotments clearly indicate that the land-settlement projects were designed, in part, as an attempt to stabilize farm labor through colonization. The Land Settlement sold the tracts on a 5 per cent down payment, financed 40 per cent of the costs of improvement and provided for amortization payments over a twenty-year period. So successful was the experiment at the outset that, in a short time, all available allotments had been exhausted.

In 1918 the State appropriated $1,000,000, and expanded its holdings by purchasing a tract of land at Delhi, in Merced County. This last tract was of "very sandy soil of undulating topography and low agricultural value," but the agricultural experts were of the opinion that, by careful planning, it could be improved to the point that its operation would be successful. The cost of improving the tract amounted to far more than the planners had anticipated, due to the character of the land. It was also discovered that it had been financed on a very narrow margin. For example, the land cost the State $92.50 an acre; it cost $17 an acre for water charges; an additional $60 an acre was required to develop a main pipe-line system to bring water to the land; $10 an acre had to be charged for interest during the time the land was being developed prior to sale; and $5 an acre was set up as a charge for taxes and water assessments during the development period. Thus the land had cost the State $185 per acre and the average selling price was $200 an acre, leaving a small margin for operating expenses.

Despite these difficulties, however, both Dr. Elwood Mead and Mr. Walter Packard reported to the Commonwealth Club in 1921 that the Durham and Delhi projects were a success.[3] The projects were, in fact, regarded as a daring innovation in American land policy. Reporting the experiments for *Collier's* magazine (July 29, 1922), George P. West found that the land-settlement idea was "sweep-

[3] *State Colony Settlements,* Transactions of the Commonwealth Club, November 1921, No. VIII, Vol. XVI.

ing the country." Both the Delhi and Durham projects, in fact, attracted worldwide attention. Delegations visited both projects from Europe, from Idaho, from South Carolina, and from many other States; in every case, the delegations were enthusiastic.

In some respects, both Delhi and Durham had been carefully planned. The research facilities of the University of California, for example, were placed at the disposal of settlers; community life was well developed, visitors noting that the "old-fashioned word neighbor was being given a new meaning." A large measure of co-operation was introduced, both in marketing and in purchasing. The administrators and sponsors of the projects were, however, social idealists and not practical economists. Their calculations had been premised upon the assumption of a constant price level. When the first evidence of the postwar deflation began to be apparent, the settlers were naturally affected. Their position was made particularly difficult by reason of the fact that the State Land Settlement Board had purchased the land at wartime prices and before the deflation had set in. The economic naïveté of the sponsors of the project had thus exposed the colonizers to the perils of the business cycle.

Both projects were, moreover, thinly financed. A bond issue, designed to refinance both projects, was defeated at the polls in 1921; and a similar bond issue was defeated again in 1923. By 1925 colonizers in the Delhi settlement were delinquent in their payments to the State to the extent of $293,000, and a legislative report of that year stated that "the project as a whole has been and now is a financial failure." Both projects were in a state of virtual receivership by 1927 and, by that time, the politicians were active in trying to duck responsibility for the "failure" of the land-settlement agency. The administration of both projects was transferred from one State agency to another, and nothing was done to avert the collapse. Soon the settlers became disgruntled; strife developed among the colonizers; and a voluminous litigation resulted. On May 28, 1930, the State made settlement with the purchasers and liquidated both ventures, and in a report issue in 1931 [4] stated: "After some thirteen years of costly demonstration, we are forced to conclude that the theory of State controlled land colonization will not work well in practice." The officials in charge of the liquidation took advantage of the occasion to deliver a few homilies on the frailty of human nature and the folly of economic planning: "Few human beings," reads the report, "are fashioned from sufficiently rugged fiber to withstand the weakening influences of paternalism."

The condemnation of both projects, judged by the final results, would seem to be justified. But no such condemnation can fairly be made. The men who planned both projects were idealistic social philosophers, but they were not realistic economists. They had drafted inspiring blueprints, and sketched the outline of a new rural economy, but they had been innocent of the implications of the business cycle. Both Delhi and Durham were launched at the high point in the wartime boom, which had carried over into the early twenties; the projects had originated during the fat years. From 1919 to 1930 the price of farm commodities steadily declined and the deflation, which accompanied the fall in prices, cut heavily into land values. When the State re-

[4] *Final Report Division of Land Settlement*, June 30, 1931.

fused to expand its financial aid to the projects in order to meet the situation, both projects were, of course, doomed to failure. Business interests in the State, hostile to the breath of socialism, promptly seized upon the situation to point the finger of scorn and to pronounce the projects failures. In high glee over the distress of the colonizers, they set up a chorus of reaction and worked hard to seal the doom of Delhi and Durham.

But, in addition to the lack of economic insight, the sponsors of the projects were subject to other criticisms. The agricultural experts who had reported favorably on the soil at Delhi seem to have been animated by a quixotic desire to prove that they knew more about soil properties than local residents. They seem to have taken a boyish delight in selecting the tract because of its unsuitability; they wanted to prove a theory. Actually, it was admitted at the outset that Durham was "a malarial marsh unfit for human habitation" and that Delhi was "a wind-swept desert of shifting sand." It was upon these two unlikely and distinctly unfavorable sites that the State had launched its experiment in social planning. Later, apologists for the projects stated that the reason these inauspicious sites had been selected for social experiments of such great importance was that no more favorable sites could be purchased. The land monopolists controlled the best land and refused to sell at prices that the administrators of the land-settlement agency could afford to pay, given the restricted budget which had been provided. Consequently they had been forced to select a desert and a malarial swamp as the locale for an experiment which, had it been successful, might have had far-reaching social implications. Given all these unfavorable circumstances, it is interesting to note that both projects were, from a social point of view, successful. One visitor, as I have indicated, found at Delhi that "the old-fashioned word neighbor was being given a reincarnation"; [5] while another visitor inspecting both Delhi and Durham said that the occupants of the farm-labor allotments were happy and prosperous, that none of them were in default, that they had huge gardens, and that they seemed to be contented and satisfied.[6] Similar reports were made by other observers as late as 1925.

But quite apart from what has been said above, the failure of the Delhi and Durham projects is basically traceable to a consideration which was not mentioned in the condemnatory reports. Had it not been for the "Japanese Menace" which existed in 1919 and 1920 in California, it is quite likely that the State of California would never have entered, even half-heartedly, upon a program of land settlement under State control. The tract of land at Delhi, in Merced County, was actually purchased by the State in order to prevent its acquisition by a group of Japanese settlers.[7] The feeling against the Japanese was so strong in California at the time that the State was willing to exploit the idealism of Dr. Elwood Mead, and his colleagues, in order to curb further Japanese aggression in landownership. By 1925 or thereabouts, however, the Japanese threat, in the field of landownership, had been definitely curtailed. Consequently, the land-settlement projects, which had been launched in California with such overtones of lofty social

[5] *Pacific Rural Press*, July 31, 1920.
[6] *Pacific Rural Press*, January 1, 1921.
[7] See *California and the Oriental*, 1922, pp. 137-138.

idealism, were promptly sabotaged. At a time when the Japanese were taking over entire rural communities, such as Florin and Livingstone,[8] it seemed expedient to balance State-subsidized communities against the encroachments of the "patient slant-eyed little people." Both Delhi and Durham, incidentally, were strategically located so as to offset Japanese expansion. It is this political consideration which accounts for the fact that the projects were ever undertaken, and, at the same time, explains their "failure."

Ignoring the realities which doomed both projects, Tory opinion in California has for years pointed to Delhi and Durham as awful examples of the inequity and the folly of State planning and social control. During the campaign of 1934, when Upton Sinclair was a candidate for Governor, the newspapers throughout the State carried lengthy accounts of the Delhi and Durham experiments, pointing to the projects as object lessons in socialist theory and practice. Yet today, surveying the projects in the light of subsequent developments, it is apparent that neither project can be pronounced an unqualified failure, despite the fact that neither project was a fair test of what might be accomplished under State planning. With the "collapse" of Delhi and Durham, the land-colonization idea, as a means of stabilizing farm labor, was temporarily abandoned; in fact, it was not to be revived until the creation of the Resettlement Administration. Had these initial ventures been carried through, and not jettisoned, it is quite likely that an important first step in the solution of the State's old, old problem of farm labor might have been effected.

[8] See *Survey*, May 1926.

## CHAPTER XIII

## THE GREAT STRIKES

WITH the depression came a sharp decline in California farm wages. Wage rates steadily declined after 1929, reaching levels which, even in California, were all-time lows. Agricultural production, on the other hand, continued to mount, and the gross value of agricultural products continued to increase. These circumstances, coupled with the fact that housing and living conditions went from bad to worse, after the resignation of Simon J. Lubin as Chairman of the State Immigration and Housing Commission, gave rise to a profound wave of discontent and unrest which swept through the ranks of migratory labor in the State. This unrest, breaking out in spontaneous strikes, was given added impetus when the Roosevelt Administration took office, as farm labor, like industrial labor, pinned its hopes on Section 7-A of the NIRA.

The years 1929 to 1935 witnessed in California a series of spectacular strikes, which, for the purpose of this study, have to be described in some detail. Beyond question, the strikes of these years are without precedent in the history of labor in the United States. Never before had farm laborers organized on any such scale and never before had they conducted strikes of such magnitude and such far-reaching social significance.

### Early Attempts at Organization

Prior to 1929 many attempts had been made to organize farm and cannery labor — and the two types of labor in California are closely related and overlap to a very great extent — by the American Federation of Labor. I have mentioned several such attempts beginning with 1901 and continuing through the war period. None of these efforts were successful. Briefly, the failure of the A.F. of L. to organize this important, and large, group of workers, may be traced to a number of factors: the methods employed by the A.F. of L. were not suited to the occasion; the dues demanded of the workers were excessive; and the leadership of the A.F. of L. was, at heart, hostile to the idea of organized farm labor. This observation is particularly true of the San Francisco labor leaders of the period, most of whom were reactionary political bosses. The attitude of the A.F. of L. towards farm labor was aptly summarized by Paul Scharrenberg, for years its official spokesman in California, in a statement quoted in the New York *Times*, January 20, 1935: "Only fanatics are willing to live in shacks or tents and get their heads broken in the interests of migratory labor." I have mentioned the activities of the I.W.W. among farm workers, but, by 1929, the I.W.W. was merely a tradition in the labor movement; it had no influence and, for all practical purposes, was defunct. There had been, of course, racial groups, organized among the Japanese as protective associations or clubs, and, among the Mexicans, as trade unions organized on a nationalistic basis. Such, in general, was the background of organizational activities among farm workers in California prior to 1930.

### 1. The Trade Union Unity League

Two strikes took place in the Imperial Valley in the year 1930: one in January of that year, and the other in February. Both strikes were spontaneous movements among Mexican and Filipino workers employed as vegetable and fruit pickers in the fields, and of American workers employed in the packing sheds. The strikes were provoked by wage reductions; at the same time, the strikers made certain demands for wage increases, improvement in housing conditions, and the adjustment of grievances. The Trade Union Unity League, then in existence, seized upon the strikes as an occasion to attempt the consolidation of the agricultural workers into a union, industrial in character, that would embrace the Mexican, Filipino, American, and other workers of the valley in a single organization. During the strikes in January and February, organizers of the T.U.U.L. entered the valley and succeeded in establishing a union known as the Agricultural Workers Industrial League, which affiliated with the T.U.U.L., and set up headquarters in Brawley, and began to enroll hundreds of workers. The organizers, during the strikes, were arrested on suspicion, and their activities carefully watched, but no prosecutions resulted at the time. After the strikes — which were lost — the union sent out a call for a conference of all agricultural workers of the valley to be held April 20, 1930. Every ranch and shed was asked to select delegates to the conference. On April 14, residences and public-meeting places were raided throughout the valley. Over a hundred workers were arrested, in this general round-up, and held for trial with bond fixed at $40,000. Later certain individuals were released, but a large group were placed on trial, charged with violation of the Criminal Syndicalism Act — the first use of the Criminal Syndicalism law against farm organizers in California. Eight defendants were convicted and the convictions, with the exception of one defendant,[1] were confirmed on appeal. These defendants served time in San Quentin, the last defendant to be released being Lawrence Emery, who was paroled on February 21, 1933. The convictions were obtained, of course, by the use of stool pigeons and agents provocateurs, and by methods, on the part of the prosecution, which have characterized all Criminal Syndicalism prosecutions in California. The effect of the prosecution was to cripple the union, but, at the same time, it aroused a considerable feeling of solidarity and gave workers some experience in organized action.

## 2. Formation of the Cannery and Agricultural Workers' Industrial Union

In 1931, the Communist Party once again launched an effort to organize agricultural workers. This time they enlarged the scope of their activities and included cannery workers in the proposed organization. A small group of organizers was sent into the fields. Their strategy was to follow the spontaneous strikes. Wherever a strike was reported, or wherever a strike was rumored, they would appear and attempt to organize the workers. In 1931 and 1932, the organization existed merely as a name; in fact, it existed by reason of the will of a small group of organizers to make it exist. There was a sprinkling of small, spon-

[1] *People* v. *Horiuchi,* 114 CA 415.

taneous strikes throughout the summer of 1932, culminating in a strike of fruit workers at Vacaville, California, in November. This strike was the first organized effort of the C.A.W.I.U. Some four hundred workers, under the leadership of Communist organizers, held out for a period of about sixty days against formidable intimidation, beatings, and persecution. The strike is described in some detail by Orrick Johns.[2] "In the first week of December," writes Mr. Johns, "when the strike was a few weeks old, a masked mob of forty men in a score of cars, took six strike leaders out of the Vacaville jail, drove them twenty miles from town, flogged them with tug straps, clipped their heads with sheep clippers, and poured red enamel over them." When a C.P. delegation arrived, to organize a defense program, the town was in a state of martial excitement: 180 deputized vigilantes were under arms, scabs were equipped with gas pipes and pruning shears. It was during this strike that the Rev. Fruhling, a local Presbyterian holy man, harangued his congregation on the Sabbath, urging them to drive the strikers out of the community. When the congregation did not respond, he bellowed at them: "There isn't a red-blooded man in this church: you're all yellow." Although the Vacaville strike was broken, the stiff resistance put up by the workers indicated that the time was ripe for organized action. As one worker expressed it to Mr. Johns: "We would have to starve working so we decided to starve striking."

After the Vacaville strike, a wave of protest began to develop, with strikes occurring throughout the year as the various crops matured. A general strike of pea pickers oc-

[2] *Time of Our Lives*, 1937, pp. 329–333.

curred in April, 1933, in the De Coto–Hayward section, involving approximately 3000 workers, who were striking in protest against a wage rate of 12 cents an hour. The same tactics were of course employed: wholesale arrests, floggings, general intimidation. But, despite these tactics, the strike was a success. The price per "hamper" (a hamper is about thirty pounds) was forced up from 10 cents per hamper to 17 cents and 20 cents per hamper. Mr. Johns has a few words about this strike: "The strike colony consisted of a hundred broken down automobiles, in each of which four or five people slept. There were a few tents, and some cauldrons where the daily stew was cooked. That is, if there was any to cook. When we sent food or supplies to these people, the trucks would often be wrecked or confiscated. Ten men were lying in beds in neighboring cottages, badly beaten. The roads were patrolled by deputy sheriffs, with orders to shoot anybody who tried to talk to the scabs. . . . As night fell, the pea pickers of De Coto assembled around a flat truck, some two or three hundred of them. We built a fire, selected speakers from their own ranks. One could feel the temperature rise. . . . A few days later the strike was settled, with definite gains for the pickers, but one man was dead, and many injured." In discussing his experiences during this season, Mr. Johns writes: "In remote garages and sheds, hastily made over into halls by a few wooden benches, the workers would be huddled together under a single light, discussing their problems with remarkable coolness. Looking over those halls of swarthy men and women, I saw faces that reminded me of the ruined faces in Michelangelo's Day of Judgment on the walls of the Sistine Chapel. Sometimes they would meet in their tent camps, out of doors, half of them living in battered old Fords. They were a desperate and courageous people, compelled to exist as primitively as the aboriginal Indians, and asking little." As to the impression made by the people involved in these strikes, I can confirm Mr. Johns. I have addressed such meetings, and, at one of them, a meeting of women employed in the walnut factories in Los Angeles, I saw faces which I shall never forget. It was a huge meeting, with a dozen or more nationalities being represented. The chairman was a Russian girl, eighteen years old, who used a hammer for a gavel, and presided as a veteran. The remarks of the speakers had to be translated into many languages: Russian, Armenian, Spanish. But the impression I carried away from the meeting, as of many similar meetings, was of superb faces, a sea of faces: strong, impressive, unforgettable.

From the pea pickers, in April, the strikes spread into the cherry pickers at Mountain View and Sunnyvale, where 1000 workers went on strike. The leaders of the strike were Pat Calahan and Caroline Decker. Miss Decker, a young girl, charming and intelligent, became an organizer for the C.A.W.I.U. after the pea strike. When Pat Callahan went to a large ranch to present the strikers' demands to the owner, a number of men, hiding in trees, jumped down on him and gave him a merciless beating. His jaw was broken and he was kicked and driven from the premises. The usual arrest followed. But, in general, wages were increased. When the apricot season followed, wages were raised without a strike. But, in the peach strike, at Merced, Sacramento, and Gridley, a strike was called, and again wages were raised. And, in the grape strike, at

Lodi and Fresno, where the intimidation was very great, some gains were made. When the pear crop followed, in August, 1933, in the Santa Clara Valley, the workers and organizers, profiting by their experience, planned the first carefully prepared strike. The district was mapped out; picket lines were formed; picket patrols were organized. The workers asked 30 cents an hour (they had been getting 20 cents) and, for the first time, when their demands were settled at 25 cents an hour, they marched back to work as a group. Here, where some 1200 workers were involved, mostly Italians, considerable progress was made in organizing and disciplining the strikers.

At the conclusion of these strikes, the first convention of the reorganized C.A.W.I.U. was held in August, 1933 (the second and last convention was held April 29, 1934), in Sacramento. At this convention, the union was set up along industrial lines. Membership was open to "any worker in the agricultural industry, including workers in the fields, canneries, and packing sheds," with no discrimination as to sex, race, color or belief. The basic unit was the local, with section and district organizers, secretaries and committees. Monthly dues were fixed at 25 cents for employed and 5 cents for unemployed (A.F. of L. dues were usually fixed at $1 a month). It is interesting to note the objectives of the union, particularly in view of the charges made against it in the press. These objectives were 75 cents an hour for skilled labor, an eight-hour day, time and a half for overtime, decent homes and sanitary conditions, payment of wages by the hour with abolition of piecework and contract labor, equal pay for women workers and the abolition of child labor in agriculture.

On August 14, 1933, the workers at Tagus Ranch, in the San Joaquin Valley, went out on strike under the leadership of Pat Chambers. Chambers, who for several years was the favorite *bête noir* of the California press, is a small, quiet, soft-spoken man, but a person of great courage and genuine ability as a leader. The Tagus strike had particular significance, in view of the circumstances. The ranch itself, one of the largest fruit ranches in California, owned by the Merritt family, was regarded as the citadel of reaction. The workers were carefully policed and guarded. When the strike was won, "all hell broke loose," to quote one employer. Strikes came so fast that they could not be co-ordinated or planned, or properly timed. The resentment of generations was suddenly voiced and a wave of strikes swept the State, with strikes at Oxnard, Tulare, Fresno, San Jose, Merced, Chico, San Diego, Gridley, Sacramento. On September fourth, the grape pickers struck at Fresno, with 6000 workers out, and the strike soon spread to Lodi, with the *San Francisco Examiner* on October second carrying a banner headline: "Night Raiders Call Farmers to Battle Reds." Vigilante groups were formed at Lodi, under the command of Colonel Walter Garrison, the Führer of the California farmers, and so many arrests were made that it is impossible even to summarize them. But the movement was just getting started; the culmination of the wave of strikes came in October in the cotton fields.

## 3. The Cotton Strike

For some years prior to 1933, the cotton growers of the San Joaquin Valley met at Fresno each fall and fixed the

Workers' reaction to armed force in the 1933 Cotton Strike in the San Joaquin Valley.

*Paul S. Taylor Collection, Bancroft Library.*

Women and children on the picket line during the Cotton Strike.

*Paul S. Taylor Collection, Bancroft Library.*

Calling cotton workers from the fields during the strike.

Formation of the picket line for the Cotton Strike.

price for cotton picking. Previously the price had been 40 cents a hundred pounds; and, on September sixteenth, the growers agreed to establish a price of 60 cents, in contrast to the union demand of 90 cents a hundred pounds. The union, in the preceding months, had followed the practice of organizing the workers on the job, after they had started to work, which had been the practice of the I.W.W. in earlier years. But so great was the resentment of the cotton pickers in the fall of 1933 that they refused to report for work and instead boycotted the ranches. A final conference was held October first, but no agreement was reached, and, on October 4, 1933, a strike was voted. Five thousand workers, assembled in Corcoran, California, were asked by the growers to go to work; they refused, and the fight was on. The boycott spread throughout the valley, and approximately 18,000 workers joined the strike. The magnitude of the strike may be indicated not only by the number of workers involved, but by the fact that the strike embraced the entire San Joaquin Valley, with the union attempting to picket, by patrols, a string of cotton plantations extending down the valley for 114 miles. In the entire valley, at the time, were four organizers. These four organizers were the spearhead of the great Communist Party "conspiracy," as it was described in the press, to seize control of the valley.

The first act of the workers was to rent a small forty-acre farm on the outskirts of Corcoran, and there establish headquarters. Five thousand men, women and children made up this amazing camp community. Streets were staked off; guards were established at the entrances and only workers, or those with passes, were permitted entry; two trained nurses were obtained; sanitary conditions were carefully supervised (so as to prevent the health authorities from intervening — a favorite strikebreaking device) and committees of workers were set up to govern the camp and its activities. Considerable local support was obtained for the strike, in view of the resentment of the small growers against the cotton-gin companies and their usurious practices. One local minister, carrying a Bible and a C.P. membership card, and likewise a union card, urged the workers to carry on. "We'll win this fight, by the aid of God and a strong picket line," was his slogan. At first the relief authorities took the position that relief would only be given the strikers on condition that they return to work "pending arbitration," but, when this condition was vociferously rejected, the relief authorities, responding to pressure, began to furnish some relief. At the outset of the strike Pat Chambers was arrested after leading a march of strikers to Tulare to demand relief for the workers.

On October twelfth, a group of workers were assembled in the Union Hall at Pixley, California, at about noon. As they were leaving the hall, a large number of cars drove up, men stepped out, and posted themselves behind the cars. Suddenly the union building was riddled with rifle fire. This was the "riot between strikers and growers" described in the press at the time. Two workers were killed, and several more wounded; and, at Arvin, a near-by community, another worker was murdered the same day. Seventeen strikers were arrested at Pixley, and, after much equivocation, eleven ranchers were arrested and charged with murder. Their trial was a delightful farce and they were promptly acquitted, despite positive identification of their participation in the Pixley murders. Three thousand workers assembled for the funeral of the Pixley dead, and marched through the streets of Bakersfield in an impressive and orderly procession.

Despite every conceivable type of pressure the strike continued, with about 18,000 workers out and the cotton industry throughout the valley paralyzed. National Guard units were mobilized at Hanford and Visalia, and, according to Mr. Chapin Hall, of the *Los Angeles Times*, "The Tulare County fairgrounds have been turned into a stockade and the police are rounding up strikers and rioters and putting them in the stockade incommunicado. Kings County is an armed camp" (October 25, 1933). The situation, according to Mr. Hall, "demanded a modest display of guts on the part of Governor Rolph." On October twenty-sixth, Mr. Hall visited the camp at Corcoran; that is, he came as close as he dared, under armed guard, and surreptitiously spied upon this den of Red iniquity. Needless to say, he was appropriately shocked. "This camp is the danger spot. It is a dreadful place." He was alarmed, not for the strikers, but for the safety of the community, and sedulously conveyed the impression that the Corcoran Camp was the point of mobilization from which the "Reds" were going to attack the rest of the community. The camp, he said, "was a mess of corruption. 3,700 men, women and children herded in a ten acre barren field. No shade and the sun is cruel. Cold at night. With a few ragged pup tents, no tents, and three or four shallow latrines, with long lines of misery marked humanity awaiting their turn." But things even more shocking were going on in the camp, according to

Mr. Hall. "Promiscuity is unlimited. Some things are not for printing in a home-going newspaper." The strikers, according to Mr. Hall, were in "deadly fear of their leaders," i.e. 5000 workers in the camp were being terrorized by Caroline Decker. Mr. Hall was frenetic with rage over the lack of violence and inveighed against the "bungling, pussyfooting, milk and water policy" of the State officials.

The truth of the matter was that the camp was surrounded by an army of special deputies, State Highway Police and guards. The Government, seeking to end the strike, sent Mr. George Creel to the camp, but the workers would not admit him. A sound truck was backed up, and, as Newsreel cameras clicked, Mr. Creel besought the workers to abandon the strike. They refused. Then Mr. Enrique Bravo, the Mexican Consul, spoke, and warned the Mexicans that "grave international complications" might result, if they did not abandon the strike. Mr. Bravo was loudly booed. Then the State health officers ordered the workers to abandon the camp by a certain date. The local newspaper at Corcoran announced that the workers in the camp would go back to work, or "be jailed, deloused, and defilthed, and, finally, deported." Copies of this paper were circulated in the camp. Toward the end of October, the workers began to return to work. A State Mediation Board, composed of Ira Cross, Tully Knowles and Archbishop Hanna, took testimony on conditions, and on the basis of the compromise worked out by them, the strikers went back to work. Federal Employment Agencies, however, had previously been instructed to recruit workers, additional Mexicans had been recruited, and advertisements had been placed by the cotton-gin companies for Negroes in the South. The strike, the largest of its kind in American history, lasted for twenty-four days.

### 4. Imperial Valley

After the cotton season was concluded, the workers, following the cycle of the crops, moved to Imperial Valley, for the winter crops, lettuce, and, later, peas. Pat Chambers, released from jail, was in the valley as an organizer. On January 8, 1934, a strike was voted by the C.A.W.I.U. As workers were assembling to attend a mass meeting in El Centro, to discuss the strike, they were attacked by the usual army of special deputies, and their procession broken up by tear-gas bombs and violence. Some eighty-seven arrests were made at the time. Raids continued throughout the valley, with halls and meetings being raided. When the American Civil Liberties Union intervened and obtained an injunction in the United States District Court, in San Diego, to prevent interference with meetings, the injunction was wholly ignored by the growers, and A. L. Wirin, Attorney for the American Civil Liberties Union, was abducted from his hotel in El Centro, and dumped in the desert. When the strike persisted, a force recruited from the Sheriff's Office, the local Police, the State Highway Police and vigilantes obtained in the towns, under the command of the "County Health Officers," raided the desert camp of the strikers. The shacks in which the workers were living were burned to the ground, and the workers driven out with tear-gas bombs. Over 2000 men, women and children were forcibly evicted from the camp, and the arrests continued. A baby in the camp died as a result of the bombing.

The National Labor Board, when the trouble started in the valley, sent a commission of inquiry, composed of Dr. J. L. Leonard, Simon J. Lubin and Will J. French. Their report, the celebrated Leonard Commission Report, is one of the most illuminating documents on farm labor issued to date. The Commission found that Constitutional rights had been openly disregarded by the law-enforcement agencies in the valley; that the right of free speech and assembly had been wholly suppressed; that excessive bail had been demanded of arrested strikers; that the State Vagrancy Law had been prostituted; and that a Federal Court injunction had been flouted. One of the Commissioners, Mr. Lubin, announced that the growers were "paying less than a starvation wage. I have a tabulation of the pay checks of 204 pea pickers showing an average daily wage of 56 cents. The earnings were somewhat larger at the peak of the harvest; but never were sufficient to satisfy the most primitive needs." A reporter for the *Illustrated Daily News* in Los Angeles found that families of ten were making $2 a day. As to living conditions, the Commission found "filth, squalor, an entire absence of sanitation, and a crowding of human beings into totally inadequate tents or crude structures built of boards, weeds, and anything that was at hand to give a pitiful semblance of a home at its worst. Words cannot describe some of the conditions we saw." Mr. Chapin Hall, of the *Los Angeles Times*, on hand to cheer on the vigilante groups, complained of "temporizing" on the part of the authorities. "Why this temporizing with a condition more dangerous than the bite of a rattlesnake and in the same classification? Why? Why? The only way this cancer can be removed is by surgery. . . . The mailed fist should and must take the place of the kid glove."

No attempt was made by the growers to conceal the identity of the forces used to suppress the strike. The *Calexico Chronicle* of January 12, 1934, reported the "mobilization of the American Legion reserve — to keep down the rising tide of strike sentiment." The *Brawley News* of January 11 commended the American Legion for its readiness "to go to the bat." Chapin Hall, in the *Times* of January 15, said: "It's a secret, but the vigilantes are really Legionnaires, and do they have fun!" And the American Legion *Weekly Bulletin*, published in Los Angeles, in its issue of February third, indiscreetly carried a story under the title "The Inside Story of the Imperial Valley Lettuce Strike," quoting a past Commander of a Valley Legion Post to the effect that "the veterans of the Valley, finding that the police agencies were unable to cope with the situation, took matters into their own hands and solved the situation, in their own way. Now the Valley is free from all un-American influences." That is, the strikes were broken, and the jails were filled.

### 5. *The Round-Up*

After the Imperial Valley strike in the winter and spring of 1934, the C.A.W.I.U. moved north, with the crops, engaging in minor organizational activities in the northern part of the State, notably at Brentwood, at the farm factory of the Balfour-Guthrie Company, a large British-owned concern. On July 19, 1934, the unions in San Francisco called a general strike, in connection with the then pending maritime strike. Not a wheel moved in San Francisco. When the general strike was broken, by the intervention of the National Guard, a Statewide reign of terror was unleashed by the authorities. Under date of August 29, 1934, *The Nation* printed a summarization of the hundreds of arrests and beatings reported throughout the State during the course of this planned and co-ordinated attempt to break the rising strength of the new trade-union movement in California. I merely refer to the article for details. In raids in San Jose, in late July and August, 1934, dozens of workingmen were taken from their homes and beaten, and the facts of these outrages were publicly admitted and boasted of in the press.[3] The *San Jose Mercury-Herald* of July 20, 1934, carried this item:

Armed with bright new pick-handles, their faces grim, eyes shining with steady purpose a large band of "vigilantes" composed of irate citizens, including many war veterans, smashed their way into three Communist "hot-spots" here last night, seized a mass of red literature and severely beat nine asserted radicals.

The *San Jose News* of July twentieth boasted that "the mongoose of Americanism dragged the cobra of Communism through the good Santa Clara Valley orchard dirt last night. The *News* offers its congratulations to this committee and wishes to say to them that every time they clean up a den of Communists and lead them boldly out of the country they are accomplishing a great result and will receive the commendation of the public in general." Similar stories

---

[3] See *The Nation*, August 8, 1934.

were reported throughout the State. The campaign was timed in a manner calculated to break the maritime strike, and, incidentally, to embarrass Upton Sinclair in his campaign for Governor of California, a campaign which was, at the time, just getting under way.

On July 20, 1934, the axe fell on the leaders of the C.A.W.I.U. Raiding parties, armed with sawed-off shotguns, handcuffs, blackjacks, rubber hose, billies, riot clubs, gas bombs, and accompanied by news reporters and photographers from the *Sacramento Bee*, raided the Workers' Center in Sacramento, and arrested the leaders of the C.A.W.I.U., including Caroline Decker and Pat Chambers. Eighteen defendants were placed on trial in Sacramento, charged with violation of the Criminal Syndicalism Law, most of the evidence being related to their activities in organizing agricultural field labor. On April 1, 1935, after one of the longest trials in the history of California Courts, eight defendants were convicted and sentenced to prison. Later, after they had served nearly two years of the sentence, the judgment against them was reversed on appeal. The arrests and resultant prosecution, which was staged as an anti-Red carnival, crippled and destroyed the Cannery and Agricultural Workers' Industrial Union. Their leadership in prison, the workers were momentarily demoralized; and the great wave of strikes subsided.

The C.A.W.I.U., however, made history during the period of its existence. There is, in fact, no parallel in the history of the American labor movement for its spectacular record. Dr. Silvermaster, Director of Research for the SERA, has characterized the strikes in 1933 "as the most extensive strikes of their kind in the agricultural history of

California, as well as of the United States. For the total number of men involved, the crops affected and the number of strikes taking place, no comparison based on past experience is at all possible. Of California's 1933 commercial crops, the fruit crop amounted to $128,124,000, the vegetable crop $54,941,000, and the cotton crop $12,397,000. All these crops were involved in the strikes and they represented 65 per cent of total crop values for the year. In the 1933 strikes, approximately 50,000 workers were involved, with a total of 37 recorded strikes (the actual number of strikes was much greater). Of these strikes 24 of the 37 recorded were led by the C.A.W.I.U.; of the workers involved, 37,500 or 79 per cent were under C.A.W.I.U. leadership. Of the 37 strikes, 29 resulted in gains for the strikers; and of the 24 strikes led by the C.A.W.I.U., 21 resulted in partial wage increases, the new wage scale averaging 25 cents an hour where formerly the prevailing rate had been 15 cents an hour. The gain to the workers, in terms of money, cannot be calculated, but it amounted to millions of dollars.

## CHAPTER XIV

## THE RISE OF FARM FASCISM

FOLLOWING the great wave of strikes which swept California in 1933, the farmers of the State began to form new organizations with which to combat the instinctive struggle of the State's 250,000 agricultural workers to achieve unionization. Farmers have never lacked organization in California; in fact, they have long set the pace for organizational activities among American farmers. They were pioneers in the field of co-operative marketing. Today every crop is organized through a series of co-operative organizations, many of which are institutions of great power and wealth. For a great many years these organized farm groups have held the balance of political power in the State through their control of the State Senate. Holding a veto power on all State legislation, they have dictated to governors and defied the will of the people of the entire State. In addition to co-operative marketing organizations, the canning and packing houses have long been organized into powerful trade associations and, in 1926, the Western Growers Protective Association was formed, for the purpose of consolidating various smaller organizations of shippers and growers in the State. Shortly after the 1933 trouble, in February, 1934, American Institutions, Inc., was organized in California by Mr. Guernsey Frazer, a prominent American Legion official, for the purpose of selling the large shipper-growers a high-pressure pro-Fascism legislative program. This attempt to impose Fascism from the outside, so to speak, was not successful, but, by 1934, the large growers themselves recognized the necessity of organizing for the primary purpose of fighting labor organization. The organization which they effected, Associated Farmers of California, Inc., which today has membership in California of 40,000, has played an important role in the social history of the West. Inasmuch as it is the first organization of its type to appear in the United States, and as it has many points of similarity with organizations of a like character in Nazi Germany,[1] it warrants careful scrutiny.

## 1. "From Apathy to Action"

In 1933 the California Farm Bureau Federation and the State Chamber of Commerce appointed a joint committee to study farm-labor conditions in the State. At the conclusion of this survey the farmers of Imperial Valley — "the Cradle of Vigilantism" — formed a voluntary association known as Associated Farmers, "pledged to help one another in case of emergency. They agreed to co-operate to harvest crops in case of strikes and to offer their services to the local sheriff immediately as special deputies in the event of disorders arising out of picketing and sabotage." As soon as this group was organized, the State Farm Bureau and the State Chamber of Commerce each designated a representative to go from county to county "explaining the Associ-

---

[1] See "The Fascist Threat to Democracy," by Robert A. Brady, *Science and Society*, Vol. II, No. 2.

ated Farmers idea to local Farm Bureaus, businessmen, and peace officers." Within one year, twenty-six counties had formed associated farmer groups, and, on May 7, 1934, a convention was held in Fresno for the purpose of creating a Statewide organization. I have a stenographic report of this organization meeting. It was presided over by S. Parker Frisselle [Mr. Frisselle was the first president and served for two years; his successor, and the present president, is Colonel Walter E. Garrison], who stated that the finances for the organization would unquestionably have to come from the banks and utility companies. The initial funds were, in fact, raised by Mr. Earl Fisher, of the Pacific Gas & Electric Company, and Mr. Leonard Wood, of the California Packing Company. At this meeting, it was decided that farmers should "front" the organization, although the utility companies and banks would exercise ultimate control.

Today the Associated Farmers have their headquarters in San Francisco and branch offices in practically every county of the State.[2] Each farmer is supposed to pay one dollar a year, as membership dues, and an additional dollar for each thousand dollars a year spent in wages. In some counties, dues are levied on the basis of so many cents per ton of fruit and vegetables harvested. Every member pledges himself, "in case of trouble," to report at the local sheriff's office. "Under agreement with the local sheriffs, no volunteer farmer will be asked to carry a gun or throw a gas bomb, even if he is deputized. He is armed with a pick handle about twenty inches long. A good many of the Associated Farmers would prefer fire-arms. But they have

[2] See "The Right to Harvest," by Frank J. Taylor, *The Country Gentleman*, October, 1937.

been overruled by cooler heads who say that in the heat of defending their homes by invading strike pickets, the embittered farmers might use their guns too effectively and turn public opinion against the organization." The "idea" back of these mobilizations, according to Mr. Taylor, "is to muster a show of force when required." How effectively some of the mobilizations have been organized may be indicated by the fact that in the Salinas strike, 1500 men were mobilized for deputy duty in less than a day; in the Stockton strike, 2200 deputies were mobilized in a few hours and in Imperial Valley 1200 deputies were recently mobilized on a few minutes' notice. When one realizes that approximately 50 per cent of the farm lands in Central and Northern California are controlled by one institution — the Bank of America — the irony of these "embittered" farmers defending their "homes" against strikers becomes apparent.

An efficient espionage system is maintained by the Associated Farmers. In 1935, I inspected the "confidential" files of the organization in San Francisco. At that time, they had a card-index file on "dangerous radicals" containing approximately one thousand names, alphabetically arranged, with front- and side-view photographs of each individual including notations of arrests, strike activities, affiliations and so forth. Each reference contained a number which referred to a corresponding identification record in the archives of the State Bureau of Criminal Identification. Sets of this file have been distributed to over a hundred peace officers in the State and lists have been sent to members of the association. Local offices or branches of the Associated Farmers maintain elaborate records of a similar nature, including a "check-up" system whereby workers with a reputation for independence may be readily identified and rousted out of the locality. The State Bureau of Criminal Identification, the State Highway Patrol, and local law-enforcement agencies work in the closest co-operation with agents of the association; in a sense, the association may be said to direct the activities of these public agencies. The State Bureau of Criminal Identification had its private investigators sleuthing for the Tagus Ranch in the San Joaquin Valley and it employed, at one time or another, the various stool pigeons upon whose testimony the Sacramento criminal-syndicalism prosecution was based.

In addition to its espionage activities, the Associated Farmers maintain a carefully organized propaganda department. Regular bulletins, heavily larded with "anti-Communist" information, are sent to the members; special articles are reprinted and distributed throughout the State; and a steady flow of statements and releases are supplied to the press. In recent years, the association has begun to dabble in a more ambitious type of propaganda. One of its spokesmen, Mr. John Phillips, a State Senator, recently visited Europe. Upon his return, Mr. Phillips published a series of articles in the *California Cultivator* (February 1 and 15, 1936), on his travels. One article was devoted to Mr. Phillips' impressions of the Nazis (he was in Nuremberg when the party was in session). Mr. Phillips particularly noticed the new type of German citizenship — the *Reichsburger* — under which "you simply say that anybody who agrees with you is a citizen of the first class, and anybody who does not agree with you is a non-voting citizen." His admiration for Hitler is boundless: "I would like to tell you how the personality of Hitler impressed me and how I feel that he has a greater personal appeal, a greater personal influence on his people than many of the nations realize." "Hitler," he said in a speech on January 18, 1938, "has done more for democracy than any man before him." Some years ago, Frances Perkins, Secretary of Labor, issued a statement repudiating a circular which the Associated Farmers had distributed in which they had attempted to make out, by reference to a faked marriage license, that she was a Jewess. Throughout California in 1936 and 1937, the Associated Farmers sponsored and organized meetings for the Reverend Martin Luther Thomas, of Los Angeles, who heads a "Christian American Crusade," and who is a notorious anti-Semite and Red-baiter. As a result of Mr. Thomas' harangues, the authorities in Riverside County employed a special detective, at a salary of $1,800 a year, to spy on the "subversive activities" of school children in the Riverside public schools. Mr. Phillips, who is frequently teamed with the Rev. Mr. Thomas at anti-Communist meetings sponsored by the Associated Farmers, was, for a time, holding a county office in Riverside County, designated as "labor coordinator." More recently the Associated Farmers have sponsored Samuel J. Hume, of the California Crusaders, who has spoken throughout the State inveighing against labor organization.

Shortly after its formation, the Associated Farmers launched a campaign, in the rural counties, for the enactment of the anti-picketing and so-called "emergency-disaster" ordinances. Anti-picketing ordinances have, as a consequence, been enacted in practically every rural county. The alleged justification for the "emergency-disaster" ordinances, which provide for a mobilization of all the

forces of the community in case of a "major disaster," was
the earthquake which occurred in Southern California in
March, 1933. Today practically every county in the State,
and most of the cities and towns, have such ordinances in
effect. There is nothing in the wording of most of these
ordinances to prevent their use in case of a "strike," which,
in the eyes of the farmers during harvest, is certainly a
"major disaster." The ordinances provide, in elaborate detail, for the formation of a kind of "crisis," or extra-legal
governmental machinery, which is to come into existence,
with broad powers, upon the declaration by the appropriate
executive officer in the community that a state of emergency exists. The purpose back of the campaign for the
enactment of these ordinances has been clearly indicated.
For example, on December 18, 1936, the county counsel
in Los Angeles was instructed to draft legislation which
"would permit counties to spend funds for erecting concentration camps for use during major disasters." Thus the
governmental apparatus for a kind of constitutional Fascism
actually exists in California today.

It would be suggested, of course, that I am exaggerating
the importance of these ordinances and misstating the purpose for which they were enacted. But other evidence exists
which points to the real intention back of these measures.
Concentration camps are to be found in California today.
I described, in some detail, such a camp in an article which
appeared in *The Nation* (July 24, 1935). It is located a few
miles outside of Salinas, California. Here a stockade has
been constructed which is admittedly intended for use as a
concentration camp. When local workers inquired of the
shipper-growers why such a curious construction had been

established, they were told that it was built "to hold strikers, but of course we won't put white men in it, just Filipinos." A similar stockade at one time existed at the farm factory of the Balfour-Guthrie Company (a large British-owned concern) at Brentwood, California. During a strike at this farm in 1935, "a substantial fence surmounted by plenty of barbed wire" was built about the workers' camp, with "the entrance guarded night and day." When questioned about this camp, the growers protested that "agitators continually refer to it as a stockade, a cattle corral, or a prison, and its inhabitants as slaves or prisoners." Mr. P. S. Bancroft, president of the Contra Costa unit of the Associated Farmers, in defending the camp, said that "obviously the fence and guard were there to keep the lawless element out, not to keep the contented workmen in." When the striking workers in the Imperial Valley set up a camp and strike headquarters in 1934, however, the camp was raided by local police, because, to quote from the *Shipper-Grower Magazine* (March, 1934), "it was a concentration camp in which the workers were being kept against their wishes." The burning question, therefore, would seem to be: When is a concentration camp not a concentration camp? At the Tagus Ranch, in 1934,[3] a huge moat was constructed around an orchard in order "to protect the properties," with armed guards stationed at the entrance and with a machine gun mounted on a truck. "All roads leading to the ranch with the exception of the main entrance where guards are stationed, are blocked by barbed wire and flooded with water by dikes. Fifty old employees report nightly to the ranch manager regarding the conduct of employees under suspicion."

[3] See United Press stories for July 9 and July 21, 1934.

There is much similar evidence, all tending to show that the great farm factories of California take on the appearance of fortified camps under military surveillance whenever a strike is threatened.

Throughout the year 1934 the Associated Farmers stimulated many "trial mobilizations." On July 23, 1934, Sheriff O. W. Toland at Gridley announced that a "trial mobilization" of American Legion men and special deputies had come off perfectly: "All Legionnaires were at the hall in ten minutes and in forty-five minutes the entire assembly was present." Many Legion Posts throughout the State practised similar mobilizations which were timed to coincide with organizational activity among agricultural workers. From Merced, on July 14, 1934, came word that the California Lands, Inc. (Bank of America) and the California Packing Company had demanded forty extra deputy sheriffs, "equipped sufficiently to cope with violence." From Hanford, July 16, 1934, came the report that county officials had organized an Anti-Communist League "to co-operate with county officers in case of emergencies." Most of this vigilante recruiting has been done by elected officials, sheriffs and district attorneys, and peace officers. For example, in 1934 Sheriff Howard Durley, according to the *Fillmore Herald*, "prepared to organize a county-wide vigilante group for the purpose of handling emergencies. Approximately 200 special deputies were sworn in, chosen from prepared lists, and these will be organized into smaller units of ten men each in all sections of the county." I could quote an abundance of similar evidence.

In the following year, 1935, the strategy was carried a point further, when the growers began to order "preventive" arrests. On December 30, 1935, the Sheriff of Imperial Valley (where 4000 gun permits had been issued in the summer), at the opening of the winter harvest season, "launched a valley-wide roundup of professional agitators, Communists and suspects *to avert a possible strike* among lettuce workers." Commenting upon this move, the *Los Angeles Times* stated editorially: "Professional agitators who are busily engaged in fomenting new labor trouble in the Imperial Valley winter lettuce will find the authorities ready for them. Sheriff Ware and his deputies have *the jump on them this time*," i.e. arrests were made before a strike could be called and in advance of the season.

Needless to say, the Associated Farmers have a powerful legislative lobby in Sacramento and an elaborate legislative program. In general, they have sponsored the enactment of laws restricting labor's right to organize on the avowed theory that such legislation "would help cut down the cost of labor"; the incorporation of all labor unions; laws prohibiting sympathetic strikes; measures designed to prevent the unionization of governmental and utility-company employees; provisions limiting the right of strikers to relief; and a number of other measures, such as laws making it illegal to interfere with the delivery of food or medical supplies, outlawing the Communist Party and prohibiting all picketing. At present, the farm groups are fighting strenuously against a proposal for a unicameral legislative body in California, for, under the present system, they actually hold a legislative veto through their control of the State Senate. Until this hold is broken, democratic processes cannot function.

## 2. *Santa Rosa*

Encouraged by their success in 1934 in crushing union-ization activities among agricultural workers, the Associated Farmers determined in 1935 to stamp out the last vestiges of revolt and to prevent an organizational campaign from getting under way. As part of this strategy, they organized a systematic terrorization of workers in the rural areas on the eve, so to speak, of the various crop harvests. Without waiting for organizational activity to start, and in advance of the season, fiery crosses burned on the hilltops and wholesale arrests were made, usually accompanied by an elaborate Red-baiting campaign in the local press to build up the idea, in the mind of the community, that grave danger threatened. In February, 1935, the leaders of the Associated Farmers sponsored the formation in Sacramento of the California Cavaliers, a semi-military organization, which announced that its purpose was to "stamp out all un-American activity among farm labor." Mr. Herman Cottrell, an official of the Associated Farmers and an organizer of the California Cavaliers, publicly stated: "We aren't going to stand for any more of these organizers from now on; anyone who peeps about higher wages will wish he hadn't." As the harvest season approached, statements such as the foregoing were accompanied by overt acts of terrorization. At San Jose, on June 10, 1935, on the eve of the apricot-crop harvest, three fiery crosses blazed on the hills near a workers' camp where, two years previously, a mob of vigilantes had raided the camp, kidnaped a score of "radical" leaders, held them for two hours, beaten them and then driven them across the county line. Confident that they had the situation well in hand, the Associated Farmers, in a radio broadcast on June 14, 1935, told their members "to go ahead and don't worry about agitators this season."

In general this confidence was justified, for 1935 was marked by only one major "incident," that of Santa Rosa. In August, the workers, assembled in the Santa Rosa and Sebastopol sections for the apple harvest, voted to strike. As the season was somewhat delayed, the growers ignored the strike vote until some two hundred packing-house employees decided to join the pickers in a general walkout. On August 1, 1935, two Communist Party officials were speaking at a mass meeting of pickers and packing-house workers in Santa Rosa, when the hall was raided by a group of 250 vigilantes, who jerked the speakers from the platform, broke up the meeting, and engaged in a general free-for-all fight with the workers. As the crop matured and workers were not immediately forthcoming in the super-abundance demanded by the growers, a delegation of orchard owners went to the relief agencies and demanded that a large number of relief clients be dropped from the rolls and ordered into the orchards. A few days later, on August fifth, a committee of six men, "saying they represented 300 vigilantes," called on the local WPA administrator and demanded that "all Communists, Reds, and radicals" be dropped from the payroll of the WPA, stating that if this ultimatum were not complied with in forty-eight hours, they would take matters into their own hands. The WPA administrator stalled for time, and the committee reluctantly agreed to extend the deadline.

On August 23, 1935, "with sunset this evening set as the new deadline," a mob of vigilantes seized Solomon Nitzburg and Jack Green, together with three other men, dragged them through the streets of Santa Rosa, and, after the three men had kissed the American flag on the courthouse steps and promised to leave the community, released them. Nitzburg and Green, refusing to comply with the demand, were kicked, beaten, tarred and feathered, and paraded around the courthouse in Santa Rosa, and driven out of the county. In seizing Nitzburg, the mob fired volley after volley of rifle fire through his home, and followed up this attack with the use of tear-gas bombs. The entire evening of August twenty-third was a Saturnalia of rioting, intimidation and violence, described as "the wildest scene in the history of Sonoma County." The whole affair was carried out brazenly, with no attempt at concealment, and the *San Francisco Examiner*, which played up the incident as provocatively as possible, openly stated that "the tar and feather party was hailed in Sonoma County as a direct American answer to the red strike fomentors." The leaders of the mob consisted of the following men: a local banker, the Mayor, the head of the local Federal Re-employment Bureau, several motor cops, a member of the State Legislature, numerous American Legionnaires, and the President of the local Chamber of Commerce. Later twenty-three business and professional men in the community were indicted in connection with the riot, but were quickly acquitted; and, later, when Nitzburg and Green sued for damages, the court found in favor of the defendants.

Santa Rosa, the first major "incident" after the Cannery and Agricultural Workers Industrial Union had been smashed in 1934, was significant of the rising tide of potential Fascism in California. The division of social forces was clear-cut. On the one hand were the migratory workers in the field and the packing-house employees who were, for the most part, local residents, together with a few miscellaneous local sympathizers. Arrayed against this group were a few large growers and the packing-house companies utilizing the local townspeople as a vigilante mob to crush a pending strike. The form of constitutional government was swiftly brushed aside and mob rule openly sanctioned. This exhibition of Fascist insurrection not only went unpunished, but received open public support throughout the State and the tacit approval of State officials. The strike, of course, was crushed. In fact, the strike was crushed so thoroughly that it backfired on the growers. "The mob action," according to the United Press, "of the vigilantes has frightened away from the county so many workers that the county is 20 per cent under the number of pickers needed. Pay was increased one-fourth cent a pound, with payment of transportation, to induce pickers to come here, but the increase has had little effect in this regard." Soon the local growers were wailing about a "labor shortage" and announcing that four thousand pickers were needed immediately "to save the crop." This demonstration of the short-sightedness of employer violence, however, made no impression upon the Associated Farmers who continued to use the Santa Rosa technique throughout 1935, 1936 and 1937.

### 3. The Backyard Strike

Residents of Los Angeles, reading accounts of farm-labor disturbances in the rural counties, were formerly in the

habit of regarding these riotous affairs as a peculiar manifestation of rural backwardness, a phenomenon restricted
to the "heat" counties where, in the summer, people may
be expected to act irrationally. This illusion was brutally
dispelled, however, in the spring of 1936. In April and May
of that year, tear-gas bombs began to explode and riot guns
to bark in the vacant-lot areas adjacent to golf courses; and
motorists along the highways leading into Los Angeles were
privileged to witness as ugly an exhibition of strikebreaking
as one could imagine. The occasion was a strike of celery
workers.

The strike started on April twentieth, when approximately 300 Mexican workers left the fields after the growers' association (chiefly made up of Japanese growers)
refused to meet their demands: 30 cents an hour, instead
of the prevailing wage of 22½ cents, and a 60 per cent
closed shop. Although the strikers were few in number (a
total of about 2000 workers was involved), the strike was
suppressed with typical ruthlessness. To suppress the strike,
the authorities marshalled a force of approximately 1500
armed men — policemen, deputy sheriffs and guards. When
the strikers attempted to move from their strike headquarters in Venice to the near-by celery fields, the Los
Angeles Red Squad, under the leadership of Captain William ("Red") Hynes, on three successive days broke the
caravan procession before it could get started. When the
strikers returned to their headquarters, they were pursued
by the police who tossed tear-gas bombs into the shack
with children playing on the lot outside. As workers attempted to flee from the shack, they were seized and beaten.
On April twentieth, police fired on a group of strikers as

they were leaving for the fields. One worker was shot and another was badly burned when an officer fired a tear-gas gun at his chest from a distance of five or six feet. Throughout the following week, squads of police cars toured the fields, firing volleys of shot over the heads of any strikers they could locate. In the Dominguez hills near San Pedro, in the backyard, so to speak, of the beautiful Palos Verdes estates, a miniature battle was staged when a mob of police officers and armed farmers converged on a group of strikers huddled in an abandoned barn. So many arrests were made of strikers that the newspapers could not keep track of them. I estimated that at least one third of the total number of workers on strike were arrested, at one time or another (not all of them, of course, were actually prosecuted). The practice of making wholesale arrests amounted, in this case, virtually to arresting all strikers. Strikers who were injured had great difficulty in receiving medical attention and, when they finally succeeded in getting some attention at the Los Angeles County Hospital, they were turned over, after treatment, to Red-squad officers for "interrogation." One day, during the strike, a "strike-guard" fired at persons whom he suspected of being pickets and wounded a golfer on a near-by course. The guard later said it was all a mistake: He had fired at a "rabbit."

The strike was significant in that, in this instance, many of the growers wanted to sign the union agreement but were prevented from doing so by pressure from the large farm groups in the State who ordered them "to fight it out." John Anson Ford, of the Los Angeles County Board of Supervisors, charged that funds which the county turns over each year to the Los Angeles Chamber of Commerce to advertise the general charm of Southern California were used to employ agents to visit the growers and urge them not to sign the union agreement. This interesting and lively tableau was enacted not in the Imperial or San Joaquin Valley, but on the vacant lots of suburban Los Angeles. The workers, however, received no more protection in metropolitan Los Angeles than they received in the lawless farm counties of the State.

Unlike previous agricultural strikes in California, where factual data has been difficult to obtain, the celery workers' strike is well documented. Before the strike was called, the Los Angeles County Relief Administration and the WPA, under the direction of Dr. Towne Nylander, made a survey of wages and working conditions among the agricultural workers in Los Angeles County. This report clearly reveals the basic social pattern.

A survey was made of 745 families, 93.2 per cent Mexican, 6.8 per cent white. Of this group, 88.3 per cent were employed exclusively in agriculture and received compensation from no other source. The average yearly employment for those engaged exclusively in agricultural work was found to be 30.7 weeks per year. By reference to parallel studies made in 1928, it was discovered that the average duration of agricultural employment in that year, for migratory workers of the type under investigation, was 33.1 weeks per year — indicating that the working period for migratory labor is declining. The group engaged in part-time non-agricultural employment succeeded in obtaining only 14.7 weeks per year of outside work, so that the average duration of employment from all sources was 31.7 weeks per year. The report indicated, moreover, that of the sample investigated, 75.7 per cent of the families had only one worker, contrary to reports of the employment of huge families with a large total annual family income. The nine-hour day seems to prevail in this type of employment. On this basis, the report indicates that $12 per week, during the period of employment, is the average wage, and that even the group which supplements its income by non-agricultural work succeeds in raising its pay only to $15.27 per week during the period of employment. The annual income from agricultural work for the group studied was found to be $362.01. Studies made in 1927–1928, upon a somewhat different basis, indicated an average annual income then of about $513.72. The average family income for the group investigated was $491.12. As to living conditions, it was found that 98.2 per cent live in "frame houses," of a type that, in the language of the report, could better be described as "wooden shacks," only 17.7 per cent having baths. Although the workers studied worked on vegetable farms, only 12.5 per cent received any kind of discount from their employers on the purchase of vegetables; 67.1 per cent purchased practically no milk. The report states that $7.89 is the average weekly food expenditure for the group and that the average size family is 4.7 persons. The average annual family expenditure for food alone is $412.36, or 84 per cent of the annual average gross income, leaving only $78.76 per year, or 16 per cent of the annual gross income, for housing, medical care, clothing and other necessities.

Fortunately the report on living conditions was supplemented by a report submitted by 157 farmers in the area. Of the sample, 94.3 per cent were Japanese, 2.5 per cent

Chinese, 3.2 per cent white. For the year ending September 1, 1935, the total production for this group was $1,007,217, or an average gross return for all farms of $6,415.39. Without exception each class of farm — classified as to acreage — reported a net profit for the year. For all farms, the average annual expense for paid labor was 33.3 per cent of the gross return, while average overhead expenses accounted for 50.1 per cent, of which rent, 25.7 per cent, water charges, 13.2 per cent, and fertilization, 23. 7 per cent, were the chief items (on the basis of 100 per cent for overhead charges). Most of the farmers involved, being alien Japanese, cannot lawfully own or lease agricultural land in California. This limitation has, however, been circumvented for years by various means: The land is owned by American-born children or leased in the name of a citizen. The growers' report does not indicate the facts in reference to ownership, but it is common knowledge that most of the land in question is owned by banking interests and leased, by various indirections, to Japanese growers. Even accepting the growers' figures, the survey concludes with the statement that a higher rate of wages could be paid. The report also makes an interesting statement about the manipulation of races: "Most of the friction generated in Southern California between the Mexican agricultural worker and his employers has occurred with the Japanese grower. *No racial animus* is connected with this trouble, so far as observation and inquiry will reveal. The issue is simply that the average Japanese grower sets a harder pace and pays less in proportion than the balance of the growers." The question is: Who insists that the Japanese growers pay 22½ cents an hour and no more for agricultural labor — the lowest average agricultural wage in the State — in the richest county in California? It is apparent that the interests in question are powerful enough to assure the Japanese complete immunity from the consequences of the Alien Land Law.

While the strike was in progress, Gene Masintier, "chief special agent," filed suit in the Los Angeles courts against the Venice-Palms Industrial Association, a group of Japanese growers. Masintier claimed that he had been employed to take charge of thirty-four heavily armed guards recruited from a local detective agency at seven dollars a day. "I didn't mind helping break the Los Angeles Railway strike in 1934," Masintier said, "but I wouldn't ask anyone to live like those employees of the Japanese have to. When I left it had cost the Japanese about $7,000 to keep from raising wages of their field hands. The bill for saki and beer at the headquarters while I was there amounted to approximately $600." The strike lasted for about a month, and resulted in some slight gains for the workers and the execution of an agreement which has twice been renewed. The strike was led by the Mexican Federation of Agricultural and Industrial Workers, a loosely organized union of Mexican, Japanese, and Filipino workers under the leadership of William Velarde.

### 4. Gunkist Oranges

The wave of violence, launched by the Associated Farmers in 1934, swept on into 1935 and 1936, with organized vigilante groups crushing one strike after another.

On June 15, 1936, 2500 Mexican orange pickers (organized as the Federation of Agricultural Workers Industrial Union — the same organization and the same leadership involved in the celery workers' strike) struck in Southern California, tying up, for several weeks, a $20,000,000 citrus crop. Vigilantism immediately began to flourish. Workers were evicted from their homes; Orange County was virtually in a state of siege, with highway traffic under police surveillance; 400 special armed guards, under the command of former "football heroes" of the University of Southern California masquerading as amateur storm troopers, were recruited; over 200 workers were arrested at the outset of the strike and herded in a stockade, or bull pen, in which the court proceedings, such as their arraignment, were conducted; bail was fixed at a prohibitive figure; and, when attorneys entered the county to defend the workers, they were arrested on petty traffic charges, followed about by armed thugs, and threatened in open court. State-highway patrolmen moved in and established a portable radio station, KAPA, by means of which armed patrols were directed throughout the region. Guards with rifles and shotguns patrolled the fields and "protected" strikebreakers, and the sheriff instructed these guards, mostly high-school and college youngsters, "to shoot to kill," his orders being enthusiastically headlined and warmly italicized in the *Los Angeles Times* and *Examiner*. Workers' camps were bombed and raided. When arrested strikers were brought into court (I was an eye witness to these proceedings), submachine guns, shotguns, rifles and revolvers were openly displayed in the courtroom. The *Los Angeles Examiner* spoke touchingly of the "quieting effect of the drastic wholesale arrests" while the *Times* gave a graphic account of one raid: "Suddenly, late in the night, three or four automobiles loaded with grim faced men, appeared out of the darkness surrounding the little settlement [a workers' camp]. In a few seconds, tear gas bombs hissed into the small building where the *asserted* strikers were in conclave, the conferees with smarting eyes broke, and ran out under cover of darkness and the meeting was at an end. Witnesses said they heard the mysterious automobiles and the night-riders whirring away without leaving a trace of their identity." On July seventh, in a front-page story, the *Times* joyously announced that "old vigilante days were revived in the orchards of Orange County yesterday as one man lay near death and scores nursed injuries." The *Examiner* [4] proclaimed the fact that the growers had, in addition to State-highway patrolmen, and special deputies, commissioned "bands of men, armed with tear gas and shotguns," to conduct "open private warfare against citrus strikers." No one who has visited a rural county in California under these circumstances will deny the reality of the terror that exists. It is no exaggeration to describe this state of affairs as Fascism in practice. Judges blandly deny Constitutional rights to defendants and hand out vagrancy sentences which approximate the period of the harvest season. It is useless to appeal, for, by the time the appeal is heard, the crop will be harvested. The workers are trapped, beaten, terrorized, yet they still manage to hold out. In the Orange County strike food trucks, sent by striker sympathizers in Los Angeles, were hijacked and dumped on the highways.

The provocation for this vicious assault, which was carefully directed by the local shipper-growers and the Asso-

[4] July 11, 1936.

ciated Farmers, was a union demand for forty cents an hour, together with payment of transportation to and from work, and the correction of certain minor grievances (the prevailing wage rate at the time was twenty cents an hour). It should be remembered, moreover, as the growers themselves have repeatedly conceded, that orange picking involves a variety of skilled labor. At the time of this particular strike, the growers had just received a reduction in freight rates which resulted in an annual saving of over $2,000,000 a year. The mass violence in Orange County was successful in its aim, however, and the strike was broken. At the end of the third week, the strikers began to go back to work, with slight wage increases in some instances.

At the conclusion of the strike, one citrus grower, incensed at the attitude of his fellow growers, published a revealing statement.[5] Mr. Stokes pointed out that the growers, opposing the organization of workers, were themselves the beneficiaries of many types of organized action. In California, the owners of 309,000 citrus-growing acres, valued at close to $618,000,000, sell their crops through the California Fruit Growers' Exchange. This exchange picks, packs, pools, grades, ships and sells the orange crop. All the grower has to do is to grow the crop. Through the Fruit Growers' Supply Company, members of the exchange buy automobile tires, radios, fertilizer, and other types of equipment and supplies at cost, and can obtain credit until the end of the season. The Fruit Growers' Supply Company, an agency of the exchange, owns vast tracts of timber and

[5] "Let the Mexicans Organize!" by Frank Stokes, *The Nation*, December 19, 1936.

a lumber mill, and thus buys boxes and crates at cost (over a hundred million feet of lumber are required each year for the making of exchange-box shook). As Mr. Stokes pointed out: "I irrigate my orchard with water delivered by a non-profit combination of growers. My trees are sprayed or fumigated by a non-profit partnership." The exchange even notifies the grower when he is supposed to start the smudge pots burning to protect his crop from frost. Every detail of this elaborate industrial setup has been achieved by organized action. On December 4, 1935, the winter before the Orange County strike, the fruit-exchange officials had voted themselves substantial salary increases: The general manager's salary was increased from $18,000 to $22,000 a year; the sales manager's salary was boosted from $16,200 to $18,000. Mr. Stokes made several excursions through the county during the strike: "I found scab pickers, often high-school boys, 'gloming' the 'golden fruit' in the beautiful California sunshine, while mocking birds sang on the house-tops, snow-covered Mount Baldy glistened in the distance — and armed guards patrolled the groves behind long rows of 'no trespassing' signs. Trucks came to the groves with empty boxes and went away with full ones — trucks with rifle barrels protruding from their cabs. Men in uniforms, mounted on motorcycles, dashed back and forth. Sirens screaming, everybody jittery, everybody damning the reds." The Mexicans who, according to Mr. Stokes, are as talented with "clippers" as Kreisler is with a violin, are not only exploited as workers, but as buyers. "They are looked upon as legitimate prey — for old washing machines that will not clean clothes, for old automobiles that wheeze and let down, for woolen blankets made of cotton, for last season's shop-worn wearing apparel." These are the facts, and they are stated by a grower.

### 5. Salinas

The first major test of the organized strength of the Associated Farmers came in September, 1936, with a strike of lettuce packers in Salinas. The union involved in this strike was the Vegetable Packers Association, holding a "floating" Federal Charter from the American Federation of Labor which had been issued in 1928. Membership in the organization was restricted to white workers employed in the packing sheds. The practice in California has long been to restrict shed work to white workers; and, as far as possible, to force the Mexicans and Filipinos to work in the fields. The Vegetable Packers Union migrated: six months of the year in Imperial Valley; six months of the year in Salinas. Although the union had been involved in two serious strikes — at Salinas in 1934 (settled by arbitration) and in Imperial Valley in February, 1935 (in connection with which two union members were killed) — it had come through the disastrous 1934 anti-union campaign in good shape. In fact, it was about the only organized group active in 1936. In September, 1936, when the agreement which had been won by arbitration in 1934 came up for renewal, the union was, in effect, locked out. It is quite apparent that the Associated Farmers, elated by the victories over the field groups, had determined to crush this one remaining organization. As a consequence of the lockout, the workers organized a strike and the $12,000,000 lettuce crop was paralyzed. The Salinas lettuce crop — "ice house lettuce" it is called — supplies about 90 per cent of the lettuce consumed in the United States. During the season, 35,000 carloads of lettuce, at the rate of 200 carloads a day, leave Salinas for shipment throughout the United States and Canada. Of 70,000 acres devoted to lettuce cultivation, two thirds of the acreage is controlled by a small group of powerful shipper-growers, who spend most of their time driving about Monterey County and gambling for stakes of ten and fifteen thousand dollars.

In the Salinas strike the battle lines were quickly formed: on the one side, the large shipper-growers directed by the Associated Farmers and most of the townspeople; and, on the other side, 3000 white workers, some small shopkeepers and city laborers, and about 500 Filipino field workers who joined the strike. To the amazement of local residents of Salinas, the Chief of Police and the County Sheriff seemed to abdicate their respective offices, i.e. they were conspicuous by their inactivity. For the period of the strike they were supplanted by a "general staff" especially recruited for the occasion by the Associated Farmers, acting through the local shipper-grower association. The Associated Farmers rented the entire sixth floor of a local hotel where Colonel Henry Sanborn, army reserve officer and publisher of a notorious Red-baiting journal, *The American Citizen*, was given command. Colonel Sanborn, who held no official position whatever, ordered the local officers about and organized raids and directed arrests. The expense of this particular union-smashing campaign totaled about $225,000 which had been raised by an assessment of $3.00 a car on lettuce shipped from Salinas. Colonel Sanborn was carried on the payroll at $300 a month. Strikebreaking agencies in

Los Angeles and San Francisco were employed and strike-breakers were shipped into Salinas from points outside the State. The meeting at which Colonel Sanborn had been designated as "co-ordinator" was attended by the Chief of the State Highway Patrol, six local sheriffs, and a representative of the office of the Attorney-General of California, all of whom had sanctioned the extra-legal employment of Colonel Sanborn. A large supply of tear gas was purchased from Federal Laboratories and consigned to Colonel Sanborn, and his staff. Over 200 rounds of tear-gas bombs were fired at strikers.

Extraordinary as were the activities of Colonel Sanborn, still more surprising tactics were to be used. On September nineteenth, the Sheriff emerged from his temporary retirement, and ordered a general mobilization of all male residents of Salinas between the ages of eighteen and forty-five, and threatened with arrest any resident who failed to respond. In this manner the celebrated "Citizens' Army" of Salinas was recruited. In the graphic description of the *Los Angeles Times:* "Three short blasts of the fire whistle repeated four times — the signal for immediate mobilization of the Salinas civilian army to put down riots — electrified the city. In automobiles and on foot, dragging shot-guns, rifles, and clubs, the men, all of whom have been sworn in as special deputy guards, began converging upon the National Guard Armory." At the armory, those of the volunteers who were not armed were given clubs which had been previously manufactured in the manual-arts department of the local high school. Two thousand five hundred men were mobilized, armed, and deputized in this manner.

The usual wholesale arrests followed; and the usual provoked violence ensued. As convoys of "hot lettuce" — the "green gold" of seventy thousand acres — began to move toward the packing houses, which were barricaded with barbed-wire entanglements and with special guards on the roofs with machine guns, picket lines were broken with tear gas. Automobiles with loudspeakers raced through the streets; one section of the town, on Babilan Street, was in a shambles after a police raid; faked "dynamite" and "arson" plots were hatched by the police, and the arrests continued. The *San Francisco Chronicle*, which, under the editorship of Mr. Paul Smith, was fairly and accurately reporting the strike, was virtually told to keep its men out of Salinas. Mr. Smith visited Salinas himself on September 24, 1936, and wrote an excellent story on the situation entitled "It DID Happen in Salinas." He found that the barricaded areas of the town resembled a military zone, and that vigilantes had marched to the Central Labor Council in Salinas and bombed it with tear gas, and that the same mob had threatened to lynch the *Chronicle's* photographer and reporter if they "didn't get the hell out of Salinas." But the strike continued. Strikebreakers were brought in from the neighboring communities and housed in stockades and military barracks. At the height of the excitement, Colonel Sanborn induced Colonel Homer Oldfield of the Ninth Army Corps, and Major Thomas J. Betts, Chief of the Intelligence Division of the Ninth Corps Area, to visit Salinas, and the Hearst press screamed: "Army Officers Rush to Salinas!" On October 16, with the strike still in effect, the press reported that the local jails were literally "filled to capacity" with strikers. But, at a staggering cost to the growers, the crop was harvested. Lettuce was shipped to

Los Angeles, and there, through the low connivance of local American Federation of Labor officials, was unloaded, packed, and reloaded for shipment — by members of the American Federation of Labor. After a month, the strike was crushed, the union smashed. But though they had won the strike, the growers continued their intimidation and began to "blacklist" strikers, until they were enjoined from doing so by Federal Judge A. F. St. Sure.[6] The once powerful, compact, and militant Vegetable Packers Association was no more.

At the time of the strike, the attorney for the union sent a telegram which warrants quotation, as it summarizes the situation in Salinas with apt brevity:

"Sinclair Lewis should be informed that it did happen in Salinas. It was directed from outside the affected zone of Monterey County. It embraces all civil governments, including courts. The State Militia and State Highway Patrol are directed by a civilian local committee acting as the head of a provisional dictatorship. It indicates long preparation, prior rehearsal and the work of men who know law and understand public psychology, as the average citizen is not conscious that it has happened. The plan would not be effective in large urban centers unless modified in certain respects. In semi-agricultural and semi-industrial communities it could crush any strike, however peaceful. Significant that the army of this provisional government tore Roosevelt campaign buttons off the lapels of citizens and trampled them under foot on the streets of Salinas, freely expressing their unexpurgated opinion of the present administration. Hearst's stooge, Colonel Sanborn, admits he is in command.

[6] December 21, 1936.

Organized labor will do well to investigate." Unfortunately the telegram was addressed to Mr. William Green of the American Federation of Labor, and, of course, no investigation was ordered.

## 6. Stockton

Following up their costly victory at Salinas, the Associated Farmers moved into action with renewed vigor at Stockton, California, on April 24, 1937. On February twenty-seventh and twenty-eighth, a conference of agricultural workers had been called in San Francisco, which represented the first concerted effort to map out a program and plan of action for agricultural labor. Following this conference, the Cannery Workers Union, an affiliate of the American Federation of Labor, struck the plant of the Stockton Food Products Company. Instantly the call went forth for the usual "citizens' army" and about 1500 men were quickly mobilized for action. Colonel Walter E. Garrison, President of the Associated Farmers, arrived to take personal charge of the offensive. Sheriff Harvey Odell, of Stockton, obligingly abdicated and turned over the reins of power to Colonel Garrison. Mr. Ignatius McCarthy, tear-gas salesman, was imported to provoke trouble, and, on April twenty-fourth, a bloody riot occurred. As trucks attempted to drive through picket lines, tear-gas bombs began to explode and rifles cracked. For over an hour, 300 pickets continued to fight "coughing and choking," as "vigilantes" and "special deputies" poured round after round of tear-gas bombs at them. Fifty workers were injured; the body of one striker was "riddled with buckshot from his mouth to his abdomen." More than a hundred tear-gas bombs were hurled at the picket line by State-highway patrolmen alone, and the list of injured (all strikers) assumed the proportions of a wartime casualty list. When the Governor attempted to mediate, the head of the California Processors and Growers Association told him to mind his own business; which he did. National Guard units were mobilized at Stockton, with four companies "standing by" for service. Although the Associated Farmers conducted the offensive in this strike, who were the parties at interest? Represented on the board of directors of the California Processors and the Growers are: California's Packing Company; Libby, McNeil & Libby; Barron-Gray Packing Company; Santa Cruz Packing Company; H. J. Heinz Corporation; Kings County Packing Company; and Bercut-Richards Packing Co. These are the "farmers" who, "embittered" by union invasion, elected to "defend their homes." The assault, on this occasion, was so vicious that it broke all attempts to form picket lines and the strikers were soon forced to go back to work, only to be promptly sold out, in the ensuing negotiations, by Mr. Edward Vandeleur of the State Federation of Labor. Stockton, like Salinas, was a milepost in the march of the Associated Farmers to crush union labor in the fields and packing plants.

### 7. The United Farmers of the Pacific Coast

A marked change has recently taken place in the activities of the Associated Farmers. In the fall of 1936, the maritime unions struck and tied up the Pacific Coast ports for ninety days. At the beginning of the strike, the farmers were not immediately affected, and, consequently, remained silent. But, toward the end of the strike, when farm products began to arrive in the port of San Francisco for shipment, the farmers moved into action. On January 15, 1937, the Associated Farmers announced that they had mobilized an army of 10,000 "farmers" to march on San Francisco and open the port. Promised police protection by Mayor Rossi and Governor Merriam, it is possible that the "march on San Francisco" was planned in all seriousness and, but for the termination of the strike, would have been executed. The threat was highly significant as an indication of the close co-operation that now exists between the Industrial Association of San Francisco and the Associated Farmers, the two groups functioning now as a single unit. Similar evidence of this unofficial merger has been brought to light recently in the form of recent joint conferences and united-action programs.

On December 7, 1937, the Associated Farmers held an annual convention at San Jose. At this convention it was decided to enlarge the organization and, to this end, the United Farmers of the Pacific Coast was formed. The new organization boasts a large membership in Oregon, Washington and Arizona. Representatives have been sent to organize similar groups in the Middle West and a Minnesota "Associated Farmers" unit announces a membership of one thousand. Another significant development at the San Jose convention was the concern which the growers evidenced over the problem of transportation. More and more, industrial farming is becoming dependent upon trucking; and, as this dependence increases, the interests of the "farmers" tend to merge with those of the city industrialist. The distinction between farm and city is practically meaningless in California today, and, as I have tried to show, the farms are factories. Inevitably, the Associated Farmers are being drawn into conflict with two powerful labor groups: the teamsters and the maritime workers. At the San Jose convention, a special organization, Producers Protective League, was organized for the express purpose of "controlling transportation" and keeping the "life lines" open from farm factory to city market. Today it is merely a question of time until the Associated Farmers come into headlong conflict with the teamsters' union and with the maritime unions. Eventually, the maritime unions will refuse to handle farm products as "hot cargo" and when this time comes, Californians may prepare to witness a struggle of the first magnitude.

The annual report of the Associated Farmers for 1937 contains several significant statements. The organization was formed, according to the president, to fight Communism, but today, by force of national developments, it is necessarily "opposing unionization of farm labor on any basis." Continuing, he states that the program of the organization is being converted from a defensive to an aggressive plan of action. "We cannot wait until racketeers begin organizing the packing houses and the pickers in the fields. We must oppose them now, before it is too late." The organization, he said, no longer regards itself as a temporary group formed to meet an emergency, but as a permanent organization dedicated to prevent the unionization of farm labor. "If the fight wipes out our entire crop, it would be cheap."

The new offensive program could not be explained to the members for "strategic reasons" but they were asked to accept it implicitly on the "good faith" of the leaders.

Significantly, fiery crosses began to burn on the hilltops of Central California, in March, 1938.

## CHAPTER XV

## THE DRIVE FOR UNIONIZATION

THE fact that 250,000 workers, employed in the richest industry in California, have been repeatedly frustrated in their desire to achieve organization is a matter which has long provoked discussion among labor's well-wishers and theorizers. The case for organization is, indeed, remarkably persuasive. Consider some of the favorable elements: a highly industrialized agriculture, thoroughly organized, making huge profits; perishable crops directly dependent upon transportation (two circumstances that place the industry at the mercy of a strong labor movement); wretched working conditions aggravated by racial discrimination; and, both in the past and in the present, a strong urban labor movement. These and other factors would indicate the feasibility of organization. Mention might be made, on the other hand, of a few general factors standing in the way of unionization: the militant opposition of the growers; the diversity of races making up the agricultural proletariat; the migratory character of employment; and the shortness of the season for the various crops, or industries, involved. Despite these considerations, however, the case for unionization remains, on the face of things, extremely strong. Why is it, then, that farm workers have never been able to achieve organization?

The real explanation must be sought in the consideration of a basic social question. In the last analysis, the problem involves the distinction between town and country (the economic basis of which, under capitalism, was pointed out, of course, long ago by Engels); between industrial labor, as such, and farm labor. Unless the problem of farm labor is studied against this general background, it cannot properly be understood. From a realistic point of view there is slight if any difference between labor employed in a Pennsylvania steel mill and labor employed in a California cannery; or, for that matter, between the type of unskilled labor employed in the mass-production industries and the type of field labor employed in the California farm factories. As Mr. George E. Bodle has well pointed out, "these seasonal workers [referring to the migratory farm laborers in California] are employed at an hourly or daily wage or on a piece-rate basis; they have no personal relationship with their employer; they live on wages and not on what they produce from the land; they work in close proximity to each other and in large numbers. They bear little similarity to our ordinary idea of the 'farm hand,' who lives on the ranch or farm on which he works the year around. . . . The fact that the agricultural laborer's work is seasonal does not put him in a separate category since the workers in many industries such as lumber, clothing, and construction, are employed on a seasonal basis." [1]

Not only is there no substantial difference, today, between the seasonal agricultural workers in the fields or packing sheds and the employees of our factories and industrial plants, but agriculture, as an industry, in California cannot

[1] *The Commonwealth*, Vol. XII, No. 51, p. 235.

be distinguished from any other highly organized American industry. California agriculture is monopolistic in character; it is highly organized; it utilizes familiar price-fixing schemes; it is corporately owned; management and ownership are sharply differentiated; it is enormously profitable to the large growers. Its industrial character is indicated by the fact that, in 1930, some 195,000 agricultural workers were employed in the State — four times as many as were employed in Washington, Michigan and Illinois (which are better known as "farm States" than California). A glance at the total value of farm products in California from 1928 to 1937 indicates the scale on which agricultural operations are carried on:

| | |
|---|---|
| 1928 | $646,000,000.00 |
| 1929 | 750,000,000.00 |
| 1930 | 601,000,000.00 |
| 1931 | 461,000,000.00 |
| 1932 | 372,000,000.00 |
| 1933 | 421,000,000.00 |
| 1934 | 501,000,000.00 |
| 1935 | 538,000,000.00 |
| 1936 | 627,000,000.00 |

Having every attribute of industrial organization, California agriculture continues to masquerade behind the disguise of "the farm." It is no longer "agriculture," in the formerly understood sense of the term, but a mechanized industry, owned and operated by corporations and not by farmers, and closely identified with the large financial interests which dominate industrial operations. California Lands, Inc. — the farm-holding subsidiary of the Bank of America — at one time during the depression owned or controlled nearly half of the farm lands of Northern and Central California. Still the fiction continues that California agriculture is operated by "embattled farmers" and that Trade Unions should be restricted to the industrial field, so-called, on the theory that the "farmer" is somehow immune from collective bargaining. This fiction, which has been invaluable to the interests which control California's farm factories in winning many types of exemption, legislative and otherwise, is based, as I have indicated, upon the anachronistic distinction between farm and city. In order to achieve its ultimate objectives, organized farm labor must demolish this distinction; or, to phrase it differently, farm labor, in achieving organization and in equating agricultural and industrial labor, will eventually eliminate the artificial distinction between farm and factory. The abolition of this distinction is the root of the farm-labor problem. Standing in the path of the organization of farm labor (and the important consequences which organization, in this case, involves) is the unrealistic and inaccurate division of industry into urban and rural categories. So deeply entrenched is this distinction in the institutions and laws of California today that it constitutes the pivot around which the various economic group interests compete for power. The prime reason that organized labor in California has tended to remain aloof from the farm-labor problem is that Trade Union officials, themselves entrenched in power, have feared the democratizing effect of the organization of farm labor. These petty Trade Union satraps, through their control of the political machinery of the Trade Union movement, have occasionally been able to strike a legislative bargain by throwing their support behind the industrial groups against the farm groups, or vice versa. The farm industrialists, on the other hand, have been able to perpetuate the anachronistic distinction between urban and rural industry, by forcing the city industrialists to bargain with them over control of the Legislature. For at all times the farm groups, through their control of the State Senate, have held a veto power on legislation. Our system of legislative representation is, of course, based on the idea of a balance of power between industrial and agricultural interests. Thus the present system of control is self-perpetuating and will continue until the organization of farm labor brings about a merger or fusion of agricultural and industrial interests. It is in this general alignment of social forces that the real reason for the backwardness of organization among farm workers must be sought; yet despite the entrenched position of the farm industrialists, and despite the crushing effect of the anti-union campaign of 1934, the herculean task of organizing farm labor in California continues. Present trends, in the line of organizational activities, are traced in the following sections.

### 1. Farm Labor "Joins Up"

Following the collapse of the Cannery and Agricultural Workers Industrial Union in 1934, organizational activity among field workers in California practically disappeared. Some of the organizers of the C.A.W.I.U. were, however, left at large; and the drive of the workers themselves toward unionization continued, through spontaneous action, and through such surviving organizations as the Salinas shed workers and the various racial groups. Out of the discussions carried on in 1935 and 1936, some of the shortcomings of the C.A.W.I.U., from an organizational point of view, became apparent. These shortcomings may be summarized as follows: (*a*) the C.A.W.I.U. was an independent union and, in consequence, was largely isolated from the trade-union movement; (*b*) while nominally including both shed and field workers, the emphasis of the C.A.W.I.U. was almost exclusively upon field workers and twenty-five years of experience had demonstrated that field workers cannot be organized alone; and (*c*) the C.A.W.I.U. had no roots in the small towns in the rural counties, and was thus excluded from several sources of possible support and assistance. The importance of these criticisms is made more apparent in light of the fact that, after 1933, strong labor groups affiliated with the American Federation of Labor began to develop in a few of the small towns and lesser cities. In those communities in which shed or cannery workers lived, notably San Jose, Salinas, Stockton, and El Centro, the presence of the shed workers gave an impetus to the unionization of shops and stores. The wives of many shed workers, for example, work in shops and restaurants, and they naturally carry the drive for unionization with them wherever they go. Consequently, when a general summing up began to take place after the debacle of 1934, it was fairly obvious that a movement should be launched to organize both field and shed workers into a single Statewide organization affiliated with the American Federation of Labor.

The first step in this direction was a call for a conference of agricultural workers which was held at Stockton, California, June 6 and 7, 1936, for the purpose of setting up a federation of cannery, agricultural and packing-house workers within the American Federation of Labor. Some two hundred delegates and observers attended this conference. Among other measures adopted at the conference was a resolution condemning the piece-rate method of payment, establishing a three dollar daily minimum wage (with guarantee of twenty hours' work a week), an eight-hour day and payment for overtime. Although the purpose of the conference was to organize a federation through which some 250,000 unorganized workers might be brought into the American Federation of Labor — a rather juicy plum for the A.F. of L. one would think — nevertheless the officials of the A.F. of L. were hostile to the idea from the start. Mr. Edward D. Vandeleur, of the State Federation of Labor, warned at the outset: "We will not tolerate any sort of organization but an orderly one." The Associated Farmers likewise viewed the conference with the utmost concern and, while the conference was in session, issued several threatening statements and protested vociferously that a daily wage of three dollars would immediately bankrupt the largest industry in the State.

Both before and after the conference, various farm-labor locals were formed and given Federal charters under the American Federation of Labor. It was quite apparent that these Federal locals would have to be organized into some kind of Statewide organization in order to give strength to the drive for membership and to impose some degree of centralized control. Accordingly a conference was called, this time in the name of the State Federation of Labor, in San Francisco for February 27 and 28, 1937, to set up a Statewide organization and to petition the American Federation of Labor to form a new International Union of Agricultural Workers. A continuation committee, established by the conference, proceeded to draw up a tentative organizational outline of the proposed International and to adopt a program for immediate action. On March 21, 1937, this committee met with the executive council of the State Federation of Labor, in Sacramento, and submitted its plan of organization. The hostility of the American Federation of Labor officialdom, which had been veiled in 1936, was now clearly revealed. The plan was rejected (Harry Bridges, then a member of the executive council of the State Federation of Labor, voted to accept the program) and the State Federation announced that it would continue to organize field workers in Federal locals, but that it would not consent to the organization of field and cannery and shed workers in a single union. It also insisted upon a strict control of the Federal locals by the State Federation of Labor. (The motivation behind this program was revealed during the Stockton cannery strike in April, 1937, when the cannery workers, isolated from the field workers, were sold out by the officials of the State Federation of Labor who intervened, at the request of the cannery owners, to "negotiate" a settlement.) Naturally the continuation committee, headed by such a rank-and-file leader as George Woolf of San Francisco, rebelled. Still another conference was called by the rank-and-file group, this time in Bakersfield,[2] at which it was decided to form a federation of cannery and agricultural workers and to appeal to the American Federation of Labor over the heads of the State officials for an international charter. In the meantime, the drive for in-

[2] April 25, 1937.

dustrial organization began to make itself felt among agricultural workers throughout the country. As a consequence, when the first national convention of agricultural workers ever held in the United States met in Denver, July 9 to 12, 1937, the group voted unanimously to join the C.I.O. From this convention came a new national union, the United Cannery, Agricultural, Packing and Allied Workers of America. The necessity for national organization was clearly demonstrated at the convention, as it developed that most of the workers were migrants and frequently crossed State lines in search of employment. Today, the new union has some sixteen locals in California and is proceeding, with commendable caution, to organize field and shed and cannery workers. Most of the previously existing racial organizations have voted to join the new union which is, at present, the only organization attempting to organize field workers in the State. The American Federation of Labor still has a foothold in the canneries and packing houses, but, as a result of its notorious failure to support these unions, it is steadily losing ground.

The significance of the appearance of the United Cannery and Agricultural Workers Union can hardly be over-emphasized. It has a potential membership in California alone in excess of 250,000 workers. If these workers can be organized, the union will be the largest in the State and one of the largest in the West. The militancy and courage of the workers involved, and their great capacity for organized effort, has been eloquently demonstrated in the past. Numerically, the cannery and agricultural workers can control many small towns and rural communities if their members can be induced, through the influence of the union, to establish local residence for voting purposes. Throughout the State, the potential political significance of the union is equally apparent. It is understandable, therefore, that the battle line has been drawn so sharply. Industrial agriculture in California will never permit the organization of farm labor without a fight to the finish. The situation, as it is developing, is extremely dangerous. It is my opinion that the Associated Farmers, and their allies, will wage civil war in the farm counties to prevent the organization of farm labor under the C.I.O. It is for this reason that farm labor in California is a matter of national importance. And it is precisely for this reason that the drive toward Fascist control has probably been carried further in California than in any other State in the Union. If measures are not taken immediately to mitigate the force of the struggle which impends, it will likely require Federal intervention to maintain order in California. Nor am I alone in this opinion. "The large growers' groups," writes Mr. John Steinbeck, "have found the law inadequate to their uses; and they have become so powerful that such charges as felonious assault, mayhem and inciting to riot, kidnaping and flogging cannot be brought against them in the controlled courts." They practise "a system of terrorism that would be unusual in the Fascist nations of the world. A continuation of this approach constitutes a criminal endangering of the peace of the State."

## 2. Mechanization and Other Factors

Numerous factors, some potential, some actual, have contributed to the drive for unionization. The introduction of labor-saving devices has everywhere accelerated the tendency to unionization, and California agriculture is well on the way to being thoroughly mechanized. The canneries, which can be regarded as an adjunct of the orchards, are highly mechanized. By way of illustration, the Anderson-Barngrover Mfg. Co. at San Jose has perfected a pear-peeling machine which peels, cores and splits pears, the machine operating at the rate of about forty pears per minute. The development of this and similar types of machinery is destined to mechanize the entire canning industry. The citrus industry is, likewise, highly mechanized.[3] In September, 1937, hop-picking machines were introduced in California. By using these machines, 400 men can do the work of picking, dyeing and baling that, without the machine, would require 15,000 men for picking alone. In the areas where the hop-picking machine has been introduced, regular flat wage rates have been substituted in the place of hourly or piece rates. A machine has been now invented which washes, grades and pre-cools various vegetable commodities, such as lettuce. The Vesey System, used in the lettuce industry, for crating and sorting, only requires the employment of eight men per unit, where, under the former system prevailing, some forty men were required for the same operation. The value of farm implements and machines, per acre, in California agriculture has mounted from 29 cents in 1860 to $4.46 in 1930. A cotton-picking machine, developed by the International Harvester Company, was used in Arizona, in 1937, and will be used, also, in California. Mechanized beet thinners have been introduced and, likewise, mechani-

[3] See *In the Matter of the North Whittier Citrus Association before the National Labor Relations Board* for a detailed description of the mechanized process by which oranges are sorted, washed, colored, waxed and packaged.

cal cotton choppers. In certain types of agriculture, it will be some time before serious displacement of labor by machinery occurs, due to the nature of the operations involved, as, for example, in fruit picking. But the eventual mechanization of most types of agriculture is a foregone conclusion. Field observers have already noticed that farm labor resents the introduction of machinery and instinctively senses the necessity of organization. Many dust-bowl refugees complain, for example, that they were "tractored out" of the Middle West. Faced with the same conditions in California, it is reasonable to assume that they will tend more and more toward unionization as the introduction of machinery is expanded.

Another factor which must be weighed is the political position of farm labor. Agricultural labor, as distinguished from urban industrial labor, has long been discriminated against. It is still generally assumed that farm labor is not entitled to the same protection which various types of social legislation have accorded labor in general. This is particularly true in California. The State Minimum Wage Law for women is, in practice, inapplicable to women engaged in agricultural labor. The officials who are supposed to enforce the Act restrict their activities to cannery labor. Agricultural labor is excluded from the provisions of the Social Security Act and from the provisions of the National Labor Relations Act, both Federal measures, to be sure, but measures having important intra-State implications. Many similar items of discrimination might be pointed out. The effect of such discrimination will unquestionably be to encourage organized action among agricultural workers to achieve the same type of protection afforded labor in general. With various liberal and progressive groups drafting legislation designed to improve the status of agricultural labor, it is reasonable to assume that farm workers will organize if only for the purpose of furthering such legislation.

As an illustration of the type of legislation proposed, I might refer to the California Agricultural Labor Relations Act, drafted by a minority of the Commonwealth Club committee on farm labor and printed in the proceedings of the Club (Vol. XII, No. 51, December 22, 1936). There is, in fact, strong sentiment in California today for the passage of such an act, or, at least, for the establishment of a mediation board for farm labor. It is quite likely that some such legislation will be enacted in 1939. There is, in fact, precedent for this type of legislation. Arbitration was resorted to in order to settle the cotton strike of 1933 and an arbitration board has been created, by agreement, in the Santa Maria–Santa Barbara area, for certain crops, and the experience of both groups with the arbitration procedure has been, on the whole, satisfactory. This particular board has been in existence for two years and has settled several important issues. If a State Mediation Act were to be adopted in California, it would give a marked impetus to organizational activities. When labor is backward, as in farm labor, it seems to require some type of legislative foothold before it can establish itself. Legislation of the type proposed has the effect, moreover, of giving a qualified recognition to trade unions and enhances their prestige and importance in the eyes of the workers.

The most important factor furthering the drive for the unionization of farm labor in California today is the possibility of Federal intervention. Officials of the Department of Agriculture have long been interested in the problem of farm labor in California, and, wherever they could, have tried to intervene for the purpose of raising wages and improving conditions. Until recent years, the possibilities of Federal intervention have been slight, but with the stabilization program under the AAA a practical occasion for intervention has been provided. Many millions of dollars were paid to the large growers by the Federal Government in 1935 and 1936, in the form of benefit allotments, without any effort being made to force the growers to raise wages. But, with the passage of the Sugar Act of 1937, the Secretary of Agriculture was given power to fix rates of pay for laborers employed by those sugar-beet growers who applied for subsidies under the Act. Public hearings were recently held in California for the purpose of fixing this rate of pay. When it was finally fixed at 55 cents an hour, the sugar-beet growers, who had been growing rich at the expense of the Federal Government without in any manner attempting to raise the pay of their employees, began to yell about ruination, dark disaster and imminent bankruptcy. This type of Federal intervention has great potential importance. It not only results in immediate pay increases for the workers, but it indirectly stimulates organizational activity. At the recent hearings, for example, the unions were invited to be present and to introduce evidence. The mere opportunity which such hearings afford to get the facts about the condition of farm labor before the public is invaluable; moreover, to invite the unions to participate in such hearings is, indirectly, to give them a kind of tentative official recognition.

The most important possibility of Federal intervention at

the moment, however, consists in the interpretation placed on the National Labor Relations Act by the United States Supreme Court. Agricultural labor, as such, is excluded from the Act. But how is agricultural labor to be defined? In the Santa Cruz Packing Company case, decided by the Supreme Court in April, 1938, the Court upheld the application of the National Labor Relations Act to a packing company only 37 per cent of whose total products entered the stream of interstate commerce. The decision is broad enough to bring practically all shed and cannery workers in the State under the protection of the National Labor Relations Act. Once the shed and cannery workers are given this protection, they, in turn, can force the unionization of the field workers upon the employers. The drive for unionization will "march inland," in the phrase of the maritime unions, from the packing shed to the fields. This development is of particular importance in view of the fact that most of the co-operative marketing agencies employ the field labor which picks the crops of its members. If these agencies are subject to the Act, which now seems to be settled, then the Board may very likely rule that operations such as picking are merely incidental to the process of manufacture, and thus field workers will be brought within the protection of the Act.[4] Of great importance, also, is the proposed amendment to the National Labor Relations Act which would, if adopted, give the Board jurisdiction over all persons and firms which receive subsidies from the Federal Government. The amendment, bitterly opposed at the present time by the Associated Farmers, is broad enough to bring a substantial portion of the larger farm factories di-

[4] See *In the Matter of the North Whittier Citrus Association.*

rectly within the Act. Given the protection of the National Labor Relations Act, farm workers in California would flock to the unions.

The tendency to unionization will increase as the necessity for controls of various types becomes more urgent in agriculture. The one activity is a reflex of the other, just as the trade union is, in a general way, a social phenomenon associated with the rise of the corporation. In August, 1933, the Legislature adopted a Pro-Rate Act for California agriculture.

Under the provisions of this Act, a certain percentage of the growers in a given area, engaged in the production of a particular crop, may petition the Pro-Rate Commission to approve a schedule of production. Hearings are held and, the necessary consents being forthcoming, the schedule is officially approved and machinery is provided for its enforcement. The Pro-Rate Commission is, as one might expect, entirely controlled at present by the large growers. And the Act, as administered, has improved the position of the large grower at the expense of the small farmer. The mere existence of such a measure, however, will stimulate union organization. Eventually the unions will seek representation on the Commissions (if the Act is not repealed) and will demand a voice in the hearings at which the schedule of crop limitation is determined.

The California farm industrialists are, as I have pointed out, the most highly organized farm group in America. The degree of centralization which has been established in the industry over a period of years is startling. The canneries, for example, have a central association which controls the entire industry and admittedly engages in price-fixing programs. The same interests that own the large orchards also control the canneries; consequently, the small orchardist is wholly at the mercy of his competitor. It is these central-control organizations which, ultimately, are responsible for the shockingly low wage levels in California agriculture, for they are the ones who fix the prices at which farm products are sold. Monopoly practices such as these necessarily result in unionization. The one development encourages and, in a sense, is responsible for, the other.

As indicative of the character and extent of centralized control in California agriculture, consider the California Fruit Growers Exchange.[5] The Exchange is the largest agricultural co-operative in the country; it markets 75 per cent of the California citrus crop and, in 1936, its gross sales totaled $107,000,000. It has several large subsidiary and by-products corporations. The Exchange is organized as follows: at the base, 13,400 growers; these growers in turn belong to some 210 packing associations in the various regions; above the packing-house associations are some 26 district exchanges; and over the district exchanges is the California Fruit Growers Exchange. Through this mechanism, the Exchange dominates and controls the entire citrus industry in California (the second largest industry in the State). Theoretically a "co-operative" association, the Exchange operates, in fact, like any private corporation. It is in effect a huge holding corporation, with the affiliated "co-operatives" as subsidiary corporations. It is the Exchange, through its co-operative subsidiaries, that employs, not only the packing-house labor in the citrus industry, but also the field labor, that is, the labor involved in picking, harvest-

[5] See *Fortune*, July, 1936.

ing and fumigating the crop. It is, therefore, somewhat amusing to find *Fortune* stating that "labor trouble is pretty much unknown in the citrus industry" [6] — and that labor, in the citrus fields, is "quite contented."

Lastly, other groups are beginning now to support farm labor in its drive for unionization. On November 6, 1936, the Simon J. Lubin Society of California, Incorporated, was formed. This group, which now has a fairly large membership throughout the State, is made up, for the most part, of liberal professional people. It takes its name from Simon J. Lubin, a distinguished California liberal, who was responsible for the creation of the California Immigration and Housing Commission. The Society has performed an invaluable service in giving wide publicity to the problem of farm labor in California; in raising money for relief and organizational purposes; and in drafting a legislative program for farm workers. Through its activities, the entire liberal and progressive movement in California has been made keenly aware of the condition of farm labor. Today the Society is working industriously to bring about a reformation of the Farmers' Union in California. The Farmers' Union, in California, is headed by Mr. R. V. Garrod, who is a member of the State Board of Agriculture under appointment of Governor Frank Merriam. Mr. Garrod, who frankly announces his alliance with the large growers, has converted the Farmers' Union into a subsidiary of the Associated Farmers. His leadership is, however, seriously threatened. Once the Farmers' Union can be liberated from the dominance of the Associated Farmers, it will be possible to rally the small farmers and the small growers into

[6] See page 249, sub-chapter on *Gunkist Oranges*.

an organization which will genuinely represent their interests, and not the interests of the banks, the insurance companies and the utility corporations. If this can be done, the work of organizing farm labor can be greatly facilitated.

## CHAPTER XVI

## THE TREND TOWARD STABILIZATION

FROM an early date, the farm industrialists in California have occasionally voiced the opinion that agricultural labor should be stabilized. Over a period of forty years, one can find, in the farm journals of the State, repeated references both to the desirability and to the necessity of working out some method of operation by which the employment of farm labor might be regularized. Suggestions of this kind have taken various forms. The idea of colonization, for example, has been frequently advanced (it was advocated by the *Los Angeles Times* in the late nineties as a possible solution of the farm-labor problem), and isolated growers have even experimented with some forms of colonization. Again, the centralization of employment through "labor pools" has been a major plank of the State Chamber of Commerce for many years. But, in general, these various schemes have never been put into practice. Several factors have stood in the way of stabilization. In the first place, the structure of California agriculture is essentially irrational, that is, unplanned. The demand for farm labor has constantly fluctuated within wide extremes. When labor has been scarce, the growers have become thoughtful and discussed stabilization; when labor has been plentiful, they have abandoned social theory. Powerless to impose any order (that is, "order" from a social point of view) in their own industry, they have been equally powerless to rationalize their methods of employment. In the second place, a basic contradiction has at all times confronted the growers. Theoretically it is desirable, even from the growers' point of view, that the supply of farm labor be stabilized; practically, as one grower put it, "farm labor won't stabilize." Under existing agricultural operations, farm labor must be migratory in character, that is, it must move from county to county, from crop to crop. The growers would doubtless like to have an adequate supply of farm labor permanently located in the immediate vicinity of their farm factories, but, in the absence of local industrial activity sufficient to absorb the workers in the non-harvest season, it has been impractical to stabilize employment. The introduction of new crops, however, has made it possible, in theory, to extend the period of employment throughout the year, but only on the assumption that farm labor will remain migratory in character, that is, that it will follow the crops. The policy pursued, therefore, has been one of drift and chaos animated by a blind drive for profits. A marked trend toward stabilization, however, has become apparent of late years. It has come about, however, not through the efforts of the growers, but because of the more or less fortuitous intervention of the Federal Government. Federal intervention has been manifest, first, in the operations of the various relief agencies, and, second, through the establishment of camps for migratory labor.

## 1. The Relief Agencies

The passage of the Federal Emergency Relief Act of 1933 altered the basic factors theretofore involved in the problem of farm labor in California. It was apparent, almost from the outset, that the administration of Federal relief would have a direct and vital bearing on the business of recruiting farm labor. The importance of the relief situation was emphasized in California by reason of two collateral considerations: first, the growing militancy of farm labor, as indicated by the strikes of 1933 and 1934; and, second, by the dramatic exodus of the Mexicans. It has been estimated that, in the period from 1928 to 1933, close to 160,000 Mexicans either left the State or were repatriated. In 1933 the Mexicans constituted not more than a fourth of the total of migratory farm laborers in California. Faced with a "labor shortage" and an awakening labor consciousness on the part of the workers, California agriculture was immediately concerned with the administration of relief.

The reality of this concern was abundantly demonstrated in 1933, the first year in which Federal relief was provided. Residence was essential in order to obtain relief and this circumstance, from the outset, tended to check the mobility of farm labor. Throughout the State, workers were quick to realize the situation and attempted, wherever possible, to establish and to maintain a permanent local residence. The cotton strike in the San Joaquin Valley in 1933 illustrated another important consequence of Federal relief. There the workers had been able to win a partial victory largely because of the fact that they were able to obtain some assistance from the local relief agencies during the strike. When the significance of these two developments — permanency of residence and aid to strikers — began to dawn upon the growers, a bitter fight was launched to wrest control of the relief agencies from the Federal Government and to place this control in the hands of county officials and State agencies directly under the dominance of the shipper-growers. The fight for control, launched in 1933, still continues in California.

To understand the background of this struggle, one further fact must be mentioned. Both the Federal Government and the State maintain unemployment services. For many years both of these agencies, as operated in California, have been controlled by the large growers. In fact the Federal Unemployment Service and the State Unemployment Service have functioned as the labor-recruiting personnel of the farm industrialists. Consequently after 1933 the growers used the employment services, which they controlled, as clubs to beat the relief agencies into line. The established practice has been somewhat as follows: In advance of each particular harvest, the growers start a great hue and cry in the press about a "labor shortage" and "crops rotting in the fields" in order to assist the employment services in bringing pressure to bear upon the relief agencies (*a*) to cut relief to the bone and (*b*) to force relief clients into the fields. Conceivably the relief agencies might question the authenticity of these recurrent "acute labor shortages" if they were directly approached by the growers; but, when the demand for workers comes from other Governmental agencies, they have had to give it full face value.

For the first few months after Federal relief had been inaugurated in 1933, the relief agencies managed to remain fairly neutral, but by the spring of 1935, reports appeared in the press, throughout the State, that relief clients were being forced off the relief rolls and given orders to report for work in the fields. In the period from 1933 to 1935, the growers had endeavored to accomplish the same end by demanding that the relief allowance be cut to such a low point that its recipients would quit in desperation. Failing in this effort, they began to demand that the relief agencies deliver workers to them and, by and large, the relief agencies succumbed to this pressure. On April 23, 1935, the State Emergency Relief Administrator, F. C. McLaughlin, entered into a written agreement with the head of the National Re-employment Service in California, and Roy Stockton, representing the State Employment Co-ordinators, "to supply whatever labor might be needed in the fields." In May, 1935, 2396 persons were "turned over" by the relief agencies to the growers in the San Joaquin Valley alone. The growers were immediately elated and various chambers of commerce throughout the State passed resolutions in praise of the new cheap-labor mechanism. (See a report on "The Suspension of Relief in Agricultural Areas," August 29, 1935, prepared by Mr. David Ziskind, for the Department of Agriculture, on this entire subject.) Seeking to ward off the demands of the growers, relief administrators in Los Angeles County, in June, 1935, appointed a citizens' committee to hold hearings and to fix a scale of hourly pay by which the various relief agencies might be guided in determining whether, in a given case, workers should be forced to accept employment. It was revealed at these hearings that in the citrus industry, second richest industry in the State, the average period of yearly employment was only about

150 days and that the annual average wage was about $300. Although finding that agricultural wage conditions in California were "deplorable," the committee fixed the prevailing wage at 30 cents an hour for field workers in the citrus and avocado industries, 25 cents an hour in other types of orchard work and 22½ cents an hour in all types of agricultural employment except orchard labor, and the relief administrators then instructed their clients to accept these wages or to get off the relief rolls. Throughout the State in the spring and summer of 1935, thousands were struck from the relief rolls and ordered into the fields, and, in most cases, no attempt was made, as in Los Angeles, to fix a prevailing wage. A former relief worker has told how some 4000 men were taken off the relief rolls in Northern California and ordered to work in the Sonoma orchards and vineyards. These men were corralled in "concentration camps" described as "pest holes without tents," with open latrines and a total absence of sanitation. Hundreds of cases of dysentery, hop poisoning (a skin disease) and influenza were reported in the camps. In Solano County workers were ordered into the fields and, in cases where they refused to work for the wages offered them, they were automatically and permanently removed from the relief rolls. This procedure was highly praised by the growers. "It enables us," they said, "to get our share of available unemployed labor without having to impossibly compete with union wages." [1] Even this marvellous co-operation failed, however, to satisfy the growers. They continued to demand that the relief agencies "jar labor loose"; and protested that relief administrators were "unwilling to send out a Mexican worker if he

[1] *Pacific Rural Press*, March 9, 1935.

has a sore thumb or an ingrowing nail." [2] Throughout 1935 and 1936, the prevailing hourly rate for farm labor in California was 20 cents an hour or less. In the face of this compulsory Governmental scabbing, the few unions left in the State were powerless to maintain the gains achieved in 1933 by strike action.

In the fall of 1935 the relief situation became even more aggravated. Over a thousand workers were dropped from the relief rolls in Los Angeles County and told to report for work in the San Fernando Valley. In a short while, the Los Angeles County Relief Administration was deluged with protests and complaints. Some of these complaints [3] indicated that one man worked 29 hours picking tomatoes and earned $1.60; that a married couple worked in the fields ten days and only made $9; that the head of a family of five, who had been getting the lucrative sum of $15.57 on relief, was only able to earn $7.50 in five days in the fields; and that hundreds of workers who had reported in the fields (at their own expense) day after day had been unable to secure any employment whatever. When the cotton harvest started in the fall of 1935, the growers demanded that 4000 workers be cut off the relief rolls in Los Angeles and ordered to report for work in the cotton fields of the San Joaquin Valley (at a distance of some two hundred miles and at their own expense). The County Relief Administrator frankly stated that "we have to solve the farmers' problem, even if it does work hardships." When questioned concerning the type of worker being sent to the cotton fields, he replied: "Well, of course, the growers prefer the

---

[2] *Pacific Rural Press*, March 21, 1936.
[3] Summarized in the *Los Angeles Evening News*, October 17, 1935.

larger families because they make more money that way." [4]
In August, 1935, relief workers were sent to work in orchards in Northern California which were five hundred
miles removed from their homes. Similar reports continued
to appear in the press throughout 1935. Wherever relief
clients failed to accept work orders in the field, they were
permanently dropped from the rolls. The net result of this
system was, of course, that the tax burden was lightened for
the growers and that farm wages were lowered.

Under these circumstances, naturally, it was not long before the growers began to see that the relief situation had
real possibilities. On November 7, 1935, they sponsored a
conference which was held in the Biltmore Hotel, in Los
Angeles, to consider the matter (I attended this conference
as an observer). At this meeting, relief officials boasted of
the efficiency with which they had "co-operated" with the
farm industrialists. One relief administrator told how he had
cut 600 families off relief in Los Angeles and ordered them
to work in Imperial Valley (250 miles distant) and that, to
insure their docility, he had also sent 1000 Filipinos into the
valley, advising the white workers that if they did not hold
their jobs in the fields the Filipinos would take their places.
Despite this touching evidence of the subserviency of the
relief officials, and despite an unprecedentedly prosperous
year, the growers continued to howl about the relief situation, and, in conferences held later in the year at Santa Cruz,
became more insistent in their demands and informed the
relief administrators, in no uncertain language, that they
were to step lively when the whip was cracked.

The same general situation continued throughout 1936,

[4] *Illustrated Daily News*, October 15, 1935.

the only difference that could be noticed being that the whole process was better co-ordinated and more thoroughly rationalized. The growers began to urge that the relief agencies and the unemployment services be merged so as to bring the whole relief situation more firmly under their control. That they were already entrenched in the relief agencies, however, was indicated by the fact that Mr. F. C. McLaughlin (head of the State Emergency Relief Administration) sent out confidential instructions to his lieutenants in various parts of the State that, henceforth, they were to "co-operate in labor matters with the Associated Farmers." On March 5, 1936, at the commencement of the season, a conference was held in Los Angeles between the growers and the relief officials (needless to say, the workers were not represented). The relief administrators were excessively conciliatory: "We realize we cannot dictate wages to farmers," was the theme of their remarks. One relief administrator, asked what would happen if a relief client who took a field job were to be discharged, replied: "We will not take them back. We shall be vigilant to make certain that they do not get back on relief. We are just as anxious to get them off relief as the farmers are to take them." One relief worker stated to me privately: "These workers are getting a raw deal. The growers will cut wages to a starvation level. If the men cannot hold up under the grueling ten-hour day, they will get fired. Where can they go? They can't get back on relief. Industry cannot absorb them. Will the California highways be strewn with emaciated dead in the next year?" Throughout 1936 workers were taken off relief rolls in Los Angeles County and ordered to report for work in the fields as far north as Sacramento, Stockton and Santa Rosa. With considerable ingenuity, the farm groups convinced the relief administrators and the WPA officials that few if any work projects would be located in the rural regions, the purpose being to keep workers on direct relief during the off seasons so as to be able to force them instantly into the fields during the harvest. In fact, the relief administrators and the unemployment-service officials worked out a plan for short-term projects involving some 60,000 workers, the completion of the projects being timed to coincide with the commencement of the harvest season. "We will close down our projects," said Mr. McLaughlin, "whenever there is a shortage of labor in the farming sections" (March 17, 1936), meaning of course "whenever the farmers want a superabundance of workers to force wages still lower." Every effort was made in 1936 "to facilitate the transfer of relief workers to the farms," and the whole relief administration was tightened up. For example, the State Relief Administration announced that it would no longer give assistance to strikers in the agricultural areas, and, in Los Angeles County, workers were told that they must employ their children to assist them in the walnut harvest; otherwise relief would not be granted.

Throughout the highly prosperous farm years of 1936 and 1937, the growers were able to keep farm wages at a low point (at a time when wages generally were increasing and the cost of living mounting) and, at the same time, to frustrate organizational activities, by using relief workers to supplement their labor supply. So successful was the stratagem that the growers sent forth hosannas of praise (the Chamber of Commerce in Fresno, September 4, 1937, passed resolutions endorsing the relief program as administered), at the same time continuing to grouse about the shortage of labor. On September 3 and 4, 1937, in response to their urgings, Governor Frank Merriam issued an ultimatum that all able-bodied workers receiving State relief "must help the State's harvest or get off the dole." This order was headlined in the press as a "Work or Starve Order." Officials of the unemployment service went through the relief rolls, and selected the names of those whose work had proven satisfactory the previous year, and these people were ordered into the fields. The entire quota of hop pickers was recruited in this manner; and the same applies, more or less, to the orchard and miscellaneous field crops of 1937, and, to a considerable degree, to the cotton crop. The basis of Governor Merriam's order, in September, 1937, was the existence of an "acute labor shortage." Yet, in July, 1937, thousands of farm laborers were out of employment in the San Joaquin Valley, and the spokesmen of the Associated Farmers, who had raised the "labor-shortage issue," testified before the Farm Tenancy Commission a few months previously that the State was being inundated with dust-bowl refugees at the rate of six thousand a month. Despite the overwhelming evidence of an actual over-supply of labor, the dirty business of shanghai-ing relief clients continued. On September 21, 1937, the director of the WPA in Ventura ordered all men on relief projects "into the tomato fields or else."

In a number of instances, relief workers attempted to rebel. When relief workers refused to chop cotton in the San Joaquin Valley, in April and May, 1936, for 20 cents an hour, their action was denounced by the growers as a "Communist conspiracy," and when thirty clergymen — Protestant, Catholic and Jewish — remonstrated on behalf of the workers, after investigating conditions, they in turn were roundly denounced for having "stepped out of their pulpits" and for "lining up on the side of professional agitators." In May, 1937, several hundred men who had been ordered to pick peas in Sacramento returned to relief headquarters and protested against "intolerable conditions in the pea fields under which no white man, Mexican, or oriental or any other human being should work." In this instance, the WPA director upheld their action: "We do not intend," he stated, "to force these workers to become peons or slaves to the pea-picking contractors." Men ordered into the cotton fields from Los Angeles in the fall of 1937 rioted at local relief offices. In the summer of 1937, ranchers in Sonoma County flooded Los Angeles County officials with telegrams demanding that 20,000 workers be detached from the relief rolls and sent north to work in the orchards. At this juncture, the *Los Angeles Evening News* sent Mr. Tom O'Connor to Sonoma to investigate conditions. He reported that, originally, there had been no labor shortage; that the growers could get all the labor they wanted if they would pay a decent wage; that hundreds of migratory families were destitute; that the State unemployment service was openly co-operating with the large growers in jailing union officials and in terrorizing the workers; and that, when the Resettlement Administration had attempted to build a migratory labor camp in Sonoma, the growers had protested: They feared that a semi-permanent labor supply might be easily organized. The failure of the relief officials to co-operate, in this instance, provoked a storm of protests from the growers, who demanded that all relief be shut down.

"Starve them out!" bellowed L. M. Meredith of Santa Rosa, on behalf of the State Chamber of Commerce and the Associated Farmers.

Today the growers are becoming increasingly insistent that the whole relief program be turned over to them for administration. In Riverside County — citadel of farm reaction — a committee of growers, calling themselves the "tax division of the citrus section of the Riverside Farm Bureau," has made such a request to the local board of supervisors; and has demanded that it be permitted to name the County Superintendent of Indigent Aid. The extremes to which these groups are prepared to go is indicated by the fancifulness of their propaganda. They are now charging (February 24, 1938), that relief clients are being "forced to accept relief," and that the farmers must rush forward to their rescue. In the background of the struggle for control of the relief agencies in California, the powerful industrial interests of the State have so manipulated the situation that the relief burden is constantly being reshuffled back and forth, in never-ending confusion, between various agencies. The net result, however, of this campaign has been to place more and more responsibility in the hands of local officials, who are amenable to influence.

The operation of the relief system has brought about, however, a marked degree of stabilization. Stabilization was at first an indirect consequence of the relief system; it is today a conscious objective. In Arizona, for example, the State relief administration has issued an order to the effect that no family on relief is to be allowed to travel about in their car without written permission of the relief officials. "A part of the plan for stabilizing migrants,"

Ten dollar a month habitation occupied by agricultural
laborers in Brawley, California.

Tent camp for agricultural workers in California

Bathroom in a camp near Fresno, California.

*Ira Cross Collection, Bancroft Library.*

Home of an agricultural worker in Hooverville, outside Bakersfield, California. The house, constructed of palm leaves, scrap tin and tree limbs is on a lot purchased for $125; $3 down, $3 per month.

*1939 photo, California Division of Immigration and Housing.*

reads the order, "is that we take from them the easiest mode of transportation, which is the automobile." From now on the worker is to be riveted to his job, a practice which bears a striking similarity to conditions in Nazi Germany.

## 2. The Migratory Camps

Closely related to the relief situation, and in a sense arising out of it, is the matter of the migratory-labor camps. In 1931 the transient problem, so-called, was already acute. The Governor was memorialized by the Los Angeles Chamber of Commerce to call out the National Guard in order to turn back transients at the State line; and the Legislature was considering ways and means of barring further transient emigration. To cope with the problem, a committee was appointed for the purpose of establishing a series of "labor camps" for unemployed single men. During the years 1931 and 1933 approximately fifteen thousand men were "sheltered" (i.e. concentrated) in some 250 labor camps throughout the State. The "applicants" were forced to work on various public-improvement projects, as a condition of receiving shelter, and for this work they received no wages whatever. The operating cost of the camps, per man per day, was something like 60 cents, and the scantiness of the relief afforded is indicated by the fact that fourteen men died in the camps in one winter.[5] As part of this program, and for the purpose of housing relief clients who had been ordered into the fields, the State Emergency Relief Administration established "two

[5] See *Newcomers and Nomads in California*, 1937, by William T. and Dorothy E. Cross.

demonstrational migratory-labor camps," one at Marysville and one at Arvin. Under the SERA these camps were simply temporary tent cities designed to house relief clients working in the fields. It was obvious that the program had some merit, but the SERA lacked the funds and the initiative to develop the idea. Consequently, the Arvin camp was turned over to the Resettlement Administration in November, 1936; the Marysville camp in February, 1937. Thereafter the Resettlement Administration proceeded to put both camps on a more or less permanent basis and to construct four similar camps at Winters, Shafter, Coachella and Brawley (with four additional camps being constructed at the present time). Each camp is strategically located with reference to the movement of migratory labor. The Arvin camp, for example, is located near the southern entrance to the San Joaquin Valley; the Brawley camp — which cost $100,000 and has accommodations for two hundred families — in Imperial Valley. Within the last year, the administration of the migratory camps has been surrendered by the Resettlement Administration to the Farm Security Administration. In theory, the migratory camps represent one of the first constructive attempts to solve the problem of farm labor in California, and, for this reason, they merit detailed consideration. Since they have been taken over by the Federal Government, the camps have become more than mere temporary bivouacs for migrants; they have tended to become small subsistence homesteads — a new type of rural community.

The growers were quick to sense the importance of the camps and the dangers which might arise from their establishment. It should be pointed out, once again, that the

California farm journals over a period of forty years have advocated various colonization projects as a method of coping with the problem of farm labor; many large growers are on record in favor of projects not altogether dissimilar to that proposed by the Resettlement Administration. Once the suggestion assumed concrete form, however, the growers were instantly hostile. When the program of the Resettlement Administration was first announced, the growers called a special conference in Los Angeles to formulate their position. At this conference (November 9, 1935) they went on record as follows: 1. They wanted the camps to be so limited as to accommodate, in each case, not more than three hundred people and to be located on *private property*; 2. They insisted that the facilities of the camp be as meager as possible so as to emphasize the transient nature of the shelter (for example, they wanted tents and not houses; at this conference I heard one grower argue eloquently that outdoor privies were good enough for farm laborers); 3. They demanded that the supervisor of each camp should be under the control of a local committee of growers; and 4. that the camps be strictly regulated so as to prevent the spread of subversive ideas (when the Marysville camp was established, the local growers warned the manager to "clear the camp of Reds or we will level it to the ground"). They were also insistent on the point that legal residence in a particular county could not be acquired by transients registered at the camps. In general, the growers have adhered to this program and have consistently opposed the migratory camps.

The reasons back of this opposition are obvious. In

every strike of field workers in California, the growers have resorted to wholesale evictions as a strikebreaking device. In those cases where workers were housed on company premises, as at the Tagus Ranch, eviction could be summarily obtained; in those cases where the workers were congregated in improvised camps, or jungles, the camps could be raided on the theory that they constituted a menace to the public health. With the camps located on property owned by an agency of the Federal Government, an entirely different issue is presented. State and county agencies, for example, are powerless to act; and, in the case of a strike, United States Marshals might conceivably be induced to protect workers housed in the camps from the vigilante practices of the growers. On this question of migratory camps, as in many other matters, the growers adopt what appears to be a contradictory attitude. Theoretically they are in favor of farm labor being stabilized, i.e. anchored to the ground in a kind of feudal bondage; practically, they oppose stabilization if it involves conferring legal residence (which would carry with it the right to vote and to be eligible for local relief) upon the workers. This, then, was the situation: a Government agency was offering at its expense (the program involved not one cent of expense in so far as the growers were concerned) to provide housing accommodations for the workers of an industry, with the organized forces of the industry opposing the idea with every resource at their command. The growers want, of course, the impossible: stabilization without its consequences; a regular labor supply without responsibility for its maintenance; privately controlled camps operated at public expense.

Upon the insistence of the Associated Farmers, many rural cities and towns joined in the campaign against the migratory camps. They, too, were concerned with the consequences which might follow upon the stabilization of farm labor; for example, they might have to assume the expense of providing school accommodations for the children living in the camps (there are 165 children at the Arvin camp). In the face of this opposition, the work of the Resettlement Administration has been greatly handicapped. The construction of the first six camps had to proceed at a snaillike pace. Once the camps were constructed, however, much of the local opposition in the small towns began to disappear. In one community, the local townspeople rallied behind the Resettlement Administration and urged the construction of a local camp in the face of strong opposition on the part of the large growers. Although admittedly inadequate, the camps which have thus far been established are highly important institutions and foreshadow the appearance of a new rural social order in California.

In practical operation, the camps may be described as small collective communities. Applicants to the camp must present a card showing that they have registered for work with the United States Employment Service. If admitted to the camp, they are assigned living quarters for which they pay a rental fee of ten cents a day. The camps are laid out, in sections, as small communities. The living quarters consist of platform tents, with kitchenettes and outdoor pantries. Diesel heating units provide hot and cold water. The general buildings consist of a utility unit, an isolation unit, a "delousing" unit, assembly room, nursery, first-aid unit and child clinic (a resident nurse is supplied by the United States Public Health Service), library, a garage pergola and grease rack (residents are encouraged to keep their antiquated jaloppies in some state of repair), office and living quarters for the resident manager, a warehouse, pumphouse, hose-cart shed, incinerator, shower baths and sanitary units, laundry units and clotheslines. It would be difficult to overemphasize the importance of the fact that the camps provide migratory workers, for the first time, with an adequate supply of decent drinking water and proper sanitation.

The managers have been carefully instructed to establish a large measure of self-government in the camps. What they have attempted to do is to introduce the "town-hall" type of government. The Campers' Committee, for example, attends to all matters of discipline and law and order within the camp, and settles all controversial issues. Under the manager's supervision, each person is expected to contribute two hours' work a week toward the upkeep of the camp, and, in cases where a family cannot pay the ten-cents-a-day fee, they are supposed to work two hours a day. A Recreation and Entertainment Committee has charge of various social and athletic activities (recently an impromptu program was broadcast from one of the camps). A Child Welfare Committee and the Good Neighbors Committee have charge of various aspects of camp life. Every effort is made to induce the campers to solve their own problems. The Good Neighbors Committee, for example, collects and repairs old clothes for those in need. Without exception, the resident managers report that their methods meet with an excellent response on the part of the workers, who

show, when encouraged, great capacity for self-government.

I have been privileged to study a series of weekly reports
submitted by Mr. Tom Collins, manager of the Arvin Camp,
to his superiors. In addition to being social documents of
the first importance, these reports make fascinating reading. To take a sample week, Mr. Collins tells of the arrival
in the camp of a woman so filthy that she resembled an
animal: She had been living for two months on a vacant
lot. The whole camp is excited over the arrival of a baby —
the first to be born in the camp. Again, Mr. Collins is busy
instructing mothers on the technique of trimming toenails,
and the general advisability of the procedure, and the
use of toilet paper (many of them had never used toilet
paper in their lives). He then has to turn his attention to
the Baby Clinic, which is well attended, and to the lectures
sponsored by the Good Neighbors Committee for the
women living in the camp. A baseball game has to be supervised; the weekly dance organized; and committees must
be put to work cutting weeds and painting. He notes with
approval that the residents soon change their diet; "the
old reliable sow belly" is being replaced by fruit and
vegetables. In reading these reports, one can see a whole
new community coming into existence as these courageous
people, who have suffered untold privation for years,
slowly begin to rehabilitate themselves with the slight
assistance, guidance and support that is given them. Of
the utmost importance is the fact that the workers are
permitted to meet in the assembly hall and discuss their
problems. No attempt is made to organize the workers,
but the managers all recognize that the residents of the

camp, as American citizens, are free to join any organization they desire. It is strictly up to them, as individuals, whether they want to join a union or not. Potentially the camps provide the measure of stabilization from which organization will unquestionably develop. While living in the camps, the workers can hold meetings; they cannot be evicted; and a measure of protection against vigilantism exists.

In much of the current writing on the problem of farm labor in California, the migratory camps have been hailed as a solution of the farm-labor problem. But the migratory camps are not a solution: They are merely demonstrations of what might be accomplished. At the present time, the camps are wholly inadequate; they provide shelter for only a small portion of the workers involved. It should be pointed out, moreover, that the camps enable the residents to work at very low wages and, to this extent, they have probably tended to keep farm wages at a sub-subsistence level. The solution of the farm-labor problem can only be achieved through the organization of farm workers. The chief significance of the migratory camps is that they provide an agency through which organization can be achieved. Quite apart from this consideration, however, they are social agencies of great practical importance and they demonstrate that the stabilization of migratory labor can be accomplished. Already it is planned to augment the camps by granting five-and-ten-acre tracts to the residents at nominal prices. The Farm Security Administration has also taken over the experimental co-operative farm which the Resettlement Administration planned at Mineral Kings, California, and this experiment will be watched with great interest. California agriculture would lend itself admirably to collective control and operation, and the long-range significance of the migratory camps consists in the fact that they represent an initial step toward a collective agricultural economy. At first regarded as temporary makeshifts, it is now generally conceded that the migratory camps are here to stay.

## CHAPTER XVII

## THE END OF A CYCLE

IN 1937 it became increasingly apparent that a basic change had taken place in the character of farm labor in California. Although the change had been taking place for some time, it was suddenly realized in 1937 that the bulk of the State's migratory workers were white Americans and that the foreign racial groups were no longer a dominant factor. The change had, in fact, commenced about 1933, at the bottom of the depression. At the end of 1934, the Commission of Immigration and Housing estimated that roughly fifty per cent of the labor-camp population was native white American, with about one third Mexican and the balance made up of Filipinos (eleven per cent), Japanese (three per cent), and Chinese (three per cent). The first reaction to this discovery was rather naive: "Our Race Problems Vanish," editorialized the *San Francisco News*, pointing out that the possibility of a "permanently stratified society in California" would probably cease with the elimination of the minority racial groups. But the pattern of exploitation has not been altered; it remains exactly the same. The established pattern has been somewhat as follows: to bring in successive minority groups; to exploit them until the advantages of exploitation have been exhausted; and then to expel them in favor of more readily exploitable material. In this manner the Chinese, the Japanese, the Filipinos, and the Mexicans have, as it were, been run through the hopper. From what source, then, was the latest army being recruited? The answer was soon forthcoming: from the stricken dust-bowl areas, from Oklahoma, Texas, Arkansas. The new recruits were refugees from drought and disaster. The circumstances of their misery made them admirable recruits. They came in without expense to the growers; they were excellent workers; they brought their families; they were so impoverished that they would work for whatever wage was offered. They came, moreover, in great numbers. The growers naturally seized upon these workers as a providential dispensation. But they failed to perceive that, with the arrival of the dust-bowl refugees, a cycle of exploitation had been brought to a close. These despised "Okies" and "Texicans" were not another minority alien racial group (although they were treated as such) but American citizens familiar with the usages of democracy. With the arrival of the dust-bowl refugees a day of reckoning approaches for the California farm industrialists. The jig, in other words, is about up. To see this development in proper perspective, a few words of explanation are essential.

### 1. Tramps and Migrants

The first consideration to be kept in mind is that the influx of dust-bowl refugees differs qualitatively and quantitatively from previous migrations. As I have shown in earlier chapters, the California growers themselves set in motion the currents of migratory labor: first, by expropriating

the small settlers and squatters; second, by deliberately encouraging and soliciting "tourist" emigration through the
activities of the California Development Association and
similar organizations; third, by recruiting, particularly in
the nineties, out-of-state workers; and, fourth, by fostering the "Dirty Plate Route" along which the tramps, bindle
stiffs, bums and hoboes of former years used to plod their
way on foot and by freight cars. In fact, the tramp as
such, the authentic hobo of California tradition, has never
passed out of existence. Stubble-bearded, with his roll of
blankets, he can be seen today plodding along the highway
trying to thumb a ride. The old current of migration,
which the growers set in motion, still circulates. Likewise,
the custom of recruiting out-of-State labor for specific
purposes, such as breaking a strike, is still continued. For
example, on April 11, 1938, forty-six Mexican strike-
breakers from Uvalde, Texas, were escorted into California under an armed convoy and taken to a strike area
near Bakersfield, the armed guard being furnished by the
Associated Farmers. Another refinement must be noted:
The professional "fruit tramp" still exists. Mr. William
Plunkert, in an admirable social document, has traced
the life history of a family which has "followed the crops"
in California for twenty-four years. Thirty-five members
of this family, directly and indirectly related, follow the
crops in California today. Workers of this type have
grown up, so to speak, with California agriculture. They
have no habitat; they are permanent migrants, with their
own traveling equipment, possessing an intimate knowledge of the ebb and flow of the crop harvests. They require no bulletins for their guidance. They know instinc-

tively, for example, when cherries are ripe in the San Joaquin and when the peach harvest starts in the Sacramento Valley. Without a fixed place of abode, these workers are nevertheless Californians. They constitute, however, a factor of diminishing importance. They really belong to the past. It should be pointed out, also, that families from Texas and Oklahoma appeared in the valleys as early as 1921,[1] primarily as cotton pickers.

But the migration which began in 1933, and which rapidly increased throughout 1934, 1935, 1936 and 1937, has been of an entirely different character. The presence of these latter-day emigrants was not altogether solicited (although many of them say that they had read advertisements for work in California); they came like grasshoppers driven before a storm. They have come, moreover, in such numbers as to constitute a major migration somewhat comparable to the great influx of '49. During the year 1935–1936, 87,302 migratory workers entered California, of whom nine tenths were white persons and over a third of whom were from Oklahoma, Texas and Arkansas. It has been estimated that a total of 221,000 have entered the State since 1933 (the Farm Security Administration, on April 5, 1938, announced that it was attempting to provide for 45,500 destitute dust-bowl refugees in California who had been "burned out, blown out, eaten out"). On November 20, 1937, 3000 pea pickers entered the Imperial Valley from Arizona. The caravan of cars made up four lines of traffic along the highway, with as many as thirteen people to the car, the largest single influx of its kind ever noted by local authorities. *Business Week*, for July 3, 1937,

[1] See *Pacific Rural Press*, October 21, 1921.

estimated that 30,000 *families* had entered California from the dust bowl and aptly characterized this shift in population as "one of the greatest inter-State migrations since the gold rush." "This," commented the *Pacific Rural Press* for May 22, 1937, "is not a bindle stiff movement."

The new migrants have come, for the most part, in dilapidated flivvers and incredibly ancient jaloppies. They have migrated as families, bringing their possessions with them, and they are in search of homes. Most of them are in California to stay. They are, in general, white Americans. "Long lanky Oklahomans with small heads, blue eyes, and surrounded by tow-headed children; bronzed Texans with a drawl, clean-cut features and an aggressive spirit; men and women from Arizona, Arkansas, New Mexico, Missouri, and Kansas." Some 43,000 men, women and children entered the State in the six months ending December 15, 1935. Once within the State, these emigrants have not come to rest; they have been necessarily swept along by the established currents of migratory farm labor. Entering, for the most part, through the Imperial Valley, they have worked their way north following the crops. To-day they are scattered throughout the State and constitute, needless to say, one of the gravest social problems facing the people of California. Their presence has completely altered the farm-labor equation. Before discussing the new situation, it is important to stress the fact that two types of migration are involved in California farm labor: migration *into* the State and migration *within* the State. To some extent, as I will point out, the first type of migration has been checked; but migration within the State is, so to speak, functional. The alternation of the crops in different sections requires wholesale mass movements from county to county: a constant ebb and flow, with families moving, during the harvest seasons, every few weeks.

## 2. *The Border Patrol*

The acute social problem presented by this amazing emigration was soon accentuated by other factors. On September 20, 1935, the Federal Emergency Relief Administration ordered the liquidation of the Federal Transient Service, which had, at one time, provided relief for 38,815 transients in California: 13.5 per cent of all transients in the country. With the abrupt discontinuance of Federal assistance, the local authorities became wildly hysterical. The methods by which they have ever since attempted to cope with the problem have been, to say the least, curious. The first step in this direction was the creation of the Los Angeles Committee on Indigent Alien Transients, headed by James E. Davis, Chief of Police. In flat disregard of constitutional provisions, this power-drunk functionary of the Los Angeles Chamber of Commerce proceeded to establish some sixteen border patrols staffed by the Los Angeles City Police, the patrols being located in counties hundreds of miles removed from Los Angeles. Throughout November and December, 1935, and January, February, March and April, 1936, some 125 policemen stationed at these various points of entry stopped all cars that looked as though they might contain "unemployables" and turned them back. When a court action was brought in the United States District Court by the American Civil Liberties Union, to test the constitutionality of this procedure, the Chief of Police detailed the head of his celebrated "Intelligence Squad" to "work over" the plaintiff in whose name the action had been commenced. Not only was the plaintiff himself intimidated, but his wife and child were threatened and browbeaten by police officers (one of whom has since been convicted in Los Angeles of attempted murder); and, ultimately, the plaintiff was "induced" to drop the action. The patrol unquestionably checked the influx of refugees, but the effect of the blockade was to "back up" the refugees and temporarily delay their entry into California. Repercussions of the blockade were felt as far East as El Paso.[1]

Recourse was had to other time-honored stratagems to stem the tide of migrants. A bill was introduced in the Legislature to bar all transients from the State; stiff vagrancy sentences were given "alien transients"; transients failing to meet the three-years' residence requirement for relief, were left to starve; many were rounded up by the relief officials and shipped out of the State; and, in the rural counties, transients were shifted back and forth from one county to the other, in the vain and foolish hope that, somehow, in this elaborate reshuffling process, they would suddenly disappear. By these and other methods, the influx was somewhat checked (the border patrol was, for example, given wide publicity in the Middle West); but the transient problem remained. Nothing was done, of course, to settle the matter and the transients were left to fend for themselves. An obliging people, they continued to starve until

[1] See *Monthly Labor Review*. December 1936.

a series of major revelations focused public attention on a problem that could no longer be ignored.[2]

### 3. Nipomo

The first revelation to attract widespread attention had to do with 2000 pea pickers marooned in Nipomo, a small community north of Santa Barbara. For two preceding seasons, labor contractors, licensed by the State of California, had been permitted to advertise in Arizona newspapers for "thousands" of pea pickers, promising work "for the season." In response to these appeals, 2000 workers had assembled at Nipomo in the spring of 1937 only to discover, of course, that there was work for but a third of their number. To complicate matters, rain destroyed a portion of the crop and flooded the camp of the workers. Those who had any funds at all moved on; some sold what belongings they had and tried to escape. But about 2000, trapped in their miserable camp, were actually starving when a representative of the Federal Surplus Commodities Corporation discovered their plight. Local authorities admitted that there was "some distress" but tried to duck responsibility. Federal agencies rushed in supplies of food and medicine, and managed to help the workers along until the other crops matured. The pictures taken at this camp, by Federal representatives, are almost incredible in their revelation of the plight of 2000 starving, dirty, utterly dejected men, women and children. I know of nothing com-

---

[2] See "Towards a National Policy for Migration," by Eric Beecroft and Seymour Janow, *Social Forces*, May, 1938; and "Labor on Wheels," by Frank J. Taylor *Country Gentleman*, July, 1938.

parable to these pictures except the scenes of the famine areas in postwar Europe. But irony must be added to misery in order to complete the picture. When the pea pickers who remained in the camp until the storms were over and the picking started attempted to strike on April 15, 1937, for decent wages, the local sheriff told them to go to work or leave the county or face arrest on vagrancy charges. To back up this ultimatum, he proceeded to swear in over a hundred special deputy sheriffs. Needless to say, there was no strike.

A bad situation, indeed; but precisely the same tragedy occurred in the spring of 1938. On March 11, 1938, the press announced that six hundred families were again stranded at Nipomo, where labor contractors for the third year had overestimated the number of workers required. In this instance, the fact of destitution was admitted. Local authorities conceded that the workers were starving; and even the *Los Angeles Times* reported that both children and adults were suffering from malnutrition and that one child had died from starvation. But the local authorities and the newspapers have short memories. For, according to both sources, "an acute labor shortage" had existed in 1937 and again in 1938. The Santa Barbara newspapers, for example, had headlined stories in 1937 about "Supervisors Make It Possible For Growers To Attract Help," going on to point out that the county had opened a camp for workers (incidentally, at the prohibitive rate of one dollar a day per individual) by way of encouraging additional migratory workers to assemble for work. (The effect of maintaining such a camp at public expense was, of course, to assume a portion of the obligation which rightly belonged to the growers and, by so doing, to further lower existing wage rates.) The *Los Angeles Times* in 1937 had carried stories of a "Crop Crisis" in Santa Barbara and had demanded that the relief authorities rush workers to the harvest areas. Yet when a real crisis, not a crop crisis but a crisis affecting two thousand people, developed, these same agencies adopted an ostrichlike attitude, and, for a time, pretended to hear no cries of distress and seemed unable to see or to acknowledge human misery. This same stupid and brutal hypocrisy has been revealed in numerous similar "crises." When authorities in the coastal counties (San Luis Obispo and Santa Barbara) finally realized that they had a problem to solve, they resorted to a childish stratagem: Two thousand dollars was jointly appropriated to buy gasoline for the stranded workers in order to dump them into the lap of the inland counties. The idea being, of course, to get rid of these burdensome workers, who had just picked a bumper crop at sub-subsistence wage rates, at any cost. Nor was this the end of the episode: At the conclusion of the 1938 season, Santa Barbara County announced that it had erected "a legal fence" of officers to keep unemployable transients out of the county — that is, of course, until the next harvest.

## 4. The Crisis in the San Joaquin

In July, 1937, Californians were shocked by a sensational address by Mr. Harold Robertson, national field secretary of the Gospel Army, who charged that 70,000 transients were starving in the great valley of the San Joaquin. Speaking from personal observation, Mr. Robertson announced that "people are seeking shelter and subsistence in the fields and woods like wild animals" and that children were working in the cotton fields for 15 cents and 20 cents a day. Lured to the valley by announcements that 25,000 additional workers were required to harvest the 1937 cotton crop, a vast army of transients had assembled there to starve. Under the impetus of this forceful address, the social agencies got busy and conducted an investigation which amply confirmed the charges. The *Los Angeles Times*, taking cognizance of the crisis, sent a special correspondent into the San Joaquin areas who confirmed the findings of Mr. Robertson and added a few grim details based upon his own observations. Although everyone in California conceded that a grave crisis existed in the summer of 1937 — the point of maximum employment — nothing whatever was done to guard against the obvious consequences. The transients, herded together like cattle, were permitted to eke out an existence in the fantastic hope that they would ultimately disperse, vanish into the sky or march over the mountains and into the sea or be swallowed up by the rich and fertile earth. But they did not move, and with the winter season came heavy rains and floods. Soon a major crisis was admitted to exist, with over 50,000 workers destitute and starving. The situation was tided over, for the time being, when the Farm Security Administration assumed the burden of supporting the transients. But the problem has not been solved: It has merely been shoved forward. And the army of transients continues to camp in the San Joaquin.

From an investigation conducted by the State Relief Administration in 1936, and from later investigations in

1937, supported by some excellent stories in the *San Francisco News* by Mr. John Steinbeck, Mr. Theodore Smith, and Miss Tessie Williams and a series of articles in the *San Francisco Chronicle* by Mr. Robert E. Girvin, it is possible to summarize the actual condition of migratory labor in California with reference to housing, health and sanitation, education and employment. The facts may be summarized briefly; but they are illuminating and require neither emphasis nor elaboration.

With the exception of one or two large ranches, the investigators agreed that the housing situation was indescribably wretched. One investigator reported that he had found a two-room cabin in which forty-one people from Southeastern Oklahoma were living; another described a one-room shack in which fifteen men, women and children, "festering sores of humanity," lived in "unimaginable filth." The State Immigration and Housing Commission on December 3, 1937, ordered thirty shanties near Visalia condemned as "unfit for human habitation." Most of the boasted "model camps" maintained by the growers were found to be without baths, showers or plumbing; in most districts, the workers bathed in and drank from irrigation ditches. Eighteen families were found living near Kingsburg, under a bridge. Workers in large numbers were found living in shacks built of linoleum and cardboard cartons; in tents improvised of gunny sacks on canal banks with coffee cans serving for chimneys on their makeshift stoves; in some cases a bit of carpet or sacking had been tacked against a tree for shelter. One investigator found an entire tent city consisting of "dirty, torn tents and makeshift shacks in a sea of mud." Most of the ranches, it develops, charge from $3 to $15 a

month for the wretched accommodations they provide
the workers and sell water at 5 cents a bucket. One ranch,
taken as typical, provided a single bath house and a single
shower in connection with a block of houses capable of
housing 400 people. Along the way to the camps, "beside
the road are sights reminiscent of Death Valley, with heaps
of abandoned automobiles and farm tools, junked, rusting."
"A visit to these squatter camps," wrote Mr. Ray Zeman
of the *Los Angeles Times*, "leaves one aghast."

Health and sanitary conditions were found to be equally
appalling. Six thousand cases of influenza broke out in one
county in February, 1937, largely among migratory workers, and between 75 and 100 cases developed into pneumonia
with fifteen deaths. All the local health authorities agreed
that the presence of a vast army of destitute migratory
workers was responsible for the outbreak of numerous epidemics. "At times we have to move them along as a health
measure," was the cynical comment of one health officer.
In an attempt to protect the public health, officials in one
county lined up 7000 migratory workers, in the camps,
and conducted a mass compulsory vaccination. Most districts in the San Joaquin Valley were afflicted with various epidemics: influenza, typhoid fever, colds, infantile
paralysis, skin diseases. Fifty babies, the children of migratory workers, died of diarrhea and enteritis in one county
in a single season. Children were reported dying in Tulare
County at the rate of two a day, with 90 per cent of the
mortality being among the children of migratory workers.
In one ditch camp, 27 out of 30 children examined were
found to be defective through malnutritional diseases; some
25,000 families were reported in need of medical care and

treatment. Inspecting eighteen camps in a four-mile radius of Kingsburg, Tessie Williams found "dozens of children with horribly sore eyes; many cases of cramps, diarrhea and dysentery; fever, colds, and sore throats." She reported the case of one woman who was taken from the county hospital, after being confined, and returned with her baby to live in the shade of a tree. Many women told her that they had lost babies for three and four successive years. Everywhere the rural hospitals were overcrowded. Dr. Omer Mills of the Farm Security Administration visited the San Joaquin area on January 25, 1937, and reported such typical cases as a man, woman and child who had lived on a diet of bread and potatoes for four weeks; and the presence of hundreds of children (165 in one camp) living "like little wild animals." Local health officers attempt to render some aid in the case of infectious diseases; but they usually remain more or less indifferent to cases of non-infectious illnesses and malnutritional diseases. Observed diets were: for a family of seven, beans and fried dough; family of six, fried oatmeal; family of eight (with six children) dandelion greens and boiled potatoes. "I'm getting mighty tired of just beans and water," said one woman, "but even that may run out any day now." In cases of childbirth, prenatal care was reported as almost unknown and the presence of a doctor at the time of delivery was described as quite exceptional. In his novel *In Dubious Battle*, John Steinbeck describes a confinement in a jungle camp, the details of which were incredible to many readers. Later investigations have revealed many similar cases. An entire volume of documentation could be supplied on the subject of health and hygiene.

The picture of the educational situation was no less distressing. Local school authorities were reported as powerless to cope with the problem. During the height of the harvest season, the schools in the rural areas are extremely crowded. When the post-season exodus begins, fifty per cent of the enrollment may drop out of attendance. In one area, the investigators found a cow barn which had been converted into a schoolhouse. I quote a few lines of description (from a report of the State Board of Health): "There were no glass windows; the only openings were sections of the wall which could be propped out, and since it was winter they were closed. Some small screened openings provided all the light and ventilation. Consequently the atmosphere was dense, especially as the native effluvium of the recently washed floor mixed with other odors." A survey of the schools in Bakersfield and Taft indicated that 8515 pupils entered the rural schools of Kern County in one season and 6450 moved out, with students hailing from Oklahoma, Texas and Arkansas leading the list. Fully half of the students move twice during the school year; five, six and seven moves are not uncommon. The effect of this constant shifting is generally bad, as might be expected. Even the parents comment upon it. "There is a growing consciousness," writes Dr. Paul Taylor, "that for many of their kind the future portends, not progress from generation to generation, but retrogression." He quotes one migrant: "My children ain't raised decent like I was raised by my father. There were no rag houses then, but I can't do no better."

Most of the investigators, however, failed to realize that exactly these same conditions have existed for fifty years in California. In an article entitled "California the Golden" which appeared in *The American Child*, November, 1920, Emma Duke pointed out that thousands of children under the age of sixteen were working in the California fields; 3000 in the cotton fields alone. She noticed children five years of age picking cotton in California. She also discovered that local school board officials ignored the problem; that they seemed eager to overlook the fact that the children of migratory workers were not attending school, as they did not want to burden the schools or to detract from the educational facilities afforded their own children. Even where the local authorities were inclined to insist that migratory children attend school, the nomadic nature of the employment followed by their parents made it almost impossible to enforce the school laws. In a pamphlet on migratory child labor in California by George B. Mangold and Lillian B. Hill, issued June 28, 1929, the same conditions are described. The authors of this pamphlet state that, in 1929, there were 36,891 children reported in the school census in California who claimed no permanent residence and were migrants. A special legislative act was passed to set up some method of providing educational instruction for migratory children, but the appropriations for the department have been wholly inadequate (at one time, the appropriation was $5000 a year). Miss Hill found that migratory children were herded together in garages, school corridors and abandoned barns, with as many as 125 children for one instructor. Care was taken, also, to segregate migratory children and to discriminate against them, both as to the character and the extent of their education. Migratory children were made to attend school from 7:30 A.M. to 12 o'clock so that they might then be excused to work in the fields. The policy back of this type of discrimination was announced as an attempt to "adjust the child to the crop." Most migratory children can only attend school for a few months during the year; they are generally backward, because of lack of opportunity and fatigue, and many of them are so retarded that they fall into the second, third and fourth grades.

In two eloquent and moving articles appearing in *Hearst's International Magazine* for February and March, 1924, under the title "Little Gypsies of the Fruit," Arthur Gleason described conditions that have not changed in the intervening fourteen years, except to grow worse. Migratory existence, he wrote, unsettles the life of children. "It turns home life into a drifting gypsy existence. The family becomes wagon tramps instead of settlers and citizens. It smashes schooling into broken bits at one or two way stations each year. You can't educate a procession. Even a sailor and a drummer have somewhere to return. A street gamin has a block and a slum tenement. But these children have no fixed center. They are children of the crops. They are born in the crops. The crops condition their lives, bring them into a ranch, send them on to another county, and pull them back just one year later." Interviewing these children, he asked one of them: "Where is your home?" and received the reply: "Home? We're cotton pickers." He found one girl who was the fastest grape picker in her section, but a village doctor told him the youngster was "so keyed up that she can't sleep nights." Most of the crop children, who reported at the migratory schools, were definitely retarded; he estimated, in fact, that 50 per cent of them were "hopelessly retarded." "In the prune country," he writes, "a friend of mine went into the shack of the Meronda family at eight o'clock in the evening. The twelve-year-old boy was in bed asleep. His hands were moving ceaselessly in sleep, traveling across the sheet and picking at it. 'What is the matter?' asked my friend. And the boy's mother answered: 'He does that sometimes when he's asleep. He thinks he is picking prunes.'"

The investigations of 1937 revealed that migratory workers were receiving incredibly low wages. Dr. Omer Mills found wages in the cotton district to be as low as 50 cents a day and that they were tending to decrease; he also found that some workers were making $2 and $3 a week and were attempting to support families on these earnings. Dr. Paul Taylor estimates the average annual income for migratory workers at between $350 and $400. The State Relief Administration estimates that most agricultural workers only have employment for six months in the year or less; and that the average yearly earnings per family group dropped from $381 in 1930 to $289 in 1935. In the same study, the S.R.A. estimated that each family, in 1935, should have had at least $780 to eke out an existence. The average period of employment for migratory workers is nowhere more than thirty weeks a year. In the summer of 1937, during the height of the harvest season, 6000 migratory workers applied for relief in the San Joaquin Valley alone. In 1932 there were 181 agricultural workers for every 100 jobs offered; in 1933, 185; and for the first seven months of 1934, 142. The same report indicates 60,000 unemployed agricultural workers as of April, 1935, in the face of the growers' insistence that an "acute labor shortage" existed.

Most of the investigators agree that the new migrants, the dust-bowl refugees, are here to stay. Mr. Ray Zeman estimated that at least 95 per cent of the transients who had come to California from the dust bowl had no intention of returning: "They are mobile only in following the seasonal work north and south in the valley." Most of them lost their residence in the States from which they fled and are determined to acquire legal residence in California. The prejudice against the migratory worker has always been intense, white migratory workers being treated in exactly the same manner as their predecessors, the Mexicans and the Japanese. As most of the migrants have not acquired legal residence, and therefore cannot vote, they can be discriminated against with political immunity. The "Okies" and the "Texicans" are looked down upon by the Californians and this curious condescension is reflected by the local officialdom. Mrs. Joan Pratt, county welfare departmen director in Tulare County, complains: "You can't change the habits of primitive people from the Southern and Middle Western States. You can't force them to bathe or to eat vegetables." A local police officer gives his view: "A shiftless stock and inclined to petty thievery and shirking of work." The field investigators, however, are unanimous in reporting that the dust-bowl refugees are orderly, neighborly — a patient and kindly folk — and that they "quickly assimilate new habits."

## 5. The Future

There is no longer any equivocation in California: The problem of migratory labor, dramatized and intensified by the influx of dust-bowl refugees, has forced public recognition of an acute social problem. But, as in the past, the same fumbling remedies are suggested. It has been advocated, for example, that the States, by interstate pacts, should regulate the movement of unemployed transients; that the Federal Government should once again directly assume the burden of housing, feeding and transporting the transient population; that California should force the Eastern States "to put their own house in order" — whatever that may mean — before admitting any further transients into the State. The press has, in fact, been inundated with other, and sillier, remedies and proposals.

The significance of the present situation is that it is now theoretically possible to solve the farm-labor problem in California. With the influx of thousands of transients, we now have a superabundance of skilled agricultural labor. The race problem has, in effect, been largely eliminated. The growers themselves, through their various labor exchanges and pools, have demonstrated that the demand for farm labor can be estimated with sufficient accuracy for purposes of regulating the supply. The migratory camps have proved that a measure of stabilization can be achieved or at least that large groups of workers can be stabilized within a definite area. The introduction of new crops has now made it feasible to extend the period of employment almost throughout the year, assuming that the supply of labor is regulated. But these developments are merely signposts along the way. The real solution involves the substitution of collective agriculture for the present monopolistically owned and controlled system. As a first step in the direction of collectivization, agricultural workers must be organized. Once they are organized, they can work out the solutions for most of their immediate problems. They can, for example, regulate employment through hiring halls similar in operation to those used on the waterfront with such great success. With public encouragement and assistance, they can solve most of the immediate problems of housing, education and health conditions. A partial solution will be achieved when subsistence homesteads have grown up about the migratory camps; such an arrangement should bring about a large measure of permanent stabilization. But the final solution will come only when the present wasteful, vicious, undemocratic and thoroughly antisocial system of agricultural ownership in California is abolished. The abolition of this system involves at most merely a change in ownership. The collective principle is there; large units of operation have been established, only they are being exploited by private interests for their own ends. California agriculture is a magnificent achievement: in its scope, efficiency, organization and amazing abundance. The great farm valleys of California, rescued from sagebrush and desert, are easily among the richest agricultural regions of the world. The anachronistic system of ownership by which they are at present controlled must be changed before the valleys can come into their own. That day, as it now seems, is far distant. In the meantime, the dust-bowl refugees, unlike the pioneers of '49, have made the long trek West to find not gold but labor camps and improvised shantytowns. It is just possible that these latest recruits for the farm factories may be the last, and that out of their struggle for a decent life in California may issue a new type of agricultural economy for the West and for America.

# BIBLIOGRAPHY

This bibliography is a list of general sources for further reading prepared for the first edition. Following the SOCIAL CONDITIONS category is a general updated bibliography prepared by the author for the 1971 edition.

## CALIFORNIA AGRICULTURE

*Agricultural Inquiry*, April 1917, University of California

*Agricultural Labor in the United States, 1915–1935*, Dec. 1935, Bureau of Agricultural Economics

*Agricultural Labor in the United States*, 1936–1937, Bureau of Agricultural Economics

*California Farm Labor*, April 1936–Dec. 1935, Paul S. Taylor and Tom Vasey

"California Farm Labor Problems," April 7, 1936, Commonwealth Club, Vol. XII, No. 14

*California's Fruit Growers and the Labor Supply*, Dec. 1902, Transactions of the Twenty-seventh State Fruit Growers Convention by H. P. Stabler

*California Fruit Growers Exchange*, July 1936, *Fortune*

*Di Giorgio*, Aug. 15, 1937, *Los Angeles Times* — Kenneth Crist

"Farm Labor," May 1918, Commonwealth Club, Vol. XIII, No. 3

*Farm Management*, Chapter XXII: "Farm Labor," 1921, R. L. Adams

"Getting Together," July 10, 1920, *California Cultivator* by A. L. Spellmeyer

*Harvest of the Years*, 1927, Luther Burbank

*History of California Labor Legislation*, 1910, Lucille Eaves

*Preliminary Report on the Economic Situation of California Agriculture*, February 1938, Simon J. Lubin Society

"Reducing Labor Costs," Sept. 19, 1921, *California Citrograph*, G. B. Hodkkin

*Report on Agricultural Labor*, Jan. 14, 1935, N. Gregory Silvermaster to National Labor Mediation Board

*Seasonal Labor Requirements for California Agriculture*, July 1938, University of California Bulletin No. 623 by R. L. Adams

*Something about Sugar*, 1917, George M. Rolph

*Sugar*, 1897, Herbert Myrick

Transactions of the California State Agricultural Society, 1882, 1885, 1886

### FICTION

*Afoot and Alone*, 1872, Stephen Powers

*California Gringos*, 1930, H. A. Van Coenen Torchiana

*Casa Grande*, 1906, Charles Duff Stuart

*Feud of Oakville Creek*, Josiah Royce

"Fruit Tramp," July 1934, Daniel Mainwaring, *Harper's Magazine*

"*Golden State*," Oct. 29, 1938, David Lamson, *Saturday Evening Post*

*Grapes of Wrath*, 1939, John Steinbeck

*In Dubious Battle*, 1936, John Steinbeck

*Octopus, The*, 1901, Frank Norris

*Of Mice and Men*, 1937, John Steinbeck

*Ramona*, 1884, Helen Hunt Jackson

*Seed of the Sun*, 1921, Wallace Irwin

*Wild Orchard*, 1927, Dan Totheroh

### LABOR DISTURBANCES

"Autopsy on the General Strike," Aug. 1, 1934, Miriam Allen de Ford, *Nation*

"Battle of Sacramento," July 20, 1935, Bruce Minton, *New Republic*

"California Casualty List," Aug. 29, 1934, Lew Levenson, *Nation*

"California Justice," Feb. 12, 1935, *New Masses*

"California's Embattled Farmers," June 8, 1934, Commonwealth Club, address before, by Ralph H. Taylor

"Can the Radicals Capture the Farms of California?" March 23, 1934, Commonwealth Club, address before, by Simon J. Lubin

"Farm Labor Disputes Board, A," Dec. 22, 1936, Commonwealth Club, Vol. XII

"Fascism on the West Coast," Feb. 28, 1934, Ella Winter, *Nation*

*Free the Imperial Valley Prisoners*, Pamphlet. Introduction by J. Louis Engdahl refers to Imperial Valley situation in 1930

"General Strike – Labor Bids for Power," July 18, 1934, Miriam Allen de Ford, *Nation*

"Gunkist Oranges," Carey McWilliams, *Pacific Weekly*

"Lettuce – with American Dressing," May 15, 1935, James Rorty, *Nation*

"Marysville Strike," April 4, 1914, Inez Haynes Gilmore, *Harper's Weekly*

"Mexican Strike at El Monte," July–Aug. 1934, Charles B. Spaulding, *Sociology and Social Research*

"Porterhouse Heaven and the Hobo," Aug. 1914, Walter V. Woehlke, *Technical World*

"Red-Baiters' Holiday in Sacramento," March 13, 1935, Frances Clement, *Nation*

"Removing the Cause of Labor Unrest," Dec. 8, 1934, Ernest E. Behr, *California Cultivator*

"Salinas," Sept. 21, 1936, Citizens Welfare League Report

"San Diego I.W.W.," July 6, 1912, Walter V. Woehlke, *Outlook*

"San Francisco's Labor War," June 13, 1934, Evelyn Seeley, *Nation*

Statistical Information on Agricultural Strikes in California in 1934, N. Gregory Silvermaster, Director of Division of Research and Surveys, CSERA, to National Labor Mediation Board

"Terror in San Jose," Aug. 8, 1934, John Terry, *Nation*

"That California Dictatorship," Feb. 20, 1935, Norman Mini, *Nation*

"Trial by Vigilantes," Feb. 14, 1935, Bruce Minton, *New Masses*

*Union Smashing in Sacramento*, Aug. 1935, Herbert Solow (pamphlet)

"Wheatland Riots," May 16, 1914, Travers Clements, *Outlook*

### LANDOWNERSHIP

*Cattle King* [Biography of Henry Miller], 1931, Edward F. Treadwell

"Farm Colonies of the Salvation Army," Sept. 1903, Commander Booth Tucker, Bulletin of the Bureau of Labor

"Farm Tenancy," Feb. 1937, Report of the President's Committee

"Feudalism in California," May 24, 1919, W. J. Ghent, *Survey*

Final Report, Division of Land Settlement, June 30, 1931, Report of the Committee on Swamp and Overflow Lands, State of California

*Fraudulent California Land Grants*, 1926, Clinton Johnson

*Great American Land Bubble*, 1932, A. M. Sakolski

"Land Tenancy in California," Nov. 1922, Commonwealth Club, Vol. XVII, No. 10

*Patrons of Husbandry on the Pacific Coast*, 1875, Ezra S. Carr

*Poor and the Land, The*, 1905, H. Rider Haggard

Report of the Commissioners of the General Land Office, 1885, State of California

Report on Land Colonization and Rural Credits, Nov. 29, 1916, California State Printing Office

Report on Large Landholdings in Southern California, 1919, W. J. Ghent, California Division of Immigration and Housing

*Romance and History of California Ranchos*, 1935, Myrtle Garrison

*Single Tax Movement in the United States*, 1916, Arthur Nichols Young

"State Colony Settlements," Nov. 1921, Commonwealth Club, Vol. XVI, No. 8

### MIGRANTS AND TRANSIENTS

"Drought Refugees and Labor Migration to California, June to Dec. 1935," Feb. 1936, Paul S. Taylor and Tom Vasey, *Monthly Labor Review*

"Labor on Wheels," July 1938, Frank J. Taylor, *Country Gentleman*

"Lean Time Ahead for Migrants," May 23–24–25, 1938, *San Francisco News*

"Mexican Children," Aug. 1, 1928, Martha Walter, *Survey*

*Migratory Labor in California*, July 11, 1936, State Relief Administration

"National Policy on Migration," May 17, 1938, Jerry Voorhis, *Congressional Record*

"No Jobs in California," November 2, 1930, *Saturday Evening Post*

"Nomads of the California Farms," Feb. 4–19, 1938, *San Francisco News*

*San Francisco Chronicle*, March 14, 1937, Herbert E. Girvin, series of articles beginning noted date

"Squatters," July 25, 1937, Ray Zeman, *Los Angeles Times*

*Survey of Kern County Migratory Labor Problems*, July 1930 to July 1937, Dr. Joe Smith

"Survey of Labor Migration," July 1937, N. A. Talles, *Monthly Labor Review*

"Towards a National Policy for Migration," May 1938, Eric Beecroft and Seymour Janow, *Social Forces*

*Transients and Migrants*, Feb. 27, 1939, Victor Jones, Bureau of Public Administration, University of California at Berkeley

*Transients in California*, Aug. 3, 1936, State Relief Administration

Unemployment and Relief, Feb. 8, 1938 through April 8, 1938, Congressional hearings

"What Shall We Do with Them?" April 15, 1938, Commonwealth Club, address before, by Paul S. Taylor

## MINORITY GROUPS

### GENERAL

*Alien Americans*, 1936, B. Schrieke

*California and the Oriental*, June 19, 1920, State Board of Control of California

"Colony Life in Southern California," Nov. 1886, George H. Fitch, *Cosmopolitan*

*Common Sense Applied to the Immigrant Question*, 1869. C. T. Hopkins

*Immigrants in Industries*, Vol. II, Part 25, Page 69

*Industrial Commission of Immigration*, 1901, Vol. 15, Page 500

"Land, Crops and the Oriental," May 1926, Elliot Grinnel Mears, *Survey*

*Report of the Industrial Commission on Immigration*, 1901, Vol. XVI

*Sociology and Social Research*, Vol. 14, Page 53; Vol. 16, Page 149

"Third Biennial Report," 1887–1888, Bureau of Labor Statistics, Page 318

ARMENIANS

*Armenians in America*, 1919, M. Vartan Malcom

FILIPINOS

"Exit — the Filipino," Sept. 4, 1935, Carey McWilliams, *Nation*

*Facts about Filipino Immigration into California*, April 1930, Department of Industrial Relations, State of California

"Filipino Immigration," Nov. 5, 1929, Commonwealth Club, Vol. V, No. 45

"Filipino Labor Cycle," Benico Catapersan, *Sociology and Social Research*, Vol. 14, No. 61

"Filipino Labor in Central California," Donald Elliott Anthong, *Sociology and Social Research*, Vol. 16, Page 149

HINDUS

*Caste and Outcast*, 1923, Dhan Gopal Mukerji

*Hindustani Workers on the Pacific Coast*, 1923, Rajani Kanta Das, published by Walter de Gruyter and Company, Berlin

"Rag Heads — a Picture of America's East Indians," Oct. 28, 1922, Annette Thackwell Johnson, *Independent*

"Tides of Turbans," June 1919, Herman Scheffauer, *Forum*

JAPANESE

"California Uproots the Jap," March 1, 1924, Robert Welles Ritchie, *Country Gentleman*

Description of Japanese Communities in Florin and Living-
stone, California, May 1926, *Survey*
*Japan and the California Problem*, 1921, T. Iyenaga and
Kenoske Sato
*Japanese in the United States*, 1932, Yamato Ichihashi
*Japanese Problem in the United States*, 1915, H. A. Millis
"Quota on Exclusion for Japanese Immigrants," Dec. 20, 1932,
Commonwealth Club, Vol. VIII, No. 51
*Real Japanese Question*, 1921, K. K. Kawakami


MEXICANS

*California Cultivator*, Feb. 15, 1930, May 8, 1926, May 5, 1931,
May 20, 1931
*Mexican Immigration and Its Bearing on California Agricul-
ture*, Nov. 1929, Dr. George P. Clements
*Mexican Labor in the United States*, 1929, Paul S. Taylor,
University of California Press
*Mexicans in California*, Oct. 1930, Department of Industrial
Relations, State of California
"What of the Bracero?" June 1925, Charles A. Thompson,
*Survey*


MISCELLANEOUS

*Agricultural Labor on the Pacific Coast States: A Bibliography
and Suggestions for Research*, Aug. 1935, Social
Science Research Council, Regional Committee
"Armies of Unemployed in California," Aug. 22, 1914, E. Guy
Talbott, *Survey*
"Battalions of Life," Nov. 1918, Alice Prescott Smith, *Sunset*
"California the Golden," Nov. 1920, Emma Duke, *American
Child*
"California's Labor Camps," Nov. 8, 1919, Christina Kryste,
*Survey*
*Casual Laborer and Other Essays* (Chapter II: "Wheatland"),
1920, Carleton H. Parker
"Child Labor," 1937, Tom Ireland
"Colony at San Ysidro," Nov. 1911, John Cowan, *World's
Work*

"Food First," Oct. 1920, Walter V. Woehlke, *Sunset*

"Old and New Labor Problems in California," Sept. 19, 1914, John A. Fitch, *Survey*

"Riveted Down — and They Like It," July 29, 1922, George P. West, *Collier's*

"Sisters All," May 1919, Susan Minor, *Overland*

"Social Changes in California," April 1891, Charles Howard Shinn, *Popular Science Monthly*

"Who Says White Folks Won't Work?" Dec. 1920, Georgia Graves Bordwell, *Sunset*

## SOCIAL CONDITIONS

*Health Problems among Migratory Workers*, Sept. 8, 1938, Omer Mills, Farm Security Administration

*Migratory Child Workers*, June 28, 1929, George Mangold and Lillian Hill (pamphlet)

"Migratory Children," Sept. 1938, *Sierra Educational News*

*Study of the Health of 1,000 Children of Agricultural Laborers in California*, July 1936–June 1937, Bureau of Child Hygiene, California Department of Public Health

*Trailing Child and Maternal Health into California Migratory Agricultural Camps*, July 1937–June 1938, Bureau of Child Hygiene, California Department of Public Health

EXTENDED BIBLIOGRAPHY
1971 Edition

*Agribusiness and its Workers*, National Advisory Committee on Farm Labor, 1963

*Delano: The Story of the California Grape Strike*, John Gregory Dunne, 1967

*Dollar Harvest: The Story of the Farm Bureau*, Samuel R. Berger (foreword by Cesar Chavez), 1971

*Farm Labor Fact Book*, U.S. Department of Labor, (no date)

*Farm Labor Organizing 1905–1967: A Brief History*, National Advisory Committee on Farm Labor, 1967

*Forty Acres: Cesar Chavez and the Farm Workers*, Mark Day (intro. by Cesar Chavez), 1971

*Labor and Liberty: The La Follette Committee and the New Deal*, Jerold S. Auerbach, 1966

*LaCausa: The California Grape Strike*, Paul Fusco and George D. Horwitz, 1970.

*Los Mojados: The Wetback Story*, Julian Samora, 1971

*Merchants of Labor*, Ernesto Galarza, 1966

"The Politics of the Mexican Labor Issue," Ellis W. Hawley, *Agricultural History*, July, 1966.

*Prejudice: Japanese-Americans, Symbol of Racial Intolerance*, Carey McWilliams, 1944, 1971

*Sal Si Puedes*, Peter Mattiessen, 1969

*The Slaves We Rent*, Truman E. Moore, 1965

*Small Farm and Big Farm*, Carey McWilliams, Public Affairs Committee, 1945

*So Shall Ye Reap, The Story of Cesar Chavez and The Farm Workers' Movement*, Joan London and Henry Anderson, 1970

*Spiders in the House and Workers in the Field*, Ernesto Galarza, 1970

"Wetbacks, Growers and Poverty," Sheldon L. Greene, *The Nation*, October 20, 1969